THE
MORAL
REVOLUTION

THE
MORAL
REVOLUTION

A Christian Humanist Vision

Daniel C. Maguire

1817

Harper & Row, Publishers, San Francisco

Cambridge, Hagerstown, New York, Philadelphia, Washington
London, Mexico City, São Paulo, Singapore, Sydney

"A Theory of Justice" was previously published in *A New American Justice*, by Daniel C. Maguire. Minneapolis: Winston Press, 1981.

"The Primacy of Justice in Moral Theology" is excerpted from an article previously published in *Horizons* 10 (1983).

"Ending the White Male Monopolies" was previously published in USA Today: *Journal of the Society for the Advancement of Education* 110 (1981).

"War, Peace, and the Christian Conscience" was previously published in *The New Subversives: Anti-Americanism of the Religious Right*, by Daniel C. Maguire. New York: Continuum, 1982.

"The Case Against Violence" was previously published in *Death by Choice*, 2nd Edition, by Daniel C. Maguire. New York: Doubleday Image Book, 1984.

"The Violence of Anti-Semitism" was previously published in *The New Subversives: Anti-Americanism of the Religious Right*, by Daniel C. Maguire. New York: Continuum, 1982.

"The Morality of Homosexual Marriage" was previously published in *Challenge to Love: Catholic Views of Homosexuality*, edited by Robert Nugent. New York: Crossroad, 1983.

"The Feminization of God and Ethics" was previously published in *Annual of the Society of Christian Ethics*, 1982.

"The Feminist Turn in Ethics" was previously published in *Horizons* 11 (1984).

"The Exclusion of Women From Orders: A Moral Evaluation" was previously published in *Cross Currents* 34 (1984).

"The Moral Revolution in Health Care" was previously published in *Thought* 57 (1982).

"Visit to An Abortion Clinic" was previously published in *National Catholic Reporter* 21 (1984).

"The Freedom to Die" was previously published in *Commonweal* 96 (1972).

"Catholic Ethics in the Post-Infallible Church" was previously published in *Absolutes in Moral Theology?* Washington, D.C.: Corpus Books, 1968.

"A Moral Creed for All Christians" was previously published in *Anglican Theological Review*, Supplementary Series, 1976.

"Service on the Common: A Portrait of the Ethicist" was previously published in *Religious Studies Review* 10 (1984). The editors of *Religious Studies Review* commissioned a "retrospective essay" on all of Maguire's work and invited him to add the short essay given in this chapter by way of self-portrait.

"Pigeon Ethics: The Moral Philosophy of B. F. Skinner" was previously published in *Living Light* 9 (1972).

"The Knowing Heart and the Intellectualistic Fallacy" was previously published in *Journal of Religious Ethics* 10 (1982).

Library of Congress Cataloging-in-Publication Data

Maguire, Daniel C.
  The moral revolution

  1. Christian ethics—Catholic authors.   I. Title.
BJ1249.M164   1986   241'.042   85-51826
ISBN 0-06-254539-6 (pbk.)

86   87   88   89   90   RRD   10   9   8   7   6   5   4   3   2   1

Contents

Prologue

Moral norms do not come down to us from mountain tops or from oracles or infallible gurus. To know what is *moral* (befitting persons in all of their preciousness) we have to think and feel, listen and agonize. That effort, in academic circles, is called ethics. In ordinary life it is called wisdom. In any context, it is hard and lively work.

Moral value judgments touch our identities as well as our most intimate needs and wants. Ethics, therefore, is highly charged with emotion. Often it is strangled by traditions which no longer fit and bedeviled by authorities who think they know what they do not. It is never far from controversy. Moral values are enfleshed in life: in sex, in business, in money dealings, in politics, in religion, and in justice-claims and power-plays between sexes, classes, and races.

This book looks at all of that and attempts to do some honest and sensitive thinking. Such a book must be serious, given the mortally serious matters it treats. But such a book should also not be dull. Ethics serves on the common of life where the mysteries and questions of living meet. May the reader find stimulant and service in these pages.

Part 1

DOING JUSTICE TO JUSTICE

Justice is the linchpin of the social life, and yet ignorance about its nature abounds. Neither American philosophy or political theory offers a coherent theory of justice. Chapters One and Two speak to this need and offer the framework of a justice theory suitable to modern realities. Chapter Three applies this justice theory to the redistribution of wealth, power, and privilege in the United States.

CHAPTER 1

A Theory of Justice

Justice is the permanent passion of public life. Every policy maker and litigant claims it. Everyone points to it to justify his or her claims. And, yet, only rarely do we pause to ask the most fundamental question of our political experience: *what is justice?* You can do a lot of work with electricity without knowing what the essence of electricity is and still not get hurt, but this is not the way with justice. Ignorance about justice hurts and even kills. In political life, justice is crucial. The conception we have of it controls our judgments and our political judgments control lives.

To speak of justice is to reach for the foundations of human existence. Justice is not one virtue among the lot. It is the cornerstone of human togetherness. To survive and thrive a little we need justice like a body needs blood. To try to define justice is to address the most profound questions ever to challenge the human mind. The American approach has been to dodge these questions. Our public philosophy does not contain an explicit theory of justice. All our laws are, of course, expressions of some concept of justice, but those laws exist in a matrix of confused and contradictory concepts of justice. American scholars have not paid their debts to justice theory. This leaves a gaping hole in the center of our polity.

What I offer here owes many debts to some classical Greek, Hebrew, and medieval theories of justice. There is richness in these theories to be mined and refined and so they are a solid foundation for the theory of justice I develop here. The classical definition of justice begins with deluding simplicity: *Justice is the virtue that renders to each his/her own.* "To each his/her own" is the persistent core formula for justice that has spanned the literature from Homer through Aristotle, Cicero, Ambrose, Augustine, and Roman law, and it is still seen as the axiomatic core of justice theory. (The Latin for "to each his/her own" is *suum cuique* which is neither sexist or clumsy. Our his/her is linguistically ungraceful but morally imperative since justice is all-inclusive and must not be defined in sexist terms.) The simplicity and consistency of this definition are welcome as a start, but it is only a start. It is like the skin which must then be peeled away to reveal the layers of reality beneath.

Justice is the first assault upon egoism. Egoism would say: "To me my own." Justice says, "Wait. There are other *selves*." Personal existence is a shared glory. Each of those other subjects is of great value and commands respect. The ego has a tendency to declare itself the sun and center of the universe. Justice breaks the news to the ego that there are no solar gods in the universe of persons. Justice is the attitude of mind that accepts the others—all others—as subjects in their own right. Justice asserts that one's own ego is not absolute and that one's interests are related. In the simple concession that each deserves his/her own, the moral self comes to grips with the reality and value of other selves. Justice is thus the elementary manifestation of the other-regarding character of moral and political existence. The alternative to justice is social disintegration because it would mean a refusal to take others seriously.

But let us peel away another layer. When you say, "To each his/her own," you face the question "Why?" Why take others seriously? Why not just "To me my own"? The move from pure egoism to justice is nothing more or less than the discovery of the value of persons, or, in the common term, the discovery of "the sanctity of life." Justice implies indebtedness. You *owe* his/her own to each. But indebtedness is grounded in worth. The each is worth his/her own. Justice is thus founded upon a perception of the worth of persons. We show what we think persons are worth by what we ultimately concede is due to them. Talk of justice would sound like gibberish if we had no perception of the value of persons.

All of which leads to a jarring conclusion. If we deny persons justice, we have declared them worthless! Justice, you see, is not the best we can do in reaction to the value of persons. Friendship is. Aristotle did well to point out that friends have no need of justice. In friendship a higher, more generous dynamism is operative. You don't tell newlyweds they owe one another signs of affection in simple justice. Love will take care of that.[1] Justice, however, is the least we can do for persons. It is the first response to the value of persons, the least we can do in view of that value. In friendship and in love we respond lavishly.

Justice is concerned with the minimal due. Less than this we could not do without negating the value of the person. To be perfectly consistent, if we deny justice to persons we ought to kill them because we have declared them worthless. Their liquidation would be perfectly in order.

These are grim tidings in the political order. Love does not make the political world go around; justice is the most we can achieve. Love can flourish at the interpersonal level, but it would be a mad romantic who said that, at this point in moral evolution, love can be the energy of the social order. In the political realm, only justice stands between us and barbarity. In this realm, when justice fails, persons perish. In different words, justice is incipient love and the only form love takes in political life.

Notice, I started out saying "To each his/her own," with a warning that there is more to the phrase than meets the eye. This led to the worth of persons as the only reason why we should acknowledge the other *eaches* and render them at least their minimal due. Denying that implies they are worthless, and is thus murderous in intent. And this leads to the next key question: How does *need* relate to justice?

Most would concede that justice means giving to each what each deserves. Justice, in other words, is based upon deserts. Here quickly the ways part between individualists and the defenders of genuine social justice. The individualist would say that your deserts and entitlements come from your own achievements or as gifts from other achievers. The theory of social justice concedes this but goes on to say that you also *deserve* in accordance with your *needs*. Needs too give entitlement. The essential needs of each are also "his/her own."

When Needing Is Deserving

"To each his own" translates into "To each according to his/her merits and earned entitlements" *and* "To each according to his/her needs." I contend further that not only is the latter formula a solid dictate of justice but that it can even at times override the entitlement formula. In other words, we might have to yield some of our fairly merited entitlements, in view of the needs of others. This yielding might even at times involve not only what we have but even life itself in the case of the supreme sacrifice.

To each according to his/her need. This little formula, if you can forgive its use by Marx, has a fairly harmless ring to it. Why then the resistance of our cunning species to its use? The answer is that the formula contains a threat to self-interest. There is no immediate threat apparent in the idea that everyone should have what s/he earns (or is given), i.e., the entitlement principle, in the sense of earned entitlement. But if people have a right to what they need, that could hurt. Giving them what they have earned makes a kind of hard-nosed sense and it implies that I'll be able to keep what I earn. Giving them what they need is another matter. What I have earned may have to be balanced against what they need. Thus the formula at hand is no gentle piety. What it does is bring us face to face with a major question of justice. In the process of rendering to each his/her own, might individual interests have to be sacrificed for social goals and the common good? Need raises the prospect of such sacrifice. If the need of others is in some way my business, the plot of my life is thereby greatly thickened. If I can say "To each his/her own" and concede to the other only what s/he has earned, my life has all the simplicity that individualism seductively promises. But if I owe them what they need, even if I did not cause their need, simplicity is no longer my portion and I am more bound up with others than American individualism would lead us to believe. (Individualism is the denial that we are naturally social and sharing animals who cannot survive or thrive without a justly sharing context. Individualism, often called conservatism, is a figment of egoistic imagination and it is also quintessentially American).

What then are the justice-credentials of human *need*? To open the discussion, let me make the question of the rights of need very concrete by dipping into my own personal life for an example—even though in so doing I am breaking the sacred canons of authorship which insist that one should write as though one had no personal life. The example of rights generated by needs is provided by my son, Danny, who died three years ago at age ten. Danny received many extraordinary benefits from the American political community, particularly the city of Milwaukee. We had door-to-door transportation to school by bus and, when necessary, by taxi. He thus rode in heated comfort through Wisconsin winters while other children walked. He was in an almost one-to-one teacher/student situation. Specialists were brought in to attend to his special needs. There was no public utility in any of this. Danny had an incurable, degenerative disease (Hunter's syndrome) that slowly ravaged his central nervous system and made his life a short one. His mental age was never more than eighteen months to two years. Danny could claim no distinctive merits, works, rank, or earned entitlements. He was delighted with the efforts of his teachers and passionately reached out for what they offered. He wanted to be part of this world and his teachers were a medium for contact with the world and some of its meaning. Despite his slight intellectual reach, his need for the stimulation of school was real and poignantly insistent. He looked for the school bus even on holidays and weekends. When he could still manage such a sentence, he would announce to people on the street: "I go school!" The human *need* here was essential, not frivolous. He wanted to be with us, and school—at least for a time— was one essential link.

Yet with all of this, it remained a fact that he was learning progressively less and was always forgetting what he knew. His physical problems were alleviated by the physical therapy the school provided, but that too was a losing battle. The polity invested enormously and never could get a productive citizen. The critical questions are *who* paid for all of this and *why*? And, more importantly yet, was this cost borne out of charity?

My taxes clearly did not pay for what he got. Through law-based taxation, the people of the political community were required to pay. Some of those who paid are childless and are still required to pay for the education of other people's children. Those who had children in school were also paying for Danny to get benefits that their children did not get. And those people never got any calculable return from Danny. Most never knew of his coming or his passing, and yet they sacrificed for his benefit. Still, even amid a tax revolt, such aid to the handicapped was not in principle threatened. In cases like Danny's, the ruling perception seemed to be that this little boy with blighted mind but exquisite affections deserved suitable though expensive care from the community. And the community made it a matter of *enforced* law and justice, not of *optional* charity. The outreach and care that Danny needed and I could not afford to give him was given him by the community as an expression of social justice. The "his/her own" part of the justice formula includes need—personal need as well as group need, the needs of productive as well as of unproductive persons. The community decided that Danny's "own" included the development of whatever potential he had for as long as he had it. It was not *his own* because of a deal he struck with the community, as contractarian theory would have it. It was not a reward, for he was without "merits." Neither was it reparation, for the community had not harmed him. It was also not an investment, for he was capable of no return. His own *worth* was the reason why he had a right to the essential care he *needed*. The enthusiasm and hunger he brought to his schooling showed that it was an essential need for him to stretch his potential as far as it would go for a long as it would last. Helping him to do as much as he could seemed the least that we could do. Meeting his felt need for development was his minimal due. He was worth that. The need here was essential. Essential needs are those without which self-respect and hope cannot endure. Even the retarded have such needs. Hitler's justice theory did not believe this, but then we fought a war to defeat that theory in its political manifestation. While American justice theory is not developed, American practice shows, in cases such as Danny's, that we operate out of implicit notions of what social justice entails. It is the task of justice theory to show the sense of this.

Need gives entitlement because of the worth of the needing person. The judgment housed in the law and practice of the community here is that to deny the needed care would be to deny justice. Hitler judged such life worthless, and then quite logically eliminated it. Out polity values persons, and therefore justice, differently in many respects. We have decided that the Dannys of the world are worth justice and so we render to them according to their needs. The working—if unexamined—assumption is that we *owe* things to people in strict justice because of their need. People have *rights* and *entitlements* because of their needs. Need, therefore, is a critical category of justice. Danny's case is particularly illuminating in this regard since his intrinsic worth was the only justification for meeting his essential needs. It may be socially useful to help a child with Downs syndrome since help may make the child somewhat independent rather than a future burden on the state. The Danny's of the world have rights based on need without reference to social utility—with reference only to their personal worth.

Need, of course, like all human categories, is slippery and calls out for distinctions. For one thing, need, like every term relating to persons, has both an individual and a social meaning. Both individuals and groups have rights-breeding needs. A starving individual has a right to "steal" a loaf of bread from a bakery if his death would otherwise follow. (He would not be *stealing* since he has a right to it.) A group which has been disadvantaged as a group needs reinstatement into the sharing patterns in which essential goods are distributed in a society. South African blacks, for example, have a right based on need—which in turn is based on personal worth—to a restructuring of the distributional patterns of their society. Identifiable groups have similar problems in the United States.

Furthermore, the need in question may not always be guiltless in origin. Handicapped persons whose ailment was self-induced—by drug use, for example—have needs to which society is and ought to be sensitive. If they are rendered incompetent, we don't gas them and incinerate them, which we could do if they had no rights. We see them as having rights, based on need, based on enduring worth. It is generally seen as unjust to use criminals—even those condemned to death—as guinea pigs in medical experiments. This too is another reason why capital punishment is unjust since it implies that the persons, who may indeed have lost their right to freedom, have lost all their rights and are therefore worthless. This, of course, is a gratuitous, unprovable assertion, and thus bears a burden of proof which it cannot meet.[2] Personal worth is not negated by the loss of some rights. No one can judge any human being completely worthless.

Some need is based upon mismanagement and even thievery, as when a major corporation sinks into financial distress. Sometimes it is judged that such a corporation should be allowed to die of its own mismanagement. At other times, *for considerations of the common good,* it is judged that unbearable harm would come to the economy, and a rescue operation is undertaken at public expense. If well advised and truly promotive of the common good, this is an act of justice. The common good has moral standing because that is one dimension of the good of persons. Every consideration of justice and morality is rooted in the good of persons. For that reason, the grounds for helping Chrysler and Lockheed and Danny are the same—if we presume that Chrysler and Lockheed had valid claims. All valid claims are traceable to the breeding ground of every right and entitlement—the perceived preciousness of persons.

Need sometimes relates to the dignity of an office. We provide our president with a mansion because we judge that, for practical as well as symbolic reasons, he could not serve the common good as well from an apartment on Q Street. We see this as a social need.

Also, we decide that farmers and small businesspersons might need special aid and tax breaks for a vigorous overall economy. Crop failures and other natural disasters create needs to which society responds. The details of such things are subject to infinite wrangling, but the principle is that justice entails reacting to the needs of certain individuals and groups. As we become more sensitive to the value of persons, we preceive more needs. Only recently did we decide that defendants need and deserve a lawyer even if they cannot afford one. We are still debating whether persons need minimum health care just as much as they need minimum education. In the gory past we did not judge that persons needed a fair trial, freedom from slavery or torture, "social security," the opportunity to vote or run for office, et cetera. Social progress is based on a deepening perception of the value of persons.

Because of their value, certain of their needs should not be unmet and certain things are inalienable rights. Persons should be literate; they should have safety and sufficient food; they should have some say over their political destiny; even when they are handicapped they should be able to activate their potential; if they have been ostracized by society, they should be reincorporated. They should not be tortured, et cetera. Social evolution is based on a growing appreciation of the worth of persons, which is the grounding of all moral and political life. Because of that worth, we must render to them their deserts. Deserts, however, are grounded both in their achieved entitlements *and* in their essential needs. To deny either would be to declare them worthless.

Of course persons do not have a right to everything they think they need. Some people think they need luxury. Hence the stress on *essential* need. Essential needs, again, are those without which life, self-respect, or hope could not endure. On this basis, we have guaranteed certain rights such as those contained in the Bill of Rights and provided for at least minimal health, education, and welfare. It is on this basis also that unjust monopolies should not be tolerated. This is true in the world of business. It is also true when white males have controlled all the power centers in the society from government to business to the professions in such a way that certain groups face head winds and barriers that prevent them from competing. This denies those groups both self-respect and hope and even life itself. Changing this is an *essential need* and thus a matter of simple justice.

Needs, of course, like rights, can conflict with one another. Nazi Americans might feel a need and claim a right to march in Skokie. However, the need and right of Jewish residents not to have insult added to their unspeakable injuries can outweigh the Nazi claims. In a time of acute scarcity, Danny's needs for special education could be superseded by more urgent need. Also, freedom of movement would be considered an essential need, but in the event of a rare and virulent disease, the need for quarantine might be justified. Needs and rights are not *acontextual*. They are marked by the relationality and sociality of human existence. This necessitates an eternal process of discernment and debate. The principle, however, is the thing. *Basic needs issue into rights when their neglect would effectively deny the human worth of the needy.* Or in other words, essential needs create inalienable rights.

The final point on need is this: meeting essential needs in society is not a work of optional charity or benevolence. It is often spoken of this way but this is loose and dangerous talk. Meeting essential needs does not make one a candidate for sainthood; it merely establishes one's credentials as human. It is a minimal manifestation of human-ness, the alternative to which is barbarity. If we wish to make it pos-sible for handicapped people, as far as is financially feasible, to move about in society, this is not heroic on our part. It is simply a matter of meeting essential needs of persons as best we can. As soon as we cast this obligation in terms of compassion or charity, we have declared it supererogatory and therefore dispensable. To neglect it would be ungenerous, but not morally wrong. When we are speaking about es-sential needs, such a view is nonsense. Such a view is also a radical departure from the Judeo-Christian idea of justice, which is supposedly normative for many Americans. In Hebrew and Christian thought, meeting essential needs is the soul of justice.

The Three Sides of Justice

All of justice is divided into three parts. There are three ways in which we give "to each his/her own." To miss out on even one of these is to be unjust.

Having said that, I must immediately become defensive. Persons who may have stayed with my thesis thus far might now throw up their arms and cry: "Here comes the inevitable pedantic quibble!" Per-mit me to enter a plea of innocence swiftly. What is involved here is no harmless numbers game. Errors would not be "merely academic," as that strange expression goes. If there are three ways we can be just or unjust, and if injustice may be lethal to human beings and disruptive of their environment, it is not unpractical to indulge in a little clarity on what justice is. Although it is rarely adverted to or understood, a rich variety of apparently disparate topics depends on an appreciation of the tripartite nature of justice. Though I am not considering all these issues I offer here a list of just some of the issues which require us to assume, implicitly or explicitly, a position on what justice is and how many forms of justice there are: universal health care, civil disobedi-ence and the right to dissent, using organs from retarded donors, med-ical experimentation on children, limiting sales to blacks to prevent a neighborhood from "tipping" and going all black, international income tax for economically developed nations, progressive income tax, the right to take a child from parents who refuse medical care, drafting persons for an onslaught on poverty and illiteracy, and quotas for dis-empowered groups such as women and blacks. These seemingly un-connected issues are approached in varying ways in the different disciplines. All of them, however, are hinged to a conception of justice and its several forms, although, as I have said, this is broadly missed. Implicit in any conception of justice are assumptions about the nature of personhood and the rapport between the individual and society. All of the issues just mentioned involve just such assumptions. And unexplored assumptions are at the root of all intellectual evil.

For this reason, I beseech the reader to meet the theoretical issue of justice squarely. There could be nothing more practical than this theoretical exercise.

The heart of the matter is that we are not merely individuals; we are *social individuals,* and there are three fundamental modes of sociality to which the three kinds of justice correspond. These three are *individual justice, social justice,* and *distributive justice.* These are not three different categories but rather three ways in which the one category, justice, is realized. Justice does not admit of partitioning. Failure at any form of justice is injustice.

The beginning of most confusion occurs in a failure to recognize the tripartite nature of justice. Even Aristotle, whose influence has been so controlling on this subject, never managed to get it straight as to whether there were two, three, or four basic forms of justice. The experts on his work are still divided on that count.[3] Bad faith adds to the muddle. If one doesn't want to meet the demands of justice in some way, it is self-serving mischief to define that form of justice out of existence.

Quite simply, there are three forms of justice because persons relate to persons in three different ways.[4] We relate on a one-to-one basis (individual justice); the individual relates to the social whole (social justice); and the representatives of the social whole relate to individuals (distributive). When, for example, we talk about fulfilling contracts or repairing injuries done to discrete individuals, we are speaking of individual justice. When we speak of modes of indebtedness to the social whole exemplified by such things as taxes, jury duty, and eminent domain, we are speaking of forms of social justice. And when we speak of distributing the goods and bads of society fairly (largely through the instrumentality of government) we are speaking of distributive justice. Though social and distributive justice are distinct forms of justice, both relate to the common good and are thus co-ordinates. It is an act of distributive justice for the state to collect taxes; it is an act of social justice to cooperate. It is an act of distributive justice for the state to insist on preferential affirmative action. It is social justice for citizens to cooperate and even voluntarily anticipate this redistributive need.

One may therefore speak of social-distributive justice without conflating these distinct but related forms of justice.

Therefore, it is in these three distinct ways that persons render to each his/her own. The dozens of species of justice that encumber the literature on the subject are all reducible to one of these three essential modalities of just rendering.[5]

Individual justice is basically simple in its concept. It is, after all, rather clear-cut that if I contracted to cut your lawn, I owe you a lawn cut, or if I stole your lawn mower, I owe you a lawn mower's worth of restitution. Justice at this level can often be captured in simple terms of mathematical equality. Also in individual, one-to-one justice it is only the ones who are interacting who are involved. If I made a deal to cut your lawn, that is a matter between you and me; the neighbor down the street is presumably in no way implicated. Social and distributive justice do not enjoy a similar basic simplicity. What is owed, by whom, and to whom is never as clearly delineated as in individual justice, and at the social level, justice is not reducible to simple equality since *unequal* demands may *justly* be made.

Social justice concerns individuals' debts to the common good. Fundamentally, this means that citizens owe a contribution toward making the social whole a context in which human life can flourish—a context in which respect and hope are present for all. That task is immense and never finished. No one can say he or she has cared enough, dared enough, been creative enough and thus has paid in full what is owed to the common good. The guilt of apathy and insufficient caring affects us all. Let's face it. Would whites have started the civil rights movement? Would males have started the women's liberation movement? Voting, joining citizens' lobbies, cooperating with justifiable enlistment, et cetera, do not exhaust our debts to the needs of the social whole. Racism, classism, and sexism reign. Respect and hope for all persons do not obtain and we are all debtors on that account.

The prime subjects of *distributive justice* are the agents and agencies of government. But there are other economic and institutional powers that control some of the conduits through which the goods of society flow. All of these and the individuals who support them, at least by their apathy, are also subjects of distributive justice. It is not just the "powers that be" who control distribution. Individual citizens are implicated in some way in all the workings of distributive justice. To some degree government requires a base of contentment among the people. Otherwise the rule of the rulers will be rejected and the government will toppel. Seven centuries ago Thomas Aquinas pointed out that distributive justice involves more than the princes. When the people are not rocking the ship of state, they are clearly satisifed . . . *contenti* in Thomas' term.[6] Their undergirding contentment shores up (legitimates) what the government is up to. Citizens may also participate in distributive justice by their influence on corporations. Such things as stockholders' resolutions, selective boycotts, and other forms of citizen and consumer pressure can have some influence on those corporate powers that are every day making decisions affecting the common good.

As Thomas Jefferson wrote to James Madison, whenever there are unemployed poor, "it is clear that the laws of property have been so far extended as to violate natural right."[7] To change his language but keep his point, we could say that, whenever there are unemployed poor and massive dislocations of wealth and privilege, the distributional patterns of the society are unjust. Such a condition implicates the government, the agencies of corporate power, and the apparently decent citizens who legitimate the powers of distribution with their undergirding contentment. The agents of distributive justice, therefore, are not only the persons who exercise governmental, corporate, and professional power but also the citizens who support the patterns of distribution by what they do, or, more significantly, by what they do not do.

These then, in brief, are the three forms of justice. Discussion of any issue of justice will force you to assume some stance regarding the meaning and import of the tripolar category of justice. What stance you assume, however, will be influenced and possibly dominated by your cultural context. The American context is a breeding ground for special errors in understanding justice. This presents us with the dual task of cooling the pretensions of individual justice in American culture and of mounting a theoretical defense for social and distributive justice. With this undone, private entitlements and individuals goals could not be sacrificed for broader social aims. In meeting the theoretical problems with justice that afflict American culture, I shall also be fleshing out the theory of justice in general.

The Pitfalls of Individual Justice

If you don't know what individual justice means, you will soon have ample time to ponder its meaning in jail. This kind of justice is not likely to be neglected in any society; the individuals involved see to that. It will certainly not be neglected in an individualistic society which is fixated on this kind of relationship and only reluctantly concedes the existence of other forms of indebtedness.

Fixation at the level of individual justice, to which United States individualism is gravely prone, is beset by three radical problems: 1) mistaking a part of justice for the whole; 2) fomenting lawsuits and a spirit of litigiousness; 3) ignoring the social consequences of greed and the built-in necessity for redistribution.

First of all, therefore, by mistaking a part of justice for the whole, individualism falls into the same kind of error that collectivism does in ignoring other forms of sociality and justice. At the level of logic, the American individualist (conservative) is a fellow traveler of the strict Maoist collectivist. Both are reductionists. Both simplistically bracket out the richness and complexity of human social existence.

Fixation on individual justice means that only one form of social relationship is acknowledged—the one-to-one kind. Such a fixationist could say, in fidelity to his/her own premises: "If I made a deal with you I will honor it; if I hurt you, I will make amends; but, if I did neither, bug off!" If there is only individual justice, those would be the words of a just person. The rigid collectivist is also fixated, but at the level of social and distributive justice. In the collectivist's view, individual dealings and relationships are faint shadows upon the grand substance of the common good, embodied in the state. A wife is more a political comrade than a spouse. All individual claims are subordinated to the collectivity. As the waves of the sea are but mere fleeting apparitions of the sustaining, enduring ocean, so persons in the collectivist vision subsist in the state. They have no personal rights except by concession. Individuality is subsumed in commonality.

Fixation, whether collectivist or individualist, is by its nature unjustified selectivity. There is nothing benign about such exclusionary selectivity when the subject at hand is justice because the definition of justice is nothing less than the definition of social existence. Mistakes here introduce social distortions and strip persons of what is their due. Both collectivism and individualism lead to a social structure in which some persons, at least, will not get what they deserve. Pure individualism and pure collectivism never exist without inconsistency but they do exist as dominant biases affecting national institutions and laws.

The second related problem with fixation on individual justice is that it makes for a very litigious society. Individual claims and rights assume absolute value and the peace of the society will be fractured in their defense. Rights will be interpreted in the separatist, "don't tread on me" tradition and sweeter forms of reconciliation will be bypassed. Not surprisingly, the United States has some 500,000 lawyers while Japan, with almost half our population, has fewer than 15,000. Culturally, Japan places more stress on harmony and sociality than the United States, and so a spirit of accommodation regularly limits the grasping quality of individualistically conceived rights. Indeed, the term "rights" in American vocabulary harbors a good deal of our native, countersocial litigiousness. "Rights" is heavy with defensive connotations in American parlance. "I have a right to it and you don't" is what it says. The chip is upon the shoulder and the frown upon the brow.

Beyond American usage, however, the assertion of rights implies an adversary situation. If one is receiving one's due, there is no need to assert rights. Rights talk arises in the face of a denial of rights. In the United States, most of our justice claims are likely to be couched in rights language. Most Americans would be baffled by the fact that in Chinese there seems to be no word that exactly corresponds to our word "rights." There is, of course, a word for justice and a rich tradition surrounding it in the long history of China.[8] In fact, it is of no little interest to contemplate the paralysis that would beset our moral and political discourse if we were deprived of this our most hallowed linguistic tool for justice claims! I am not suggesting that those who either forgo or disparage rights language are well advised or better off for this. Indeed the collectivist or utilitarian temptation can best be met with a healthy dose of rights-talk. But at least we should look to see what presuppositions dwell within this favored word of ours. When you marry a word, you may not want all the relatives, and the American relatives of "rights" are a mean bunch.

Professor Ronald Dworkin's description of rights shows the strengths and the weaknesses of the term. "Individual rights are political trumps held by individuals. Individuals have rights when, for some reason, a collective goal is not a sufficient justification for denying them what they wish, as individuals, to have or to do, or not a sufficient justification for imposing some loss or injury upon them."[9] Rights are "held by individuals" in a face-off with the group. Group rights are not excluded, but in an individualistic milieu they could be put on the defensive. Put such a description of rights into the hands of someone who tends to see all group claims on the individuals as guilty until proven innocent, and the legitimate claims of social justice are imperiled. (My purpose here is not to negate individual rights but to keep them in necessary tension with the legitimate and neglected claims of the group.)

The liberation of the individual from submersion in the collectivity is a distinguished modern achievement and the language of rights served it well. However, when one is talking ethics out of a simplistic individualism, such a perspective must be redeemed by a vision of social obligation and of debts owed to the many by the one. The pendulum of human thinking swings too easily from one excess to another. A socially naïve individualism easily arises from reaction to overbearing collectivism. Individualism forgets that there is more to justice than rights. There is also need and need comes in individual and group form. This point is missed by individualists, i.e., in United States' parlance, by conservatives.

This leads to the third problem with a fixation on individual justice: its incomprehension of the might of greed and the need of redistribution. Let us imagine that the private dealings of individuals in a society are one and all scrupulously respectful of individual rights. At the one-to-one level, no one seems to be cheated. Let us further suppose, what is quite supposable, that as a result of these dealings power and wealth begin to concentrate in the hands of the few superdealers. The result is that the many can be gravely afflicted even with regard to their basic goods and needs without ever being defrauded on a one-to-one basis. They are done in by the monopolistic patterns that develop in the free trade atmosphere. Of course, no society runs on a completely free or individualistic basis. There is always some tempering of individual claims. The problem is one of bias and proclivity. A society which is addicted to unbalanced individualism will tolerate enormous amounts of human misery and the power patterns that sustain that misery before it will move to the necessary redistributive restrictions upon individual "rights." No society can be totally blind to redistributive needs—poverty intrudes itself upon our senses—but an individualistically biased society will console itself with "trickle-down" and "ooze-out" theories of redistribution. Here we are at the level of faith, and bad faith at that. We are confident that if acquisitive private dealings are uninhibited an invisible hand will guide the trickle-down excess to where it will do the most good. Meanwhile, the acquisitive society busily plugs the leaks through which trickling and oozing could occur!

All of this leads to injustice by ignoring the ensconced patterns of distribution that enrich some and disempower and deprive others. It represents a readiness to include the dignity and lives of persons in the check list of acceptable losses. The ethical primitivity here is also sociologically naïve. The point usually missed is that the common good is the setting and matrix of private, individual good. It is not a hostile and unrelated competitor. This is the hard lesson that sooner or later comes home to all elites—even when those elites constitute a national majority. Fixation at the point of individual justice, therefore, is unrealistic, self-defeating, and ultimately cruel however bedecked it is with claims to democratic respectability.

With all that I have said about the evils of reducing justice to the one form of individual justice, I do not thereby disparage individual justice. Without commitment at the individual level we are unjust. The most obvious manifestations of individual justice, as I have said, are at the level of fulfilling contracts and repairing injuries.[10]

More basically, however, individual justice represents an incipient form of mutuality. It recognizes the other as a legitimate source of moral claims. It is a beginning of the essential other-regarding pattern of genuinely human life. This points beyond external exchanges. What we owe persons is not just to follow through on our dealings. We owe them respect even when a deal has not been struck. In fact, we owe them more respect than we can render, given the value of persons. Goethe was being none too cynical when he said that being a person means learning to be unjust. This is why individual justice has also been called "compensatory justice." For this reason too some have said that the principal manifestation of individual justice is restitution. We do not react to the heroic value of persons with appropriately heroic response, even in our private dealings. We may at some level of our beings agree with the Jewish philosopher Martin Buber when he said that a person "is *Thou* and fills the heavens," but we don't always respond accordingly.[11] Thus a neat scoreboard of contracts kept and torts repaired does not mean that even individual justice has been met in all its demands. Therefore, far from disparaging individual justice, I am arguing that we don't even measure up to its awesome exigencies. And on that chastening note, I turn to the forms of justice that are more demanding yet.

Justifying Social Justice

Social and distributive justice must be seen together since they represent the *to* and *fro* between persons and society. Both are based upon the pivotal assumption that persons are *social* by nature and not just *sociable*. Even the purest of individualists can concede elective sociability. Persons can interact and can even redistribute their goods on a consensual basis. To say beyond this, however, that society is the womb of personality, that persons are intrinsically and naturally social and political, is a qualitative leap beyond mere sociability. And a coherent theory of social and distributive justice is based upon that leap.

Recall that we are here comparing faith visions. The American-style individualist *believes* that rights belong only to individuals, that sharing with others is morally based upon consent, and that any forced sharing violates human rights. Individualism differs from a theory of social and distributive justice in two ways: first, regarding the nature of *personhood* and, secondly, regarding the nature of *society*. Individualism sees persons as basically separate atoms, individualized and detached entities, which relate to others only if they choose to do so and as they choose to do so. The state is not a natural reality but a voluntary contrivance of individuals. The wording of the Preamble of the Massachusetts Constitution of 1780 gives the individualist's view of society in a nutshell: "The body politic is formed by a voluntary association of individuals."[12] If the individuals did not voluntarily associate, there would be no body politic—only detached, individually compacted persons doing their own independent thing. There is no ultimate tension in this view between private good and public good, since the public or common good has no rights except those voluntarily conceded by individuals. Sacrifice of individual good for the common good makes sense only if individuals decide on it as a useful strategy. For the consistent individualist there are no debts to the common good; the common good has no rights. We can have debts only to other individuals; only individuals have rights. We are not a naturally sharing animal in this view—just an animal that might decide to share. If you carry all of this to its absurd extreme, as Robert Nozick does, even taxation is objectionable and on a par with forced labor.[13] Sharing is not natural; only being free to share or not share is natural. We are not social individuals; we are individuals who might socialize when it is in our self-interest. Dying for the common good would make no sense at all in this view and is a phenomenon that is theoretically unaccounted for in individualism.

Pure individualism is nonsense and no state ever survived or ever could survive on such a theoretical basis. (Even Nozick with his dire view of taxes undoubtedly pays them since academics are not forced to practice the nonsense they may write.) Any surviving political community has somehow come to grips with the reality of persons as *social individuals*. Some forms of social and distributive justice are found in every society. What this signifies is that there are two elements in the meaning of personhood: individuality and sociality. To lop off sociality, as individualism does, or to lop off off individuality, as collectivism does, makes for unbearable problems. A realistic theory of personhood (and justice) lives with the natural tension between individuality and sociality without apotheosizing or negating either. Such a realitic theory rests on the recognition that the human animal is.

The Sharing Animal

Human life is shared life. It is this fact that grounds social and distributive justice. It is to this fact that I refer when I speak of our natural sociality. It is to this fact also that Aristotle referred when he said that "it is evident that the state is a creation of nature, and that person is by nature a political animal.[14] Human life begins and develops sharingly or it does not begin or develop at all. This does not mean that no sharing is good sharing or that we have to share everything we have. But it does mean, among other things, that our social individuality is naturally expressed in political form and that our privately and fairly made entitlements are not absolute or immune to demands from the common good. It means that we have reached the point where individualists must choke or abandon their partiality and join us in a broader and realistic view of humankind.

It is because we are by nature the sharing animal that we cannot realistically imagine a "state of nature," as it has been called, in which self-sufficient individuals exist asocially. In this creation of deviant individualistic imagination, persons would be political by choice, not by nature. The state, in this view, would be created by a free compact made by individuals and would not be a "creation of nature." Such a "state of nature" is no more sustainable than a state of foodlessness or weightlessness. Persons flower into political existence or they wither. Obviously persons can survive without a political community longer than they can survive without food or oxygen because the need is different. It is, however, a natural need and what persons can become they will not become without the enabling matrix of a political community of some sort. Political community is not a jacket you put on if you think you need it; it is rather a body through which you live.

No coherent notion of social justice can emerge without an appreciation of our sharing social essence. From conception until death, human life unfolds under the physical law that *to be is to share*. Our social history is etched in our genes. Everything about us is social. The way we know, our language, our liturgies, friendship, sex, family—all are manifestations of unfolding sociality. And so too is the state. The formation of a political community or state is a natural and necessary law of survival and maturation for the human animal. Individualism's effort to see it as an adventitious device and not as essential and intrinsic to the human condition must implode under the pressure of its own inconsistency and unrealism. Even the rugged egoism that fuels individualism is ultimately frustrated by individualism's effort to sever individuality from its social moorings. Even private good is undone when its ties to common good are loosened or cut. The human person is by nature "a political animal." The need for a state is not negotiable since the state meets certain human necessities that will otherwise not be met.

Two general necessities are fulfilled by the state: 1) meeting private and public human needs through state agency; 2) providing persons with a medium for self-definition. The meeting of these natural necessities permits persons to survive, grow, and thrive. None of this would happen if these necessities were unmet. This illustrates the naturalness of our sharing sociality and the politicality of our being.

First then to those services to human good that are specific for the state. *There are indispensable needs that can be met only by the state. There are other needs that could be handled by the private sector but tend not to attract sufficient interest in a reliable and consistent way.* A list of some of these will illustrate the indispensability of the state. Some of the state's functions are these: the regulatory control of the physical environment; encouraging the arts and research of all kinds since the arts and research can get lost within the narrow needs of the market place; ensuring adequate health care for all; drafting individuals when necessary into military or other public service roles; sustaining literacy and educative standards; providing for the handicapped; dismantling monopolies that impede a healthy economy; protecting against monopolies of information; dealing with multinational corporations; dismantling caste and elitist structures that may develop; chastening racist, sexist, or classist power structures; controlling energy use and development; issuing money; taxation; police protection; establishing and supporting courts; husbanding resources; directing disaster aid in a systematic way; traffic control; enforcing contracts; relating to foreign nations; managing trade patterns and international finance; issuing patents and copyrights; negotiating with other nations on space and sea rights; et cetera. I have said that some of these functions can be and are assumed by private agencies, and I also concur with attorney Jethro Lieberman's comment that "the boundary between private and public can never be marked with manicured shrubs."[15] But to say that the state is an optional extra or that we could choose a state of nature and do without

the state is silly. Also, there is an incremental quality to the need for
a state. We need it now more than ever and will need it more in the
future. Our political sociality is growing. The expression of social-distributive justice is extending. In pre-industrial times, for example, the
use of one's land rarely caused harm to others and so there was a
minimal need to limit the use of one's property to avoid injury to others. Now the use of one's property might be lethal for present and
future generations and a new and inexorable need for regulation exists
in the modern state.

Increased state involvement has been the natural and inevitable result of industrialism. As Robert Heilbroner and other economists have
pointed out, government has become more and more involved in the
economic sphere in modern times simply to preserve that sphere. Government is involved in the unavoidable work of regulation in the area
of ecology, environmental impact, and pricing. Corporations are in a
sense creatures of the state, formed under state charters, governed by
state laws and tax policy, and often working on government contracts.
As Richard de Lone says: "The conceptual paradigm in which public
and private spheres are separated has crumbled."[16] No force but the
state could work toward full employment, bring about a national policy
whereby firms would be required to invest a certain percentage of their
investment capital in labor-intensive urban areas, provide for the job-
less, or enforce affirmative action. Other possibilities of even greater
government involvement in the economy are being experimented with
in other countries such as Japan. It was felt in 1973 that energy-poor
Japan would be devastated economically by the surge in OPEC prices.
Such has not been the case. Instead a new kind of "corporate state"
has been developing, involving a new and more intimate mode of collaboration by management, labor, and government. Koji Taira foresees
a time when "negotiations among national-level interest groups, with
the government's participation, may replace market forces and pluralistic (that is, free and decentralized) collective bargaining."[17] It clearly
would be more difficult in individualistic America to achieve more fruitful realizations of cooperation among management, labor, and
government.

All of the needs in my long but not exhaustive list of governmental
chores could be classed as "pragmatic." This requires a word of explanation lest it give aid and support to the individualistic idea of the state
as an incidental device. Clearly the state does have pragmatic value.
However, we can distinguish between pragmatic luxuries and pragmatic necessities. In other words, contractarian theories of state assume

that if we could find a way around it we could do without the state. That, of course, is about as realistic as saying that is we did not need to reproduce we could do without sex—missing the point that we do need and want to reproduce and that sex does a lot more in the world of persons than make babies. Similarly the state is not just a clever device to meet some needs that we happened to run into and might choose to ignore. Persons are self-transcending animals. They cannot pasture like contented cattle amid the actual; they are explorers of the possible. They are freighted with "divine discontent," which can sense the "not yet" beyond every achievement, the possible beyond the given. This self-transcending process of personal life would be frustrated and stunted if it were ripped from the enabling context of the *polis*. Thus the *polis* is a natural, not a contrived, need.

Politics, like technology, makes for a lot of messes. Abuse, however, does not invalidate use. Politics and technology can be abused. The "use" of politics, however, is natural to persons. Rejecting its naturalness and indigenous human status is a wild form of narcissistic imagination.

There are public and private needs that only government can meet. Without the empowering context of political community, atrophy would replace growth in the expansion of human potential. As A. D. Lindsay says in his *The Essentials of Democracy*, the state is the "hinderer of hindrances." The purpose of all its powers "is the setting free of the spontaneity which is inherent in the life of society."[18] The state, from this perspective, is as natural as is the setting free of our human possibilities, since these would not be set free without the state.

The second natural need met by the state is to provide persons with a medium for self-definition. By the nature of things, the state is not just a functional apparatus. It is also a system of symbols through which the members of the society interpret their meaning and destiny. Much is missed if a nation is seen only as a pragmatic agency. A nation also becomes a culture, a socially endorsed interpretation of reality equipped with an enshrined orthodoxy about what the good life entails. For this reason nationhood is always heavy with myth, symbol, and ritual. Patriotism is never a merely utilitarian emotion. If it were it could never inspire, as it does, supreme loyalty. A nation, in other words, is a creedal as well as a practical reality.

This mysterious but quite essential function of political community is illustrated by a thirteenth-century conversation between the Mongol leader Kuyuk Khan and Pope Innocent IV. Mongol expansion was threatening the Christian West. So the Pope sent a message to the

Mongol court not only protesting the massacres in Eastern Europe but also requesting that the Mongols receive baptism and submit to papal authority. Kuyuk Khan was bewildered. "This your request, we do not understand it," he wrote back to the Pope. He could not, of course, understand it. Contradictory interpretations of reality were here contending. The military successes of the Mongols confirmed them in their assessment of things. It was "by the virtue of God" that "all realms" had been granted to them. The Pope should submit to them, and if he did not, he would be guilty of not observing "the Order of God."[19] Clearly there was more afoot here than military control. Each party was demanding that the other be baptized into another worldview.

The heavily religious dressing of this exchange might make it seem an irrelevant period piece. However, as political philosopher Eric Voegelin observes, "The Communist movement is a representative of . . . truth in the same sense in which a Mongol Khan was the representative of the truth contained in the Order of God."[20] Similarly, the United States in its collision with Communism is concerned about more than markets and hard-nosed power politics. Each side wants to bury the other in the baptismal waters of conflicting creeds. Kuyuk Khan would have had no trouble understanding the rationale of the erstwhile House Un-American Activities Committee. The protection of orthodoxy was the issue and un-Mongol thoughts and activities would have been as sacrilegious to Kuyuk Khan as un-American leanings were to the priests of American orthodoxy. Contemporary clashes in Northern Ireland and the Near East could never be understood in purely legalistic or pragmatic terms. Visions of reality and even cosmologies are contending. Divergent views of meaning are vying. The separatist tensions in Canada also represent interpretational differences as much as tribal pride and the narrowness of vested interest.[21]

Obviously, all of this is dangerous. My point, however, is that, dangerous or not, it is the way we are and it is the way we *know*. Making sense of things is a political as well as private process. If we err by using the nation (or an international movement such as Communism) not as a heuristic vehicle of interpretation but as the definitive embodiment of truth, we slip into worship of the state (statolatry) and totalitarianism. If the process ceases to be self-transcending and does not point us toward a single global nation rich in diversity, then we will join the Khan and the Pope in falsely absolutizing partial visions of the real. But even if we achieve the ideal of a single planetary "nation," the knowing process will not lose its political dimension. We will still need to know ourselves through the political medium. Political community will still be a heuristic instrument of ongoing interpretation, given the sociality of our knowing processes.

In conclusion, then, social-distributive justice is based upon the fact that a person is a sharing animal. Sharing is as natural to this animal as are water and warmth to a tomato plant. This, however, isn't just an apolitical piety. It is rather the supreme political fact, the fact that makes us the "political animal." We must share politically and not just interpersonally. To some degree sharing must be public and structured as well as private and spontaneous. Societalizing (an admittedly clumsy word) or polis-making (clumsier yet) is nature's rule for the successful unfolding of human life. Human life becomes better and more human as the public and private sharing patterns do more and more justice to persons. Greedy monopolies obstruct sharing and are thus malignancies on the body social. Social-distributive justice attacks these malignancies. Thomas Aquinas came up with the conclusion that "justice consists in sharing."[22] Where monopoly causes a bypass in the proper sharing patterns a systemic problem exists that calls for a systemic solution.

But what is proper sharing? Does everyone have to get an equal share? Must we share everything—our spouses, our children, our homes? Equal shares are not necessarily fair shares since not everyone has the same merit or the same need. Neither should everything be shared. Just sharing rules out only the deprivation of others through exploitative monopoly. Exploitation is the key. Exploitation is the treatment of persons in a way that denies them their minimal due. If I deny you living quarters in my home, under most circumstances I do you no injustice. (In an emergency, it may be unjust to so deny you.)

Social and distributive justice require sufficient sharing to meet what is minimally due to persons . . . their essential needs. Again, generically speaking, the minimal need for persons is for an ambience marked by respect and hope, the essential ingredients of human life. We can do without anything, we can even lose life itself in the context of respect. When there is no respect, even the slightest inconvenience is unbearable. Insult—the absence of respect—is the cause of all rebellion. The absence of hope is also fatal for persons. Only hope moves us. Even Sisyphus had to be hoping for something or he would have left that stone where he found it. So if we would render to each his/her own, we owe our contribution to a social matrix in which respect and hope exist for all. If the plutocratic, acquisitive bent of persons has elbowed certain groups of persons out of competition by disempowering and excluding them from a fair share of the action, social and distributive justice require restoration. Disempowerment is worse than deprivation since it strikes at respect and hope. The deprived can put up with a lot if they haven't been stripped of the wherewithal to succeed. But power is the sacred souce of both respect and hope. If society has exercised its perverse bent for building wealth upon exploitation, by blocking certain groups with built-in head winds and insurmountable barriers, those groups are radically deprived at the level of power, self-respect, and hope. The evil inflicted on them is worse than anything we can achieve at the one-to-one level because group action is more powerful and more pernicious. We are meaner together than we can be alone.

This kind of situation has another urgency built into it. Since the common good is the good in which all private good is set, we attack our own good when we do not pay our debts to the common good. If we exploit and disempower certain groups, depriving them of the essential ingredients of human life, we have blighted the common good in a way that is ultimately our own undoing. If we disempower and excommunicate some, we all lose what that group, empowered, might have contributed to the common good. Social injustice saws at the limb upon which we all sit.

CHAPTER 2

The Primacy of Justice in Moral Theology

The American nation would appear to be biblically obsessed. Bibles greet us in every motel room. The "Good Book" is center stage at every political inauguration and in every courtroom. Biblical allusions regularly garnish political rhetoric. The New Right which has showed itself a significant political force uses Bible and flag as twin symbols of the American way. And yet, apparently unbeknownst to its devotees, the Bible contains a theory of justice that is radically at odds with the American system. (Indeed, it offers a vision of the just society that is at odds with every extant and past national system.) The Bible envisions the fullest flourishing of human life in its effort to give a view of the truly just society. Americans would be well advised to know the book they so facilely brandish.

Even Christian theologians have neglected the elementary message of the Bible regarding justice. The full challenge and subversive force of the biblical vision has not been met or incorporated into Christian piety. We have preferred to talk of love and friendship, rather than of justice. This allowed for a privatistic piety that settles for interpersonal goodness in an unjust society. In the social and political order, talk of love and friendship can be a prescription for disaster. There justice is the closest one can get to friendship. Justice is incipient love, and in the political order it is the only form that love takes. Privatistic talk of love is at that level unavailing, naive, and ultra-conservative in effect. Ironically, love-talk in the social-political sphere provides an ideological veil for injustice and inures one to the needs of the poor for whom justice is life blood.

Decadent moral theology was Bible-shy. Had its treatments of justice and charity been biblically nourished, justice could not have been seen as minimalistic or at odds with love. In the Bible, justice and love are hyphenated in a way that is "good news to the poor" (Luke 4:18).

The bold claim of any Bible is to a God's-eye view of things. Revelation implies gifted knowledge with God perceived as the giver and with us as God's struggling students. So what is the Bible's view of God's justice? In addressing the biblical teaching on justice, I concur with Stephen Charles Mott that "there is a unified picture of justice which appears throughout the canon and in a great variety of literary forms."[1] Furthermore the picture of justice is presented as revelational, as essentially linked to the image of God. God is a lover of justice (Ps. 99:4) who finds delight in justice (Jer. 9:23). God's holiness is manifested in terms of God's justice (Isa. 5:16). Justice is the holiness with which God would want us to be holy. It is the sacrament of encounter with God since "the decision of justice belongs to God" (Deut. 1:17). This means that in doing justice we are the conduit of God's justice and thus become holy with God's holiness.[2]

As an exegetical tool, it can be useful to understand biblical justice by comparing it to the prevailing notions of justice in the United States.[3] This is an exercise in the hermeneutics of contrast. Schematically, American and biblical justice diverge in the following fashion.

The American	*The Biblical*
Avowedly impartial	Biased in favor of the poor
Abstract (blindfolded)	Earthy and sin conscious
Reactive	Preactive
Punitive	Benevolent
Individualistic	Social
Stressing merit	Stressing need
Private property rights	Redistributive empowerment
Egalitarian (arithmetic)	Uneven (geometric)
Conservative	Revolutionizing
National	Universalist
Minimalistic	Effusive
Seeks end of litigation	Seeks Shalom
Avowedly dispassionate	Candidly passionate
Machomasculine	Feminine

Certainly this schema calls for more exposition than this chapter allows. I will proceed suggestively, relying on the energetic genius of the reader to follow through.

The partiality of biblical justice for the poor is unequivocal. As Norman Snaith said, God "has a particular regard for the helpless ones of earth." The prime biblical root for justice (*tsedeq*) "has from the first a bias towards the poor and needy."[4] From the stirring song of Hannah (1 Sam. 2:8) to the Magnificat of Mary, God is raising the poor from the dust and the dungheap. To the destitute and the failures, the prisoners, dropouts and the "unsoaped" (in Dickens' term), the biblical God says: "Blessed are you!" To the rich, this God says: "Woe to you. It would be easier to get a camel through the eye of a needle than to get you to understand that justice which is to be the hallmark of the reign of God" (see Matt. 19:24; Luke 6:20–26).

In this biblical face-off between rich and poor, it is chastening to see who the rich are. Bible-wise, one need not be a Rockefeller to be rich. In a word, anyone who knows today that he or she will not want for breakfast a year from this day is rich by Bible standards. The rich are the secure. The target of the condemnations is broad.

American justice is mathematically balanced and blindfolded. For the prophets, as Snaith writes, justice is not found "blindfoldedly holding the scales in just equality."[5] The Bible's sin-conscious advice would be to remove the blindfold and see who is tampering with the scales. With the blindfold gone, it will be seen that they do not balance. Then justice reponds with holy anger in defense of the weak.

Biblical justice, eschewing scales and blindfolds, offers in their stead the symbol of a mighty mountain stream, roaring down a ravine with enormous power, taking with it all it touches (Amos 5:23). And what is the goal of this torrent of boundless divine energy? Quite simply it is *the utter elimination of poverty.* "There shall be no poor among you!" (Deut. 15:4). "The poverty of the poor is their ruin" (Prov. 10:15), and no such blight befits the flesh that is so beloved of God (Ps. 71:12–14).

Justice in the American style reacts to injustice. It is patchwork and punitive. Ministers and departments of justice are fearsome. Biblical justice is preemptive benevolence. The biblically just are friends to the poor. They seek out the cause of those whom they do not even know (Job 29:14, 16). If your brother is weak, go find him and "make him strong" (Lev. 25:35). The prime Hebrew word for justice (*sedaqah*) "is never used in scripture to speak of God's punishment for sin. It deals with God's positive actions in creating and preserving community, particularly on behalf of marginal members thereof."[6]

American justice could only reflect the spirit of individualism that is part and parcel of our national self-consciousness. The preeminence of "rights" and "merits" in American moral discourse puts the accent not on sharing, but on what I can claim and you cannot.[7]

Undergirding this is a strong and egoistic sense of the sacramentality of material and economic success. The philosophy of John Hay is quintessentially American: "That you have property is proof of industry and foresight on your part or your father's; that you have nothing is a judgment on your laziness and vices or on your improvidence. The world is a moral world; which it would not be if virtue and vice received the same reward."[8] Thus it was commonplace in American speech to conjoin "property and character" or "property and principle." This is as cruel as it is unbiblical, for unlike the Bible, it puts the burden of proof on the poor for their poverty and makes economic success the badge of divine good-pleasure. The Bible puts the burden on the shoulders of the economically secure for tolerating the arrangements that impoverish the disempowered. God's justice is not fixated on property rights and legal entitlements. It does not cut the pie up into equal pieces. In the process of redistribution, some fare less well than others. "He has filled the hungry with good things and has sent the rich away empty" (Lk 1:53). Need outranks juridical claim.

Nowhere is this seen more clearly than in the Jubilee Year laws (Lev. 25). The Jubilee year called for the forgiveness of debts and the return of properties legitimately bought from the now landless poor, because "there shall be no poor among you" (Deut. 15:4). This revolutionary system of redistribution is of growing significance to Christians studying justice today since there is evidence that Jesus' view of the Reign of God was notably conditioned by the prophetic understanding of the Jubilee Year.[9]

American justice is conservative. It dickers amid the given with a bias for the status quo. Biblical justice condemns any adulterous dalliance with the status quo while God is not yet all in all. It calls for a new heaven and new earth. The call to Christian discipleship is a summons to revolution. Indeed, the invitation to "take up your cross" may have originally been a Zealot recruiting slogan. "If you would follow us, you will risk the revolutionary's fate of crucifixion."[10] The cross was not a matter of private expiation but the natural lot of one who would assault the social structures of injustice. Jesus was the proof of this. He could have died in his bed if there were not political and economic consequences to his mission. Both "take up your cross" and "Thy Kingdom come" are expressions that house seditious sentiments.

American justice is minimalistic. It keeps a ledger where accounts are squared. It is tidy and tight, conceding *quid* for *quo*. It is distinct and distant from charity, compassion, and effusive love. Biblical justice is richly seasoned with mercy and full of grace. Here, justice and love are coordinates. "Sow for yourselves justice, reap the fruit of steadfast love" (Hos. 10:12. The dichotomy between justice and love is spurious. The two are naturally related. Justice goes before love, insisting on the minimal prerequisites for survival. But then it makes common cause with love upon discovering that surviving without some thriving is not surviving at all. "Justice without mercy is cruelty," said Thomas Aquinas in commenting on the Gospel of Matthew.[11] Biblical justice does not rest with saying: "To each his/her own." There is a wizened spirit in that esteemed axiom that does not meet the Bible's demands. If you would be holy as your God is holy, minimalism is a sacrilege.

There is no slight illogic in this. Small wonder it jars our rationalism. In our accustomed view, a person is decent if he or she meets the minimal demands of justice. Everything beyond that is supererogatory. The Bible disagrees. Justice leads into love, and together they issue into Shalom. The wounded man who deserves a bandage also deserves oil and wine and "any extra expense" (Luke 10:29–37). Both biblical justice and biblical love know that the destiny of life is ecstasy and peace, not the mere settlement of disputes or the stopping of bleeding. God's holiness and the worth of persons require that the least we begin with become more. The result of this will be the flourishing of life that is Shalom. Shalom is so much more than the absence of conflict. It involves both material and spiritual fulfillment, a full belly and a joyful heart. Only thriving is really surviving in this optimistic and biblical view. It is to this fulfillment that both justice and love are directed.[12]

American justice is purportedly dispassionate, marked by steely but fair rationality. In fact, it contains an anti-revolutionary bias. It is for this reason that the Berrigans go to jail, but most known figures in organized crime do not. Organized crime persons are even called upon for assistance by governmental agencies like the CIA and the FBI, according to recent testimony. The reason is this: the Berrigans challenge the system and its sacred assumptions, and so these pacifists go to jail. Organized crime accepts the system as it is and works its corrupt purposes in and around it. The latter is less offensive to American "justice."

The passions of the Bible are undisguised. The biblical writing on justice is heavy with emotive words. These do not exclude anger. Thomas Aquinas is attuned to scripture when he writes that anger is concerned with "the good of justice."[13] He cites Chrysostom to the effect that "whoever is not angry when there is cause for anger, sins."[14] Thomas' point is that a lack of anger in certain situations means a lack of willed commitment to the good of justice. Thomas also insists that

anger arises from threats to one's self.[15] Thus, we can argue, the virtue
of anger (for which Thomas aptly notes we do not have a name[16]) is
missing if we do not identify to the point of anger with those who are
threatened and deprived. The deficiency here is one in justice. If American whites do not share the anger of American blacks now as the
second civil rights movement in the nation's history is being blunted
by the Reagan administration, our sin is one of injustice. Dispassionate
justice is not an intelligible concept. Biblical justice is honestly and
wholesomely passionate.

Finally, American justice is machomasculine and biblical justice is
wholesomely feminine. I argue in Chapter Nine that,[17] while not all
men are machomasculine and not all women are integrally feminine,
there are discernible ways in which women are generally advantaged
and men are not. The four feminine advantages are these: (1) women
are less alienated from bodily existence and are thus less seducible by
abstractions; (2) the affective component of moral judgment is less su-
pressed in women; (3) women have historically had more opportunity
to "go to school" on children and thus to be more identified with the
moral rhythms of minimally corrupted human life; and (4) women enjoy the wisdom that accrues to the alienated. While not all men bear
the machomasculine blight, male socialization is stamped with it. Its
principal liabilities are these: (1) a proneness to violent modes of power;
(2) an anti-communitarian, hierarchical proclivity; (3) a disabling abstractionism; (4) a consequentialist bias that can sacrifice persons to
bottom line goals, and (5) a culturally devastating and widely manifested hatred of women.

To find the revelational light amid the darkness of scripture, I have
recently suggested four rules: (1) distinguish between the descriptive
and the prescriptive; (2) distinguish *ad hoc* judgments from those of
broader application; (3) distinguish leitmotifs from chance themes; (4)
in inevitable doubt, use the criteria of fruitfulness and coherence.[18]
Clearly, one could go to the darkness of scripture and find the machomasculine blight in ebullient bloom. But if we search out the biblical
light, it force is feminine.[19] Biblical justice is embodied. It speaks to the
pains of the flesh where there is poverty and landlessness, ridicule and
tears, monopolization of wealth and orphanhood. Biblical justice is of
the earth and earthy. Only a machomasculine man could have stood
in the ashes of Ben Tre in Vietnam and said: "We had to destroy this
village in order to save it." Womanly experience and biblical justice
would choke on such words. Both are closer to the flesh and the earth
in which all moral value ultimately resides.

The socialization of women does not proscribe affectivity. Thus they are spared the burdens of a castrated rationality such as machomas-culinity would impose upon men. Biblical justice is salted with tears making the tearless poor exegetes of its message. As for children, it is in the veins of our children that the gentle rhythms run that will save this earth of ours if saved it is to be. Children have a natural hunger for Shalom. Not surprisingly, children are given a normative role in scripture. The spirit of childhood is the passport into the reign of God (Mark 10:14). Our destiny is to become "children of God" (Rom. 8:17). Children are sacraments of encounter with God.

And finally, alienation lends light. Draw a circle and cut me out of it and I will become intensely aware of reality within that circle. Women are alienated and the Bible bids us view life through the eyes of the alienated if we would know the things that are of God.

The conclusion is that biblical justice is close to the feminine and far from the machomasculine. Since so many of the biblical authors were probably men, the femininity of the bible is not anti-masculine. Male and female, in the image of God, we were made. Salvation in-volves the blending of a healed masculine and a healed feminine into an ever enriching human likeness of God. At this moment in the pro-cess, however, the feminine experience, for reasons biological and his-torical, is hermeneutically well suited for the recovery of a biblical theology of justice.

The study of justice is disquieting, for justice is the least that we can do in response to the value of persons. To fail here is to fail in humanity and to merit the term barbaric. The conclusion of this is not flattering. Reinhold Niebuhr said that original sin is the one Christian dogma that is empirically verifiable. Original sin is manifested in so-cially ensconced and individually endorsed injustice. That we are mired in such injustice is empirically verifiable. Whole classes of persons are excluded from respect and hope. We care and dare little to alleviate that. Our confession of sin is in order.

Justice is the child of hope. To the hopeless addicts of the status quo, the desires of justice seem like madness. Yet it is the desires of justice that are the seeds of moral evolution. Much that we have achieved in the United States, for example, was once dismissed as hopelessly idealistic. The first abolitionists of slavery faced charges of idealism, as did and do the advocates of feminism. Getting children out of the work force, the five-day working week, paid vacations, social security, free education, aid to the handicapped—all were chided as unrealistic and infeasible. Yet hopeful justice dreamed its dreams and progress in all these areas has been made.

Jewish and Christian religions begot a remarkable and share-able vision. They pictured humankind as called by God to love justice, and to do it, and to walk humbly and joyfully toward the reign of peace. We have scarcely begun on this journey into Shalom. But directing this journey by the path of justice is the precise and foundational calling of moral theology.

CHAPTER 3

Ending the White Male Monopolies

With all the horror that greets talk of quotas, one would scarcely guess that the United States has operated on a rigid quota system for 200 years. That quota system insisted on—and got—a 90% to 100% monopoly for white males in all the principal centers of power in government, business, the professions, and in the competition for desirable jobs at every level in church and state. From board room to pulpit, from the controllers of wealth to the writers of history, power has remained white and masculine.

Now, however, blacks, women, and other disempowered groups are at the gates begging enfranchisement in the distributive systems, and indignation against quotas or any real change in the system is ablaze in the white male aristocracy. There was a meanness in the air in the elections of the 1980's that bodes ill for affirmative action or any real effort to dislodge the white male monopolies. The Reagan elections tolled the knell of the second short civil rights movement in the history of the country. Those elections provided a referendum on social and distributive justice, and the answer was negative. A champion of white male monopoly was twice elected president. The message was clear. This language may seem too strong—even strident—but the facts cry aloud. As of January 1986, black unemployment had gone from twice that of whites to almost three times that of whites—in just five years! This is bad news for all groups who are newly aware of their outsider status.

Women are the majority group in the nation and, although they do not vote as a bloc, their spirit is rising and women's causes are of increasing political might. Blacks are an increasingly strong political minority. By 1994, one out of every five 18-year-olds will be non-white. This figure, composed largely of Afro-Americans, does not include large numbers of disempowered Hispanics who are not persons of color.

Yet, in spite of these considerations, affirmative action still is in peril. Corporations are going to court to fight affirmative action. In the wake of the *United Steelworkers v. Weber* case, a bill has been introduced into the Senate to amend Title VII of the 1964 Civil Rights Act. Much in the new administration is targeted against affirmative action. *Non-discrimination* is the new rubric. "We're all against discrimination. Let's do away with it. But affirmative action is reverse discrimination for all its noble intentions. It discriminatorily prefers some folks just because they are black or female and counts it against others that they are not. So let's stop that, but get really serious about ending discrimination in any form, and let's prosecute any instance of discrimination we may find." That has an attractive ring to it. After all, who but the hate-filled fringes of society could be against it? The problem is that such an approach is an endorsement of the *status quo* and an obstacle to any serious approach to social justice. Yet, "non-discrimination" is already the password of the well-advanced retrenchment on civil rights.

How could something so noble-sounding as non-discrimination be so subversive of civil rights? The answer is that non-discrimination focuses on one-to-one violations of civil rights and leaves the controlling systemic discrimination absolutely intact. Let me illustrate this concretely.

It has been shown that, in some companies, as many as 80% of the employees got their jobs through word-of-mouth communication about job openings from other employees; employees carry the word of prospective job openings to their local bars and meeting places. If, however, these employees are white and are returning to white neighborhoods, the information network does not reach the nearby ghetto or barrio. When qualified or qualifiable persons are brought in from ghetto and barrio by enforced affirmative action, the "old buddy" network is thereby enlarged and future openings will reach those previously unreached, and eventually affirmative action will not be necessary. Word of job openings will be carried to black bars and other meeting places and to Puerto Rican bars and meeting places. The system will have been changed in the only way it could be—by enforced preferential relief (*i.e.*, by affirmative action).

A policy of mere non-discrimination, however zealously enforced, would leave the white "old buddy system" completely intact. No overt instances of discrimination might be found. The old system would be working smoothly and successfully and those excluded from the network would not know about the jobs and thus will not be within reach of either hiring or discrimination. The employers could say in all candor that they were not conscious of any acts of discrimination, that they did their hiring among the various candidates without consideration of racial factors. There would, however, be discrimination going on—systemic discrimination that can only be cured by systemic reform. To say we can have genuine non-discrimination without affirmative action is like saying to a waterless town that we will prosecute those who take your water away, but we will not build conduits to bring you the water. To change the image, discrimination occurs at the table where the pie is being cut. Those who don't get near the table will not be helped if we ban discrimination at the table. It is the arrangements that keep them from the table that are at issue. Affirmative action addresses those arrangements.

Self-confidence vs. Inferiority

Non-discrimination is shallow in another way. It is sociologically naive to suggest that one-to-one monitoring will ever affect the evil that holds disempowered groups in its grasp. For example, studies have shown that black children, at least by age eight, receive the message from the dominant white society that they are inferior. White society, after all, is impressive. These are the people who fly to the moon and fill all the major positions of prestige and power in the nation. When black children come to perceive that this overwhelming dominant power thinks them to be inferior, the very center of self-confidence in the children is raped and wounded. Their inner map of expectations is shrunken. This tragic devastation will not be undone by superficial attention to discrimination on a one-to-one basis. This would leave the insulting structures and patterns intact, delivering their demeaning message uninterruptedly to young black minds. What is needed is enforced opportunity so that black talent becomes visibly present in all the offices and stations of the land. No child, black or white, can maintain self-respect or hope without successful role models. Black children can not think well of themselves in a world where their race is massively excluded from the most esteemed positions of the society. These precious little citizens can only gain hope if the monopolistic patterns of our society are changed. It is to that end that affirmative action works. The music of "non-discrimination" brings little solace to the broken spirit of a child.

There is, however, also an internal, administrative threat to affirmative action which works insidiously against the very structures of the program. Affirmative action was initially conceived with the plight of blacks in mind. Affirmative action is a form of aid by way of preferential treatment. No one wanted to be in the same boat with blacks until there was a whiff of preference in the air. Now, the boat is sinking under the weight of their fellow travelers. What is happening is that affirmative action is being undone by the very agencies of government assigned to enforce it—and all of this in the fair name of "equality."

The primeval purpose of affirmative action was to give preference to disempowered groups that can not be helped by the mere enforcement of non-discrimination on a case-by-case basis. Realistically, there are five—and only five—groups so systemically disempowered as to merit preferential relief: first and foremost, blacks; then women, American Indians, Mexican Americans, and Puerto Ricans. This does not mean that other groups need no special help. The handicapped and other groups do need assistance and, indeed, the needs of the handicapped should be given special attention. Inducements to hire the handicapped are needed, but, because of the differences even in the definition of "handicap," the problem of the handicapped would be best handled outside the quota system of affirmative action.

What the Federal agencies have done, in a glut of egalitarianism, is to list indiscriminately all Hispanics without noting the utterly disparate conditions of different Hispanic groups. They list all Americans of Chinese, Japanese, Korean, Aleut, and Philippine descent, along with anyone who has roots in "the Far East" or "Subcontinent India." Recent monitoring by Federal grants officers even adds "Vietnam era veterans" and, without specification, "various religious/ethnic groups." When all are preferred—and that is the absurd thrust of current policy—none is preferred. We are, after all, a nation of minorities and there is no minority that could not allege discrimination of some sort.

What are desperately needed and wholly lacking in the Federal enforcement of preferential affirmative action are criteria for eligibility. I submit that, for a group to qualify for enforced, temporary preferential aid, it must be established that a) no alternatives to enforced preference are available (voluntary measures and enforced non-discrimination must have been proven inadequate), b) the prejudice against the group must reach the level of depersonalization and c) must be entrenched in the distributive systems of the society, and d) the members of the group must be visible and identifiable as such.

Groups that meet this criteria face a patterned, systemic mode of discrimination that will defeat the best efforts of those groups. I concede, again, that other groups do meet with discrimination and appropriate measures should be brought to bear on their problems. Oriental Americans, Jews, Roman Catholics, gay persons, and new immigrants suffer different kinds of discrimination, but not of the sort, under the criteria I have suggested, that merit preferential relief. Blacks, American Indians, women, Puerto Ricans, and Mexican Americans do meet the criteria. Their plight is one of radical disempowerment requiring systemic change.

What is difficult for the egalitarian American to realize is that some groups may be worse off than others. I may be accused of introducing inequalities into the situation of the various victim groups, but it is not I who introduce them—they are there. The most salient inequality, and the one apparently most unpalatable to white Americans, is the unequally bad situation of blacks. Blacks, as a group, are worse off in this society than other groups. There is already evidence that employers would rather meet affirmative action quotas with white women than with blacks. As the list of those groups who can be counted as affirmative action achievements grows, it is easier for employers to revert to the ingrained penchant of American whites not to hire blacks—while still meeting their legal affirmative action requirements. Unless the needs of blacks which inspired affirmative action in the first place are seen as primary, other disempowered groups will move upstairs and blacks once again will watch progress from the cellar. Not to recognize the unequal and differing needs of groups would also blind us to the fact that some groups will cease to need affirmative action before others. Separate judgments will have to be made about whether a particular group has been sufficiently enfranchised within the system to survive in an equitable way without preference. Some will arrive before others.

Needless to say, the arguments against this necessary redistribution are out in force. When has a privileged group ever surrendered its privileges voluntarily! It is not just white males who offer these arguments. History shows that identification with the oppressor's interests is a common way for the victim to cope.

Arguments Against Affirmative Action

The first line of defense against affirmative action is the merit system. The implication is that meritocratic ideals have reigned up until now and we must not pervert them by preferring some persons on irrelevant grounds such as sex or race. There is no slight arrogance in this argument. By implying that merit has been the prevailing norm, it is averred that we always operated with some kind of a litmus test whereby we knew who was the best applicant to be bus driver, mail-person, corporate executive, college student, professor, president, and judge. Of course, there never was a litmus test. Subjectivity, prejudice, and connections always counted, but do not miss the implication of the new stress on merit. It says that, since merit is the norm and since white males dominate all the major centers of power, they must deserve to!

It is also charged that affirmative action is "reverse discrimination." In point of fact, it is the reversal of existing discrimination so as to end the long-tenured white male monopolies. The program will not, and indeed could not, do to whites what whites have done to blacks. It will not put whites into a position where blacks are now, with a maternal death rate triple that of whites, an infant death rate twice that of whites, and teenage unemployment triple that of whites. Neither will the program stigmatize or insult whites and their children, making many of them ashamed of the texture of their hair and the specific beauty of their bodies. It will also not confine whites to ghettos where there are more rats than people and no hope. Affirmative action is not "reverse discrimination."

To say that breaking up the white male monopolies is discrimination against the monopolizers is both illogical and hypocritical. It is true that some white males will have to sacrifice in this process of just redistribution, but sacrifice is the price of justice in the social order. Social justice may in times of war require sacrifice, even to the point of death. Affirmative action, fortunately, does not require that, but the sacrifice that it does require is a matter of justice, not of discrimination.

Some, such as Midge Decter (*The New York Times*, July 6, 1980), fret lest blacks and women, as recipients of preferential treatment, suffer "permanent and unrecoverable decline in self respect." She thinks that the reception of "unearned advantages" could lead to a "lack of a sense of self worth." It is not easy to treat such an objection seriously. At any rate, the case histories of white males, so long awash in preference, would indicate that they have come out of this long time of preference with their "sense of self worth" ebulliently intact. There is reason to hope that blacks and women will bear their temporary preference with at least equal aplomb.

However fatuous and self-serving the arguments against it, the affirmative action program of redistributive justice is in peril. Civil rights movements in this nation have short and choppy histories. If the first civil rights movement definitively ended with *Plessy v. Ferguson* in 1896, the second may have ended on Nov. 4, 1980, with the election of Ronald Reagan. Superficial analyses of that election point to Jimmy Carter's failure as a debater or to the "mudslinging" he engaged in when he quoted Reagan accurately. A deeper and more accurate analysis may be found in two books from Howard University Press: *The Changing Mood in America: Eroding Commitment?*, by Faustine Childress Jones (1977), and *Meanness Mania: The Changed Mood*, by Gerald R. Gill (1980). Their titles tell the story and it is ominous for blacks.

What is mandatory at this time is a new civil rights coalition to protect achievements such as affirmative action. The Democratic Party should know after recent elections where their most loyal support is found and respond accordingly. Christian churches, with all their current interest in liberation theology from Latin America, should see the literally lethal lower-castle status of blacks in this country as their prime liberation agenda item. The Catholic Church, of which I am a member, has never shown consistent or passionate interest in the black plight. This overwhelmingly white church should put its justice-talk into practice and turn its power and preaching for the first time in an effective way toward and protection of civil rights. Jewish support for civil rights, so distinguished in the past, must return with full fervor. After all, as Prof. Faustine Jones points out, the creation and support of the state of Israel was an affirmative action by the international community to relieve the suffering of a group of people. Humanitarians of any stripe should know that this is not the time for retrenchment. If a love of justice does not motivate, prudence, at least, should recognize that the dispossessed and disempowered among us are impatient and may not for long be peaceably contained.

Part 2

WAR AND PEACE

It is a fact of life that the habitual comes to seem good. War is habitual in the human species and we therefore allot it an undue sense of normalcy. War, however, is not the extension of politics into arms; war is the collapse of politics into slaughter. It becomes increasingly difficult in the modern age to justify any war, given the alternatives to war and given the foreseeable effects of warring in this age. What is needed is an entirely new look at our self-destructive penchant for warring. Chapter Four looks at the historical attitudes toward war and peace in the Western world. It looks to the Judaeo-Christian influences on our cultural acceptance of war. Chapter Five analyses the negative effects of options for violence. Chapter Six, looks specifically at the violence of anti-Semitism.

CHAPTER 4

War, Peace, and the Christian Conscience

Peace is one of the crowning leitmotifs of the Hebrew/Christian Bible. Peace was central to the teaching of the Hebrew prophets. The vision of what life would be when God achieved his blessed rule over our belligerent world was a vision of *shalom*, of peace. All manifestations of violence and hostility would dissolve in the peace that must come about. "They will do no hurt, no harm, on all my holy mountain" (Isa. 11:9). The lion will lie down with the lamb. "Nation will not lift sword against nation, there will be no more training for war" (Isa. 2:4). They will "hammer their words into ploughshares, their spears into sickles" (Isa. 2:4). Even the text from Joel, "Hammer your ploughshares into swords, your sickles into spears" (Joel 4:10), is spoken in irony to the nations who will not head the call of God to peace. They will, as a result, founder in war. The consistent message is that peace is God's way, and when God gets his way there will be peace. The goal and essence of the "reign of God" is a "peace that has no end" (Isa. 9:7).

The early Christians had no doubt at all about how to interpret the Bible in this regard. God is called the "God of peace" (Heb. 13:20). They used the word "peace" to greet one another and it was also their favored word in epitaphs. To say that persons had died "in peace" (*in pace*) was to say that in life they had realized what Christianity meant. It was the supreme compliment of the Christian community to a departed son or daughter.

For almost three hundred years after the death of Jesus, Christian writers were unanimously pacifistic when the topic of war and violence arose. Origen repeated the established teaching of early Christianity when he warned Christians lest "for warfare, or for the vindication of

our rights, or for any occasion, we should take out the sword, for no
such occasion is allowed by this evangelical teaching."[1] Hippolytus was
a Roman churchman who drew up a list of the rules of discipline for
Christians. Two of them concerned the question of military service.
One said that a man could not be baptized as a Christian if he were
in the army, and the other said that a candidate for Christianity who
displayed military ambitions must be rejected because this "is far from
the Lord."[2] Lactantius spoke the universal language of early Christianity when he said that killing is forbidden in such a way that "in this
commandment of God, no exception at all ought to be made, that it is
always wrong to kill a person whom God has wished to be regarded
as a sacrosanct creature."[3] Lactantius also insisted that when God forbade killing, he didn't just forbid unjust killing by brigands, but also
the kind of killing that is considered legal by most people.[4] Minucius
Felix said that Christians had such a horror of bloodshed that they
could not even bear to eat rare meat, lest they be offended by the sight
of blood. Not only could Christians not kill, he said, but "it is not right
for us either to see or hear a person being killed."[5]

In the third century, a non-Christian philosopher, Celsus, noting
that all Christians were pacifists, worried about the future of the Roman
empire if conversions to Christianity continued to increase. If everyone
were like the Christians, he said, the empire "would be left in utter
solitude and desertion and the forces of the empire would fall into the
hands of the wildest and most lawless barbarians."[6] Origen, a Christian, undertook to answer Celsus's objection by saying that if all persons in the world became Christian you would need no army, because
the spread of Christianity means the spread of peace. Also, he urged,
if it was only all of Rome that became Christian, God would protect
them, and so Celsus was not to worry.[7] Celsus's response to this is
not recorded, but the significant point is that Origen did not deny the
charge that Christians would not be soldiers. He conceded Celsus's
point that all Christians were pacifists. Strong church laws against sol-
diering and bloodshed continued in various parts of the Christian
church into the fifth century.

Early Christian pacifism was able to flourish under the protection
of the *Pax* Romana. When that peace began to crumble, Christians began to accommodate. Starting around the year 170, Christians began
to appear in the army, especially where the "barbarians" were attack-
ing. But it was in the year 312, with the victory of Constantine at the
Milvian Bridge, under the alleged auspices of Jesus, that Christians
began their epochal turn to a new morality of war and peace. As their

social status changed suddenly from persecution to preferment, a new world came into being. Imperial favor was a heady wine, and peaceful idealism staggered and began to collapse. The befriending sword need not be beaten into a plowshare. Christians crept out of the catacombs and were dazzled and beguiled by the state that had turned benevolent. Theology responded by interpreting the new events in terms of blessedness, and the peace mission of the Christians waned. The Christian Eusebius was beside himself with joy at the idea of a Christian emperor. "The God of all, the supreme governor of the whole universe by His own will appointed Constantine."[8] The Christian Lactantius rejoiced that divine power could have appointed so superior a person "as its agent and minister."[9] Constantine agreed. He said that he felt called "to lead the nations to the service of the holiest law and to spread the most blessed faith."[10] He avowed publicly to Jesus: "I love your name and honor your power." And he promised to do battle against Jesus' enemies.[11] He was as good as his word. As we read in Eusebius: "He subdues and chastens the adversaries of the truth according to the usages of war."[12]

Jesus had come full circle—from Prince of Peace to Lord of War. Jesus, as war lord, was also active on the eastern front. A fourth-century bishop of Nisibis reports that in response to prayer, the Lord routed the Persians by sending a cloud of mosquitoes and gnats to tickle the trunks of the enemy's elephants and the nostrils of his horses.[13] (Clearly, Jesus had not only waxed tough, but versatile.) The Christian abhorrence and avoidance of military service so changed that by the year 416 you had to be a Christian to serve in the Roman army.[14]

Theology, in the persons of such figures as Augustine and Ambrose, accommodated by baptizing the just-war theory of Plato and Cicero. The Augustine accommodation, however, was not complete. Augustine, while allowing war under the aegis of the state, taught that it was wrong for a Christian to kill in his own self-defense.[15] He also harkened back to the earlier Christian pacifism, praising those Christians who died as martyrs rather than fight for their lives. Had they fought, he said, they would have been so numerous that nothing could have resisted them. Instead, they followed the example of Jesus who chose nonresistance and death.[16] Still, Augustine yielded, and allowed that wars could be fought, though, he insisted, this should be done in a mournful mood. He concluded reluctantly, and with an attitude more reminiscent of the library than of the battlefield: "Love does not exclude wars of mercy waged by the good."[17] As an enduring gesture to peace, the clergy who handled the sacraments of peace were forbidden to fight. And all the way to the eleventh century, soldiers who killed, even in a supposedly just war, had to perform rigorous penances. The accommodation to war was not without tension.

This tension, however, was all but lost in the barbarian invasion. These Christians were now gripped by a lust for battle. Their God was a God of war; their saints and heroes were warriors. The barbarians admired the empire that they overran, and also found the Christian faith of that empire attractive. They converted in droves. The waters of baptism, however, did not wash away their zest for battle. St. Michael, with his sword, replaced Wotan, their former god of war, as the patron of battle. In their liturgy they praised St. Peter, who used his sword to strike at the offending Roman. (They didn't bother to record Jesus' rebuke to Peter.) These newly converted Christians infused a mighty dose of violence into the already shaken cultural and moral atmosphere of the collapsing empire. Violence began to rage like a consuming libido.

The just-war theory became an irrelevant abstraction. Battles were fought on any pretext. It is recorded that a lord declared war on the city of Frankfurt because a lady of that city had refused to dance with his uncle. Elsewhere a cook, together with his scullions and dairymaids, issued a challenge of war to the Count of Salms. Even the clergy and the religious were gripped by the fever. The Archbishop of Mainz, on one occasion, sallied forth into battle and killed nine men with a club, rather than with a sword. With clerical nicety, he explained that he had chosen the club because the Christian faith abhors the shedding of blood. In a similarly hedged spirit, St. Gerald of Aurilliac went out to fight, but always with sword and spear turned backward so as to merely clobber the enemy without killing him. By a marvel of Providence, St. Gerald always won. In the midst of all this carnage, there appears St. Edmund, who went out and faced the Vikings alone and unarmed, and was slaughtered, standing for a Christ figure absorbing violence.[18]

In a vain effort to stem the violence, the Truce of God was instituted. Starting in the tenth century at the initiative of local biships, the truce banned all fighting (under pain of excommunication) for several months around the feast of Easter, for the four weeks before Christmas, and on all Fridays, Sundays, and holy days. Church properties and the clergy were always to be exempt from violence, as were peasants and pilgrims, agricultural animals, and olive trees. From age twelve on, everyone was bound to take an oath to obey the truce and, with revealing irony, to take up arms against those who would not conform.[19]

One of these oaths comes down to us from the tenth century, in a form taken by a gentleman who merited the name Robert the Pious. Its cagey wording tells much of the state of things. "I will not burn houses or destroy them, unless there is a knight inside. I will not root up vines. I will not attack noble ladies nor maids nor widows or nuns, unless it is their fault. From the beginning of Lent to the end of Easter I will not attack an unarmed Knight."[20] Stanley Windass's remark comes to mind concerning the Truce of God: "The disease was too radical to respond to such first aid."[21]

What happened next was that the violence, which could not be contained, was, in effect, diverted into the Crusades. At the end of the eleventh century, the Crusades received formal blessing at the Council of Clermont. Their purpose: to reunite Christendom and establish Jerusalem as the center of Christian holiness. The sword had now been given first place in establishing the kingdom of God. The fury of these wars shows the danger of religious motivation for violence and recalls the dreadful dictum of John Calvin: "No heed is to be paid to humanity when the honor of God is at stake."[22] One report of the capturing of Jerusalem will convey the flavor of this sorry chapter in the medieval Christian consecration of violence.

Some of our men (and this was more merciful) cut off the heads of their enemies; others tortured them longer by casting them into the flames. Piles of heads, hands and feet were to be seen in the streets of the city. . . . In the temple and portico of Solomon, men rode in blood up to their knees and the bridle reins. . . . This day, I say, marks the justification of all Christianity and the humiliation of paganism.[23]

A cargo of noses and thumbs sliced from the Saracens was sent back to the Greek emperor, in gory witness of the crusading zeal.[24]

Heresy, too, was fought with the sword as Christian warriors struck at the Cathari in southern France. Since there was a problem distinguishing the Cathari from the true believers, the instruction given was: "Kill them all; God will know which are his."[25]

Strains of the earlier pacifism reappeared eventually in various Christian groups—the Anabaptists, the Quakers, and the Franciscan Tertiaries. The Quakers represented the most effective reaction. They resisted the Augustinian tendency to leave to the state the decision on the justness of a war, and won from the English state exemption from conscription on conscientious grounds in 1802.

This, in capsule form, is what historical Christianity says on the issue of war and peace. It is, to say the least, a mixed bag. Clearly, the closer you get to the origins of Christianity, the more pacifistic and peace-centered it is. Of course, this was a luxury that could be indulged because of the Pax Romana which rested upon the military might of Rome. Accommodation did occur as that might diminished. The accommodation descended into a consecration of violence during the crusading period, as religious orders such as the Knights Templar were founded to go out and slay infidels in the name of Jesus Christ.

What is the bottom line on all of this? At the very least it seems that there is a strong concern for peace in the Christian message, and in the Hebrew scriptures on which Christianity was bred and nourished. *To be faithful in any way to the Christian tradition means having a bias for peace.* It means putting the burden of proof on the warrior, and not on the conscientious objector. The Crusader, with his bias for war, is a heretic to the Christian vision and to the Christian "God of Peace." Some Christians today opt to go back to the pacifism of the early Church. It would be rather "hard line" to argue that every Christian must take that stance. Those Christians could scarcely be considered beyond the pale who, while maintaining their commitment to peace, allow for the mournful possibility of some violence in self-defense, when all peaceful alternatives have been exhausted. But a lesser commitment than this to peace could not be, in any meaningful sense, of the word, Christian.

War and the New Right

What then of the new Christian right? Clearly, they would not be at home in the early Church, where all war was considered incompatible with the vision of the Prince of Peace. Neither would they be comfortable with Augustine's theory of justifiable war. Augustine would still not permit killing in self-defense in a private setting. He would have opposed any gun lobby defending the right to bear arms. But the New Right is for a strong, well-armed and offensive defense at home and abroad, and are staunch defenders of the constitutional right of citizens to bear arms. They clearly are closest to the Crusaders. They do not have a horror of war; in fact they give it a sacred place in their assessment of God's plans. Theirs is the big-bang theory of the return of Jesus. War in Hal Lindsey's popular book *The Late Great Planet Earth* is written into the scenario. It has a sacral role. This is the most frightening part of the New Right's religious faith.

In *The Fundamentalist Phenomenon*, coauthored by Jerry Falwell and two of his Liberty Baptist College professors, the following pompously phrased, but important statement is made: "No correct evaluation of Fundamentalism can properly be made without a proper assessment of the development and impact of dispensationalism upon the eschatology of the Evangelical Movement at the turn of the century."[26] Behind this language we can discern that what Falwell and his coauthors see as basic to fundamentalism is the following sort of biblical interpretation, which represents the philosophy of history that undergirds the New Right. It is called "dispensationalism" because it divides history into sections—dispensations—climaxing in the return and the millennial reign of Christ. Through an imaginative reading of Daniel 9 concerning the "seventy weeks," history is divided up nicely. The seventy weeks are made to be seventy "sevens" of years—totaling 490 years. Four hundred and eighty-three of these years refer literally to the period from the rebuilding of Jerusalem as recorded in Ezra and Nehemiah to the time of Jesus. After that, things do not follow in sequence. The coming of the final seven years is interrupted by the whole history of the Church. During this time-out, all kinds of things happen, many of them allegedly predicted in the Bible. Then the final seven years begins as a kind of countdown to the second coming of Christ, who will then reign for a thousand years. The final seven years is chock-full of presaged happenings. Indeed, so much is scheduled for that time that one wonders how God will get it all in. An anti-Christ will appear and be supported by apostate churches. The "Beast" of the book of Revelation will appear as a major political power. The Jews will return to Palestine, and some of them will be converted. The Jews will then go through a terrible "tribulation." But finally, as the seven years wind down, Jesus returns with a whole army of saints to defeat the hostile forces of the world powers—the Beast and the anti-Christ—in a place in the Near East known as Armageddon.[27]

Notice that in all of this, human agency is not important. Dramatic divine interventions are the marking posts of history, particularly in this "latter-day" war to end all wars. As a result of the preannounced divine plan for war as a cleansing tool of holy Providence, this "dispensationalist" tradition has always been excited about wars that look like they could be the big one, and has likewise been wary of the prospects of a world without war. So, when the Hague Conference did not produce great promises of peace before World War I, fundamentalist writers were quick to point out that this was not surprising to those who knew the scriptures. Readers of the prophets know that true peace must await the return of the Prince of Peace. Before this second coming, any kind of peace that ensues will be of a counterfeit sort. It will be but the lull before the inevitable and necessary storm.[28] " 'Peace and safety' is what the world and apostate Christendom wants to hear. . . . The outbreak of sudden judgment will someday bring the terrible awakening."[29]

World War I was seen as potentially good news. For these people the calamities of war are promising harbingers of the blessed and triumphant return of the Lord. This same spirit had been apparent during the Civil War, which was greeted by millennialist Bible readers as "the glory of the coming of the Lord." Their excitement was exemplified by the Reverend William Gaylord, preaching to a church packed with blue-coated Union soldiers ready to depart for the front. He spoke of the day when the war would end.

On! What a day that will be for our beloved land, when carried through a baptism of fire and blood, struggling through this birthnight of terror and darkness, it shall experience a resurrection to a new life, and to a future whose coming glory already gilds the mountain tops. The day of future glory is hastening on. That day of a truer and deeper loyalty to God and to country—that day when the oppressor's rod shall be broken, when the sigh of no captive spirit shall be heard throughout all our fair land . . . the day of the Lord is at hand.[30]

As Professor James Moorhead writes in his study of this period: "What makes the 1860s especially interesting is the sheer intensity and virtual unanimity of Northern conviction that the Union armies were hastening the day of the Lord."[31] Moorhead notes how mischievous these bizarre interpretations were: "These grandiose expectations, incapable of realization in any event, contributed to a simplistic assessment of national problems and were among the many roots of America's unpreparedness to deal responsibly with Reconstruction or the legacy of slavery, let alone the other strange and bewildering difficulties on the far side of Appomattox."[32]

The noxious results of this mentality are considerable. The millennial fever, in any of its forms, leads to "a simplistic assessment of national problems," as Moorhead said, and wreaks severe problems at the level of national response. These visions give an alien interpretation of national destiny and policy. They impose a supernatural grid, into which national and international events are squeezed willy-nilly. They bring the seductive allure of simplism and divine drama to human affairs. This tendency is alive and well in the New Right.

We see it in Moral Majority's Tim LaHaye, who claims access to a detailed accounting of all the events regarding the coming destruction of Israel by Russia, etc.[33] The tribulation is coming, he warns us.

LaHaye is also worried about false and counterfeit peace. Disarmament is a threat to him. He excoriates those who endorse homosexuality and the use of drugs, along with *"disarmament and everything else that is harmful to America."*[34] Obviously, disarmament is not helpful for advancing the day of the Lord—an event that essentially involves arms and slaughter—so it ends up in his list along with abuses such as drug addiction and that bugaboo of the right, homosexuality. Falwell has only scorn for the Strategic Arms Limitations Talks.[35] The "giveaway" of the Panama Canal treaty sticks painfully in his throat. The way we won it, the feelings of Latin America on the subject, and the relationship of all this to peace simply do not compute in his mind.[36] He bemoans the "no win" way in which we fought the war in Vietnam.[37] Clearly, there is no weapon in our arsenal that Falwell would have hesitated to use to assure victory. With stunning mental topsyturvyness, he describes our current rate of arms production—which he sees as too slow—as a form of "unilateral disarmament."[38] The pace of increase of arms is not fast enough for Falwell. He even berates "peaceful intentions" as "acts of stupidity."[39]

As with the Crusaders, Falwell's God is a warrior god. He cites the participation of God in the 1967 "miraculous six-day war."[40] He describes it with great awe. There were the armies of Egypt, Jordan, Syria, and Lebanon poised and ready at the borders of Israel. Waiting behind them were the armies of Iraq, Algeria, Kuwait, and Sudan. War broke out. Israel won, but deserves little credit for it. There was simply no way they could have won, General Falwell assures us, "had it not been for the intervention of God almighty."[41] Two points are again noteworthy here: the insignificance of human agency in human affairs, and enthusiasm for war as a sacramental medium. Humans are the pawns of God in His unfolding drama—which He was good enough to first predict in the Bible and then give the secret of interpretation to the pseudofundamentalists. The militaristic return of Jesus blesses war with a salvationist purpose. Again, the bias is *for* war, not against it. Here is the *Deus vult* (God wills it) of the Crusader, with millenial madness tossed in. Nothing remains of the bias for peace of the early Church.

Hal Lindsey carries this to the extent of a biblical prediction of final nuclear war. According to the apostle John, via Lindsey, every city in the world will be destroyed. One sees none of Augustine's mournful mood in the face of war when Lindsey excitedly predicts the final big bang, "Imagine, cities like London, Paris, Tokyo, New York, Los Angeles, Chicago—obliterated!"[42] According to Lindsey, the book of Revelation says that the eastern force, all by itself, will wipe out one-third of the world's population. Isaiah, in chapter 24, predicts that the Lord will "lay waste" the earth, scorch its inhabitants, with the result that only a few people will be left. Lindsey offers us one "bright spot" in all this gloom. Among the Jews who manage to survive this Armageddon, many will be converted to Jesus as their true Messiah. "The Greatest Moment," however, comes when the "great war" reaches such a pitch that it seems that no life will be left on earth. Then Jesus will return and save humankind from total self-extinction by preserving the faithful remnant. Again, in this tradition of manhandling the Bible, these events are not in any way peripheral. They are all part of what Lindsey calls "the main event."[43]

So important is "the main event" that one out of every twenty-five verses of the Christian part of the Bible is supposedly related to this second coming of Christ. So central is it to the Bible that there are five hundred predictions of it, whereas there were only three hundred predictions of the first coming of Christ.[44] When Jesus came the first time, he came as a lamb, willing to die to take away the sins of the world. Apparently Jesus has had enough of being portrayed as a lamb. Next time he will come "as a lion."[45] And what a lion! This is no longer the fourth-century Jesus, who settled for tickling the trunks of the enemy's elephants and the nostrils of his horses. His weapons are now earthquakes and thermonuclear blasts.

Jesus will make his return to earth on the Mount of Olives, from which he ascended into heaven. But as he touches down, the mountain will split in two with an enormous earthquake. A giant crevice will open in the earth, running from the Dead Sea to the Mediterranean. (An unidentified oil company, Lindsey tells us, found a fault line running exactly along that area that could activate at any time. It is awaiting, Lindsey tells us, "the foot."[46]) Those Jews who believe in Jesus will rush into the crevice—remembering Zechariah's prediction—and use it as a bomb shelter. And what will happen as they hide there in safety? There will be thermonuclear blasts. Zechariah gives us the details: "This shall be the plague wherewith the Lord will smite all the people that have fought against Jerusalem: their flesh shall consume away while they stand upon their feet, and their eyes shall consume away in their holes, and their tongue shall consume away in their mouth" (Zech. 14:12). The biblical literalists have great imagination, but it does not take any imagination to compare this to a thermonuclear blast, which is what Lindsey does, and he adds: "It appears that this will be the case at the return of Christ."[47]

One wonders what will be left after this worldwide thermonuclear destruction. Not much, as far as the bodies of unbelievers go. Christian believers will have been lifted up in the great "rapture" to meet Christ "in the air." Jewish converts will have the crevice as a bomb shelter. As for the thermonuclear mess left everywhere, Christ will "put the atoms back together," and make a new heaven and a new earth where only *the good* will dwell.

The "good" will be a rather select group. It will not include any homosexuals, because homosexuality is a voluntary perversion, and there will be none of it in the "kingdom." There will be no Jews who prefer the religious richness of their own tradition for itself, and not as a prelude to conversion to pseudofundamentalist Christianity. There will be no liberals with giveaway programs that undermine the work ethic. There will be no noncapitalists. One would also not expect to see many Catholics, since they don't read the Bible as the saved do. There will be few poor people and fewer blacks, since in the Falwellian gospel, God "prospers" the good. Since these people haven't been prospered, they couldn't have been good—so they won't be around.

The second coming as envisioned by these accentrics will amount to a ruthless and a colossal right-wing purge. The hostility and truculence that is built into its conception is virtually without limit. With their simplistic *saved vs. unsaved* view of human life, they stand ready to write off most of humankind, commending them to death and hell. We have reached an extremity of hatred and militarism here. Early Christians would be baffled that such a terrifying scenario is presented in the name of Jesus of Nazareth, whom they found to be a person "meek and humble of heart."

CHAPTER 5

The Case Against Violence

War is an enterprise which seeks to resolve conflict of interest by violence. It is a form of death by choice which decides to kill those who do not wish to be killed. It is generally accepted that war can at times be justified. There are few absolute pacifists. The problem is that we are so habituated to wars and rumors of wars, that we have justified war too facilely. We have, in fact, tragically overestimated our moral right to wage war.

I have urged that the beginning of ethics is the question *what?* By analyzing what war is, I propose to show that it is not easy to justify war morally. Because of their nature, wars are to be presumed guilty until proven innocent. John Fitzgerald Kennedy once said that there will always be wars until the status of the conscientious objector is as honored as that of the warrior. I would add that everyone should be a conscientious objector to every war until overwhelming evidence makes them warriors. The burden of proof is on the war-maker, not the objector. That is a hard saying for a martial society to hear. Let me argue it.

In general, my position is that it is extremely difficult for violence to do more good than harm. It is not impossible that violence could do more good than harm. But it is highly unlikely. The reasons underlying that assertion are:

(1) Violence makes community building and harmony hard to achieve in the post-violence period. One of the slowly civilizing insights of slowly civilizing humans is the realization that the force of war must not blot out the opportunities of post-war peace. The force expended should be limited to the achievement of the goals of the war. This civilizing insight is difficult if not impossible to maintain in the heat of battle. Successful violence requires abstraction. The violent must ab-

stract from the concrete fleshy individuality of the enemy or the cutting edge of violence will be blunted. That abstraction is achieved either by distancing one's self from the enemy, as does the pilot of a modern bomber who never sees the enemy, or by hatred. Hatred is an abstractive force. Hatred, to sustain itself, must distort. As J. Glenn Gray says in his reflective book *The Warriors,*

In a sense, hatred is nearly always abstract to some degree, since as a passion it is unable to view anyone or anything in entirety. The hatred that arises for the enemy in wartime . . . is peculiarly one-sided, for it is a fear-filled image. The enemy is not an individual man or woman, but a hostile power intent upon destroying our people and our lives. Our unreflective response is normally total enmity for the image of evil that possesses our imagination.[1]

Violence, therefore, is rarely a happy prelude to peace. In war, the enemy must be swallowed up in abstractions such as freedom, national security, and making the world safe for democracy, or they must be experienced as subhuman and depraved. Otherwise the unambiguous vigor that violence requires cannot be mobilized or unleashed.

Harmonious peace is not the natural sequel of such an experience. Resentments that burn as long as the eternal flames that honor the killing heroes are the normal product of war. Georgia remembers Sherman. The weird anomaly of pursuing peace with the sword was noted by Augustine. The Middle East, Southeast Asia, Northern Ireland are all destined to be further pathetic exhibits to make the case for the almost inevitable counterproductivity of violence. Like a man struggling in quicksand, the more violence these lands engage in, the further they are from the good life that all reasonable human activity seeks. As the violence proceeds, the possibilities for harmony, which is the indispensable ingredient of the good life, are being pulled out by the roots.

(2) Violence is addictive. It affects the people who rely on it with the ecstasy of the "quick fix." It brings relief from the frustrations of patient and imaginative struggle. Impatient cultures are most liable to become fixated at the level of violent power. Take a society that is hyperactive, task-oriented, little given to the admiring contemplation of the slow rhythms of nature—I speak of the United States—such a society will be drawn by the promise of immediate relief that violence offers. Like heroin, violence can give a temporary sense of well-being, of achievement, of change where change is needed. Something is getting done where something ought to get done. There is an addictive exhilaration in that. And there is the tendency to believe, quite irra-

tionally and compulsively, as addicts will, that more and more of the same will make things right.

Most tragically, this addictive reliance on violence, this unimaginative equating of violence with power, is not an atmosphere in which the neglected art of diplomacy will be enhanced. Diplomacy is primarily a work of patience and imagination, of sensitivity, tact, delicacy, and ingenuity. Diplomacy learns where the doors are and learns which will open and which will not. The true diplomat views the other protagonists in the international drama in their cultural concreteness. With discerning eye the diplomat dissipates myths that becloud the reality of the other. Diplomacy at its best is the supreme act of statecraft.[2] The violent are not likely to believe this. Fingers grown rough with bludgeoning are unlikely candidates for doing needlepoint.

(3) Violence limits creativity by inducing a situation of limited options. Alternatives are part of reality. Where alternatives are unperceived, reality-contact is impaired. Humans are blessed among the animals because they are inventive and can discover the possible beyond the given. I have referred to creative imagination as the prime moral faculty. Humans can burst free from the confines of the actual, imagine what is not, and make it be.

In violence, this glory is lost. At an early stage in an altercation, many solutions are possible. As violence mounts, fewer options remain and the dispositions of the subjects are less open to whatever options there may be. As violence progresses, the goal of violence exercises a reverse telescopic effect. In the contracting power of violence, reality is shrunken, focus narrowed, vision fixated. Imagination, tender though promising shoot that it is, is the first casualty in the storm which is violence.

(4) Violence minimizes the conditions for rationality. By its nature, it is alien to nuance. For violence to be successfully mounted, there must be clear distinctions between right and wrong such as the real world does not afford. Warriors must see war as either a crusade or a crime. Their war is the crusade; the enemy's, a crime. Is it not significant that the just war theory presumes one side right and the other side wrong, even though, in point of historical fact, such a clean division of merit has never obtained.

Simplism, which is the bane of sensitive reasoning, would seem to be of the essence of violent power. Without simplism, violent force is immobilized. Violence thus does violence to reason and because of this it is unlikely to be the work of moral persons or moral society.

Let it be clear that I am not saying that for a war to be justified, it must be pure with no admixture of evil. War will always do harm, a lot of harm. It may be justified if it does more good than harm, and if there was no other way to do that good, and if the good is at least proportionate to the harm. There will be disvalues mixed with the values even in a justified war. What I am saying here is that it is difficult—indeed almost impossible—for the values to outweigh the disvalues. The abolition of the conditions for rationality is prominent among the disvalues.

(5) Violence is inherently escalatory. A harsh word leads to a shove and then a push and thence to fisticuffs. At the beginning of World War II, Hitler's bombing of population centers provoked expressions of shock from England and the United States. As the momentum of the war increased, however, the shock gave way to imitation. The Western Allies soon swallowed their moral indignation and determined that civilian morale and private property were legitimate targets of war. The British Foreign Secretary, Mr. Eden, wrote to the British Air Chiefs in the spring of 1942:

I wish to recommend therefore that in the selection of targets in Germany the claims of smaller towns of under 150 thousand inhabitants which are not too heavily defended should be considered, even though those towns contain only targets of secondary importance.[3]

A Member of Parliament voiced his approval with enthusiasm. He declared himself to be "all for the bombing of working-class areas in German cities. I am Cromwellian—I believe in 'slaying in the name of the Lord.' " To this, the Secretary of State for Air, Sir Archibald Sinclair, replied that he was "delighted to find that you and I are in complete agreement about . . . bombing policy generally."[4] These were not mere words. On the night raid on Hamburg of July 27–28, 1943, phosphorus incendiaries and the techniques of the "bomber stream" produced within thirty minutes a fire storm, several miles wide, which burned or asphyxiated from forty-two to a hundred thousand people. Fire-bombing and attacks on civilians also became American policy against Japan. In the March 9–10, 1945, raid on Tokyo, 83,800 persons are reported to have died. Then, of course, followed Hiroshima and Nagasaki, and American consciences had grown so at ease with slaughter of populations that these unjustifiable attacks were borne with complacency. Such is the way of war. Here the domino theory does seem to be a telling argument against the possibility of a moral war. In unleashing violence, we unleash a force that has a power to possess its perpetrators. The escalatory thrust of violence is not easily contained within the ridges of right reason.

(6) Violence tends to bypass the need for social and cultural restructuring such as would truly correct the aggravation at issue. With regard to social reform, violence can be superficial. When the storms of violence have passed, the myths, structures, and problems that precipitated the violence may still stand tall against the sky. Violence may change the *dramatis personae* only to discover that it is the same old show—or nearly so. Symbolically and really you may trade the Czar for Joseph Stalin.

It is the beginning of political wisdom to realize that all of our social problems have deep and tangled roots in history, in economics, and in the scarcely known regions of social psychology. Social problems are processes that do not so much admit of cure as redirection. They must be addressed with patience and a sense of intricacy. More often than not, violence pulls off the leaves of the offending weeds while allowing the roots to prosper. States too easily descend to the logic of a bully who believes that differences are best settled with a punch in the mouth.

This aspect of violence relates to the escalatory thrust of violence. As the warriors begin to sense that the violence is not a panacea, and may indeed be making things worse rather than better, there develops a frantic urgency to increase the violence as though more and more of the unavailing medicine will somehow work the cure.

(7) The violence of war represents a reversion to the primitive notion of collective responsibility. The term "collective responsibility" can mean something quite realistic and something that is ever modern and in need of appreciation. I refer to the fact that peoples are responsible for the misdeeds and culpable nondeeds of their nations, at least because of their mute apathy which allows the ruling powers to sally forth into moral crimes on the international scene.

The term "collective responsibility" here is used to describe the primitive notion that if one member of a tribe offends you, the whole tribe of the offender is guilty. Anthropologist Robert Lowie gives examples of this:

The sibless Hupa were content to kill any member of a murderer's family in order to punish the crime; among the Crow if a Fox had disgraced himself and his society by taking back an abducted wife, the rival Lumpwoods had the right to cut up the blankets of all the Foxes; and in the same tribe the grief of the parents mourning the death of a son slain by the Dakota was at once assuaged when vengeance had been wreaked on any member of the hostile people.[5]

It is Lowie's judgment that this primitive conception is still operative in modern societies. "Though this is an archaic notion," he writes, "it persists to the present day in the warfare of civilized nations, which summarily shelves the practice of determining individual guilt or innocence."[6] Lowie is both right and wrong here. I do believe the primitive myth persists in modern war, but the determination of guilt is not a question that is dismissed "summarily," as Lowie says. Efforts have been made traditionally in the just war theory to apply the principle of discrimination. Originally, when war was simpler, this principle was translatable as the principle of non-combatant immunity. Kill-power had to be focused on other potential killers only. In modern war a complicated lip service is still paid to the principle of discrimination. In theory, an effort is made in "conventional" wars to be discriminatory in the infliction of war deaths. In practice, there are Coventry and Dresden and Hamburg and Mylai. In theory, fire-power is to be directed only at militarily strategic targets. In practice, many civilians are killed or maimed or dislocated. The theory accounts for civilian deaths with such clinical terms as indirect killing and "collateral damage." If, in going after a legitimate target, some civilians are *indirectly* killed, this is justified if there is proportionate reason to allow the "collateral damage." This rule paints with a broad brush. It does not turn out to be discriminating in application. In practice, Lowie is right. Risks are taken with the lives of civilians that would not be taken if they were not implicitly swept under the archaic shadow of collective responsibility. Police would not go after a gang of criminals in New York City the way that we went after "the enemy" in Vietnam, Cambodia, and Laos. Care for civilian life would be a paramount concern in New York. It was not regularly such in Southeast Asia, where even civilian life was deemed tainted. This taint was evinced in the callously loose application of the principle of discrimination.

Of course, with regard to nuclear war, only a notion of collective responsibility in the primitive sense could motivate the use of nuclear weapons. Because of its inexorably indiscriminate effects, nuclear war was condemned in strong language in the Second Vatican Council.

Any act of war aimed indiscriminately at the destruction of entire cities or of extensive areas along with their population is a crime against God and man himself. (sic) It merits unequivocal and unhesitating condemnation.[7]

All of these considerations seem to give us a well-grounded bias against violent power as a politically and morally acceptable means toward social ends. It seems that moralists have all too facilely provided abstruse and uncritical rationalizations to justify the barbaric instinct for war which lingers unredeemed in human consciousness. It becomes increasingly obvious that war does more harm than good, that there are always alternatives to war, and that "the just war theory" bears a burden of proof that it cannot meet.

CHAPTER 6

The Violence of Anti-Semitism

Some years ago a Catholic priest, Edward Flannery, was walking on Park Avenue in New York City in the company of a young Jewish couple. They passed a large illuminated cross that was part of a Christmas display. The young woman looked at the cross and trembled visibly. "That cross makes me shudder," she said. "It is like an evil presence."[1] The pursuit of the causes of that shudder led Flannery to the writing of his book *The Anguish of the Jews.*

Anti-Semitism has wracked the Christian soul from the beginning. The break of the Christian Church from the Synagogue was a bitter one. Starting with the gospels, the Jews are cast in a grievously guilty light. They are pictured as screaming for the crucifixion of Jesus and are made to say, "His blood be upon us and our children!" (Matthew 27:26) This symbol of guilt pervaded centuries of Christian and Jewish relations. As to the question of whether Christian anti-Semitism goes back to our origins, one Christian theologian, F. Lovsky, states the case bluntly: "In the final analysis there can be no debate. There are too many signs that stake out the permanence, the importance and the gravity of Christian anti-Semitism: contempt, calumnies, animosity, segregation, forced baptisms, appropriation of children, unjust trials, pogroms, exiles, systematic persecutions, thefts and rapine, hatred, open or concealed, social degradation."[2]

Even that listing of horrors is incomplete. A look at church law is revealing, because laws express and rely upon broad consent and approval. Laws are windows into a culture. The laws of the Christian churches have enough anti-Semitism in them to make anyone shudder.

Intermarriage and sexual intercourse between Christians and Jews were forbidden at the Synod of Elvira in 309. The same synod forbade Christians and Jews to eat together. The synod of Clermont, in 535, banned Jews from holding public office. Jews were forbidden by the Synod of Orlean, in 538, to employ Christian servants or to possess Christian slaves. The same synod banned them from the street during Eastertime. The Talmud and other Jewish books were publicly burned at the Synod of Toledo in 681, which, of course, taught the faithful a starkly symbolic lesson about the hideous contents of these books. Christians could not patronize Jewish doctors (Trulanic Synod, 692). They could not live in Jewish homes (Synod of Narbonne, 1050). Jews could not be plaintiffs or witnesses against Christians in court (Third Lateran Council, 1179). The same council said Jews were not permitted to withhold inheritance from children who converted to Christianity. The Fourth Lateran Council cancelled all debts that crusaders owed to Jews. This council also reinstituted the old Christian custom of confining Jews to a ghetto and making them wear distinctive badges, which took on various forms. In France, the Jews had to wear a yellow sphere, the *rouelle*. In Germany, they wore a special hat; in Poland, a pointed hat. In Sicily, the wearing of a circular badge was mandated. The Council of Oxford, in 1222, prohibited the construction of new synagogues. Christians could not rent or sell real estate to Jews (Synod of Ofen, 1279). The Council of Basel prohibited Jews from acting as agents in contracts involving Christians, and also banned them from obtaining academic degrees.

Clearly, the Nazis had a lot to build on when they banned intermarriage, barred Jews from dining cars, limited their employment possibilites, restricted them to ghettos, kept them off the streets on Nazi holidays, imposed special taxes, limited their rights in courts, voided their wills, made them mark their clothes, homes, and stores, limited their access to universities and other schools, and seized their real estate. There is a long and terrible sequence in all this. Raul Hilberg wrote: "[the Nazis] did not discard the past; they built upon it. They did not begin a development; they completed it."[3] And as A. Roy Eckardt says, the facts of the case make "ludicrous any unqualified claim that the Nazis were the enemies of Christendom. In actuality, they were in very large measure the agents for the 'practical' application of an established social logic."[4]

Even the actual genocidal attempt of Hitler had Christian precedent. When the first Crusade began in 1066, it turned first on the Jews. As one chronicler of the period puts it, the Crusaders of Rouen said: "We desire to combat the enemies of God in the east; but we have under our eyes the Jews, a race more inimical to God than all the others. We are doing this whole thing backwards."[5] They immediately corrected themselves and fell upon the Jews, slaughtering as much as a quarter or a third of the Jewish population in Germany and northern France at that time. In Rameru in France, the famous Jewish scholar Jacob Tam "had five wounds inflicted upon his head in vengeance for the five wounds of Christ."[6] This earlier holocaust was repeated throughout later history. Starting in 1298, an army of Judenschächter (Jewslaughterers) moved through Germany and Austria on a mission of murder. They are reported to have decimated one hundred forty communities of Jews, killing as many as one hundred thousand persons.

What I have offered here is but short evidence of the poison we Christians carry in the historical marrow of our bones. As a Catholic, I grew up praying on Good Friday for the "perfidious Jews" (pro perfidis Judaeis). Only with recent Catholic reforms was this violent obscenity erased from Catholic prayer. The New Christian Right in the United States is grotesque in its anti-Semitism, all the more so since it manages to be both pro-Israel and anti-Semitic at once. The state of Israel is important for the New Right because of their eschatology and their plans for the final days. Jews are not important, except as prospects for conversion.

The anti-Semitism of the Christian right if often raw. Bethany Press in 1973 published a book entitled The Bible, the Supernatural and the Jews, by McCandish Philips. The cover shows the flames of hell arising from infernal regions and encompassing a broken tablet marked with Hebrew lettering. The author argues that the Jews, being chosen, were more powerfully evil than mere gentiles when they fell away from God. The author then goes on to implicate Jews, with their superior talent for evil, in such things as satanism, drugs, rock music, and the overall breakdown of traditional morality. A few Jews are heartened by the pro-Israel stance of the New Right. Most are more perceptive. They look at the New Right and shudder. They know the old story too well.

Most Christian anti-Semitism is not as crude as that on the New Right. The New Right, however, in this and in other respects, is a caricature of what exists in subtler forms in the main stream of Christianity. Christian indifference to Jewish suffering in the holocaust and in the myriad forms of anti-Semitism that beleaguer Jews today throughout the world, signals the presence of the disease in the Christian soul. It would seem that anti-Semitism is a low-grade fever in Christian souls which stands ready to blaze into flagrant heat.

All violence begins in the spirit of persons. It ill befits Christians—given recent and earlier history—to imagine themselves free of the violent poison of anti-Semitism.

Part 3

SEXUAL MORES AND THE FUTURE OF MARRIAGE

The sexual revolution is getting well on in years. Action, however, has run ahead of theory. Challenges to the older sexual norms have not been adequately met by thoughtful response. The two chapters of this section look at some of the modes of sexual expression that exist on the modern moralscape. Chapter Seven, offers a vision of the future of marriage. Chapter Eight looks to the sexual options of homosexual persons and argues for the applicability of the marital ideal for gay persons.

CHAPTER 7

A New Concept of Marriage

Marriage would seem implausible were it not so apparently inevitable. With all the vagaries and chaos that mark human sexual history, we have been and remain the marrying animal. Marriage, of course, takes many forms from culture to culture. Still, it stubbornly remains the most highly sanctioned and respected forum for the expression of sexuality and for the raising of children.

By my definition, marriage is the legal union of persons who are bonded in a permanent, sexually exclusive friendship. That definition may seem starkly rigid and juridical, but it actually embodies the romantic ideal of marriage. Romantic love, which looks yearningly toward marriage, is not hedged or pro-rated. Its passion is for union, complete and *tousjours*. The definition given says all of that a bit more crisply.

The inevitability of marriage as a human institution, does not mean that all people achieve it or choose it. Even many who "marry" never marry in the full sense of my definition. Many would find marriage as defined naive and unsuited to today's realities. They could argue that for much of human history, "til death do us part" meant, on the average, fifteen or twenty years, given the ancient mortality rate. Longevity is largely modern. As Professor Monroe Lerner writes:

With the rise of the early civilizations and the consequent improvements in living conditions, longevity must surely have risen, reaching perhaps 20 years in ancient Greece and perhaps 22 in ancient Rome. Life expectancy is estimated to have been about 33 years in England during the Middle Ages, about 35 in the Massachusetts Bay Colony of North America, about 41 in England and Wales during the nineteenth century, and 47.3 in the death registration states of the United States in 1900.[1]

When marriage was short-term, it was more plausible, the argument might go. But now, "permanent" and "exclusive" seem "romantic" in the soft-minded sense, and unreal.

I disagree—at the enormous peril of seeking naive, and with one quick disclaimer. I do not say that marriage as "permanent, sexually exclusive, committed friendship" is statistically triumphant or even the only humane and moral mode of human love-making or mating. I do argue that it remains a realistic ideal that has beckoned lovers from antiquity and does so into our time. I also state up front that marriage as a viable ideal is an endangered species today for many of the reasons offered by its critics. But, finally, I do insist that, amid the many alternative modes of human sexual relating—some morally defensible, some not—marriage retains its distinctive place under the moral sun.

The Alternatives to Marriage

Looking to Western culture in the American mode, it is clear that there are at least fourteen ways other than marriage in which persons choose to express, use, or manage their sexuality. This list is suggestive, not exhaustive, and is offered as a construct for discussing the variety that marks sexual mores. For better or for worse, some of the alternative modes of human sexual relating are these:

1. Violent sex, in the form of rape or sexual harrassment. Here persons force their sexuality on an unwilling partner. "Violent sex" verges on oxymoron inasmuch as sex imports "*love* making," tenderness, and play. The complexity of human personality is such, however, that sex can come under the formal sway of other and contradictory agenda.
2. Commercial sex. In this form of sex, commonly known as prostitution, persons have sex partly or mainly for financial gain.
3. Quasi-anonymous sex, or "swinging," in which persons have full sexual intimacy with minimal personal intimacy and no stress on continuity of relationship.
4. Occasional, non-exclusive sex, where persons often find one another sexually convenient but seek no bonding, cohabitation, or relational ties.
5. Occasional, exclusive sex, where persons, though not cohabiting, live with an expectation of an exclusively sexual intimacy.
6. Open marriage, where persons are legally and personally bonded but with the understanding that they may freely express themselves sexually with others without hiding those other relationships from their marriage partner.

7. Live-in, exclusive relationships, in which all the elements of marriage are present except the ceremonies and legalization.
8. Group marriage, in which more than two persons live together and are sexually expressive with one another in a non-exclusive way.
9. Live-in relationships with satellites. Here there is an informal bonding with some intention of continuity but with an explicit openness to other sexual relationships.
10. Clandestine bigamy, in which a quasi-marital, unlegalized, relationship is maintained alongside a conventional marriage.
11. Serial monogamy, in which repeated efforts at permanent and exclusive marriages are made.
12. Clandestine marriage, in which persons subjected to some external pressure such as ecclesiastical law choose a permanent and sexually exclusive union, legalized or not, that is concealed from the broader public.
13. Marriage with secret affairs, in which the semblance of permanent exclusive marriage coexists with intermittent extra-marital sexual relationships.
14. Voluntary celibacy, in which persons choose not to express themselves sexually with any other person. (Celibacy can denote the absence of marriage without reference to whether a person is sexually active or inactive. Here, I am using it in the sense of unmarried and sexually inactive.) Involuntary celibacy is a common fact of life, but in this listing, I am referring to active options in our cultural milieu.

Again, given the enormous variety that attends human sexuality, this listing is not offered with pretensions of completeness. Each of these categories admit of subdivisions. There is usefulness, however, in trying to specify the extant modes of sexual expression as we focus on one of them, marriage.

This listing is not limited to heterosexual persons, except where legalized marriage is involved. That option is not yet available to permanently bonded homosexual lovers in our society.

The Ethics of Marriage

Marriage is still central to any discussion of sex. Whether we talk of pre-marital, non-marital, extra-marital, or para-marital sex, the term of reference is marriage. Marriage is the core form of human mating.

As anthropologist, Ralph Linton, wrote with a lyrical enthusiasm un-common in the social sciences:

The ancient trinity of father, mother, and child had survived more vicissitudes than any other human relationship. It is the bedrock underlying all other family structures. Although more elaborate family patterns can be broken from with-out or may even collapse of their own weight, the rock remains. In the *Göt-terdämmerung* which overwise science and overfoolish statesmanship are preparing for us, the last man will spend his last hours searching for his wife and child.[2]

Morton Hunt, exploring the sexual revolution in his 1974 study "Sexual Behavior in the 1970s, came to this conclusion:

. . . sexual liberation has not dismantled the romantic-passionate concept of sex and replaced it with the recreational one . . . while most Americans—es-pecially the young—now feel far freer than formerly to be sensation-oriented at times, for the great majority of them sex remains intimately allied to their deepest emotions and inextricably interwoven with their conceptions of loyalty, love, and marriage. The web of meaning and social structure surrounding sex has been stretched and reshaped, but not torn asunder.[3]

Psychiatrist, Perry London reaches a rather straightforward and broadly shared conclusion: "The most important characteristic of sex may finally be that it is so deeply intertwined with affection and that it is still the chief human instrument for making progeny . . ."[4]

In a word, the unitive and procreative thrust of sex continues to point toward that stable form of bonding that we call marriage. That does not give us the last ethical word on sex. Noting the unitive and procreative powers of sex does not yield a tidy code of sexual ethics. After citing these two aspects of sex, Perry London goes on to observe that they "may suggest some limits on its exercise, though they do not reveal the content of those limits."[5] Still, marriage remains central to sexual experience. Even those who would deny the enduring value of permanent and exclusive marriage must speak to it in establishing their denial.

I defined marriage as *the legal union of persons who are bonded in a permanent, sexually exclusive friendship.* The key category in that defini-tion is *friendship*. Marriage is friendship sealed by commitment. It is not friendship based simply on drift, or happenstance, contiguity or convenience, but ultimately on choice. In marriage we choose to extend our area of primary reference to include another—and perhaps many other other's in the form of children. I speak, of course, of modern western marriage. Historically, choice has often played a minor role or none at all.[6]

Unlike many friendships, marital friendship creates a new lifestyle. Beyond the interpersonal, it has legal, social, and economic meaning. It is also a *kenotic* experience in which we die to our former selves to rise to a new identity. By its very nature, it is a conversion, a defeat of egotism. Mother, father, and siblings, the elementary and foundational referents of our experience, suddenly slip into secondary status. A new center of gravity enters the lives of the marital partners as life becomes dramatically redirected. Small wonder societies strain their imaginative powers wildly as they drape this event with varied and rich ceremonial solemnity. Marriage is a relationship without peer in the realm of friendship.

Marriage is also sexual. In marriage, friendship is the noun; sexual, the adjective. Sexuality, of course, is not just our capacity for coitus. There are many forms of human intercourse, and sexuality can affect them all. Indeed, in a sexual friendship the sexual dimension may survive and thrive even in the absence of coitus due to sickness or age. Sexuality refers to a kind of bodily intimacy and reverence which is joyfully and naturally nourished by coitus but is not constituted by it. A non-orgasmic woman or an impotent man may be truly and sexually married.

Marriage, Friendship, and Sex

Sex, like friendship, is not simple. We become wiser about marriage—this committed friendship between sexually attracted persons—as we seek to know better the mysteries of personhood called friendship and sexuality. First, to sex.

The question: "what is sex?" provokes laughter among the young. They know so well what it is and they are drawn so powerfully—and, at times, so painfully—by its gravitational pull. The young know all *too* well what sex is. Only maturity brings us to a learned ignorance on the subject. On sex, that modesty which is the mark of wisdom comes late, if at all.

From adolescence on we work out an implicit definition of sex. Those definitions, however, sin by simplism. The culturally ensconced conceptions of sex make too little or too much of it. The "hippy" mode would see it as one "cool" pastime among others. Persons might take a walk, have a beer, play a little cribbage, or have a little sex together. All are seen as qualitatively the same. Ethics is reduced to consent.

Agreement makes it good. Alas! Nothing with roots so deep in human personality and in human reproductivity could ever be so simple.

Others see sex as necessarily a total experience. One study says: "Sexual intercourse is an expression of a person's whole being, the deepest core of one's personality."[7] it may be all of that betimes. Yet if one looks to the fourteen ways listed above in which persons use their sexuality, more contextually varied language seems called for.

Sex talk is also replete with contradiction. "Sex is dirty. Save it for someone you love." Theology has moved somberly over the sexual terrain, seeing sex as everything from the tainted conduit of original sin to the sacramental power of cocreativity with God. To speak of sex then is to enter a swirling melange, where everyone knows and no one knows what are glibly called "the facts of life."

I think sex is best defined as a natural liturgy. I speak of sex here not as confined to coitus but as a pervasive vitality which looks to periodic coital refreshment in a relationship. Such sex is language. Symbolic and liturgical language.

Symbol comes from the Greek *ballo*, throw, and *syn*, with, together with. A symbol *throws together* levels of meaning that cannot be simply or verbally expressed. It's hard to *say* what a sigh can say, or to *say* what one means by a smile. Such is the power of symbol over mere word. Sighs and smiles symbolize. They encapsulate in intense eloquence what would be lost in tedious telling.

A liturgy is a coordinated series of symbols which communicate and celebrate meaning. Some are natural liturgies, found, not contrived. Sex and a meal are natural liturgies. Some liturgies are conventional. Coronations of queens, presidents, and popes, and patriotic feast days are conventional liturgies. They consist of liturgical rituals contrived for the meanings of the event. As contrivance, they vary from place to place. Natural liturgies, like sex and dining, are substantially similar for all of humankind.

A Meal As a Natural Liturgy

Let me illustrate the nature of a natural liturgy first by showing the liturgical nature of human dining. Obviously, there can be para-liturgical eating where someone "grabs a bite" on the run to meet biological needs. However, when a meal is allowed to be itself at leisure, its liturgical power blooms.

The table, after all, is not a trough. People who dine together are not just consuming proteins and carbohydrates.[8] Guests are not chosen for their hunger. A meal is a friendship event, which, like a sacrament, both symbolizes and effects friendship. (It is not surprising that the Christian religion and other religions favored the meal as a symbolic matrix and principal liturgy.) Witness the exquisite attention to detail that goes into the making of a meal. We are not just feeding our friends when we invite them; we are expressing our respect and love. The dinner table is prepared like an altar. Precious vessels of crystal, silver, and china are brought forth. The lighting is changed. Music is readied. Appropriate vestments are worn. The atmosphere is one of giving and is as splendid as we can make it. An old Irish saying advises: "When you come for a meal, don't come with one arm as long as the other." Be carrying a gift. It is a gifting time for guest and host. So much more than ingestion is going on.

Even the food is prepared symbolically. It would not be a meal if we fed people intravenously or from a vat, though they would be physically nourished. The preparation and arrangement of the food is heavily symbolic. Not all meals can become fully symbolic, but the urgency toward sociality and friendship is always there. The busy househusband or housewife who has gotten the children off to school, and sits for a bit of breakfast, reaches for the phone or the television or a magazine to ward off the aloneness that offends human eating. And if all this stress on sociality, love, and respect as essential ingredients of a meal seems too lyrical, think of what happens when you are forced to eat with someone whom you seriously dislike. The consequent indigestion will bear witness to the fact that mere foodstuffs and a table do not a meal make. If you ate beside a stranger every day at a diner counter, it would be very difficult to ward off the intimations of communication and conviviality that go with personal eating. You would have to become friends of a sort.

Sex As Natural Liturgy

Sex does meet physical needs such as distraction, relaxation, and nervous release. Sometimes when the personal dimensions are minimal, as when sex is commercialized, there may be little more to it than this. But there is symbolic power in sex which, given due chance, will assert itself. Sex and the erotic context have a power to engender and express endearing emotions and intense personal expectations. It is a compelling form of sharing that invites more sharing. In the sexual encounter, the parties are not just physically enveloping and interpenetrating one another; there is psychological envelopment and penetration as well. One is personally as well as physically naked in shared orgasmic experience. The event is truly a *revelatio*, an unveiling. The usual cosmetic defenses with which we gird ourselves about do not easily survive such liturgy. The force of the encounter is unitive. Erotic power dissolves separateness. The lover may remain only an experience, but she tends to become a way of life. The lovers have shared a secret together. They have shared a powerful symbolic event that both signifies and effects friendship. "Getting involved" is a corollary of "having sex" if it is not its prelude.

This is not to say that the symbolic aspects of sex cannot be repressed or almost extinguished in certain cauterized personalities or at lower stages of personality development. But without some manifestation of cherishing and affecting, the sexual meeting is not even going to be a sensual success. And if depersonalized sex is repeated, the personal and unitive dimensions are likely to emerge.

It is ironic to note that the romantic sexual encounter, which is certainly a high form of fun, has such a lugubrious legacy in terms of songs of broken hearts, the blues, and literary tragedies. Its unitive potential explains this to some degree. The unitive power is felt by one of the parties and not by the other, or, circumstances prevent the union that is so commandingly required by the relationship. "A pity beyond all telling is hid in the heart of love," wrote the poet Yeats, and many persons who move into a sexual encounter learn the poignant adaptations that the poet's words can have.[9]

Sometimes the power of sex can be seen only in its pathology. When sexually animated passion is frustrated, the results can be violent or psychologically devastating. Policepersons note a peculiar level of violence in sex-related crimes. The urgencies and expectations generated in the sexual encounter are not feeble. Their roots are deep in the human spirit. Their assigned roles touch on elementary forces in the unfolding of human life. Psychologist Dorothy Tennov studies the power of sexually involved love in her book *Love and Limerence: The Experience of Being in Love.*[10] She had to coin the word limerence to describe the experience of being in love since our language had no specific term for it. That, in itself, suggests neglect of a most fundamental phenomenon. The book is a useful study of the power that lies in sexually nourished love. It is highly illustrative of the unitive aspects of sex.

Sex between persons, then, tends not to be merely physical. It has a meaning we do not give it and a power that never ceases to surprise. Truncated sex, that does not flower into personal meaning, provides no basis for marriage or any stable relationship. Our vulnerabilities, hopes, and secrets come out in the sexual encounter and if they are not received into reverent friendship, pain comes to the lovers. The intensity of early sexual fervor, like any emotional intensity, does not survive as such. Sexual love takes many forms and cannot be assessed by the crude calculus of orgasmic frequency. Sex is a positive, friendship-oriented force.

What Is Friendship?

Friendship is the blending of persons through love. It is the highest tribute we can pay one another. Friendship is the supreme celebration of personal life. It is the closest we get to valuing others for all they are worth. "Friends have no need of justice," said Aristotle.[11] He was right. Justice-sharing is only the foreshadowing of love-sharing. And friendship is love-sharing. Friends share spontaneously and naturally with no calculation of oughts, debts, or recompense. Friends are those who love one another well and enthusiastically. Friendship is the essence of marriage.

We cannot say enough about friendship, but let me say something. In general, it is a forgotten subject in modern philosophy and theology. One wonders what we have found to displace the ancient attention to this cornerstone of human living.

I offer two principles for the discussion of marital friendship:

1. Marital friendship is a process, not a state.
2. If marital friendship meets the growth needs and possibilities of marital partners at many levels, it is more friendly and more marital. I do not suggest that all one's needs should be met in one's marriage. This overloads our expectations and represents a warped sense of our natural sociality—as though we were not part of a number of communities beyond the marital community. Expecting too much from a marriage is probably worse than expecting too little.

Marriage as a Process, Not a State

State comes from the Latin *stare*, to stand, to be still, to be "static." Nothing that we know is static. Even apparently immobile matter is intensely processual and active at its molecular core. Friendship, which involves the blending of at least two diverse vitalities, can be stable in its direction, but it will never be static or unchanging. To be is to be in process. To marry is to enter a process.

Ethics often takes its metaphors from the juridical order out of a hunger for simplicity. Often, in the juridical and legal order, simplistic assumptions are the only practical possibility. And so in the juridical order they can hardly entertain *process* perspectives regarding something like marriage. Either you are married or you are not. There can be no discussion before the law of how married you are, or how deeply you are into the marital process. Law is too blunt an instrument to enter into these nuanced realities of interpersonal life. And so, at law, you go from being utterly unmarried to being utterly married with benefit of clergy or duly appointed officer on the occasion of the wedding. Then, all are equally married until death or divorce. These are workable assumptions in the juridical forum. Happily, however, legality is not exhaustive of reality. There is more to everything than law with its external vision can see.

Ethics moves to the full reality as best it can. It cannot rest on generalized assumptions. And either-or, static thinking provides neat assumptions, but it is not always reflective of the real. The process of marital friendship is deep and advanced, or shallow and in recession. Though it would produce wonderment in a world held by static paradigms, there are many possible answers to the question: "Are you married?" The reply might be "Somewhat." Or "Very much." Or "More than ever." Or "Scarcely." People are not so much married as marrying. "They are not *married* people (as though the process were complete and done with): they are *marrying* people.

I recall a couple who had agreed to divorce when their last child graduated from high school. She did one morning, and the two were in the lawyer's office that afternoon. Their marrying process had clearly ended some time before. They were now in the business of making this past fact legal and public. They were announcing to the public what had happened some time before. For whatever reasons, the marrying process in which they had been involved had ended. Obligations from that marriage endured, and they were planning to meet them. Staying together until all the children had finished secondary education was part of their perceived moral debt. They judged that their togetherness had produced obligations that they could not walk away from even though substantial changes in their personal relationship had occurred. They believed that they could not love one another maritally any more. Moral debts, however, are born in history. And their marital history bore them not only children but obligations to those children and to one another. Some of these obligations may not be fulfilled until "death do (them) part," even though they may be divorced before then.

The traditional stress on the indissolubility of marriage was framed in static categories. There was (and is) truth as well as untruth in it. The truth is that in bonding maritally, persons commit themselves in an awe-filled and ought-filled way. Needs and expectations of an utterly serious nature are born with that bonding. No slight causes could ever justify ending that union. Divorce is tragic, even when justified. However, it is not unthinkable—as experience confirms; circumstances can arise, for sinful or virtuous reasons, that make continued marrying dangerous or unbearable. The ingredients are not always there—or not enduringly there—to make marriage permanent. The so-called "Pauline privilege" was one case even the Catholic Church saw as justifying divorce. Catholic marriage courts today find many other causes for divorce. Unfortunately in this time of change, honesty does not abound and these divorces are often granted on the alleged ground that there never was a marriage at all! This, of course, insults the experience of people who married earnestly, had children, raised them, and only came apart later. It also insults and bastardizes the children who know they were born in a marriage and not in a casual alliance. Current Catholic Church practice is tied to static, either/or categories. Hence, the inability to say that this marriage, which was, no longer is. Somewhere it died in the process. Juridical assumptions, not moral and ethical ones, dominate Catholic marriage court "annulment" procedures at this time. This increases the suffering of persons who while bearing the inevitable sorrow of an unraveled marriage are told they were never even married. It seems a cruel effort to save ecclesiastical face by aggrieving human beings already in pain.

The untruth in the "indissolubility" of marriage was in its assumption that all processes that begin can survive and thrive. The ideal is that they should. In Utopia, they would. Marriages are not made in Utopia or in heaven. There are marital unions that cannot endure and do not. The temptation to which the Church succumbed in the past was to turn the ideal (of no divorce) into an absolute (or, rather, almost absolute) juridical rule. This rule was then enforced without mercy or differentiation. Such juridical absolutism may be indulged in some courts of law; it should not be tolerated in the courts of conscience.

Church courts and tribunals are an anachronism. They are another example of the Church imitating the state. The state is competent to handle in its courts the effects and facts of divorce. Nothing prevents the Church from closing its marriage tribunals and attending to the work of conscience education and pastoral care to better serve those who marry.

On a more positive note, acknowledgment of the processuality of marital friendship, leaves open the possibility of deepening the union that may have begun on a superficial note. Joys and sorrows, the birth of a child, the death of a child, success and illness, maturity and the experience of aging, can all draw the marrying partners into an even deeper union. Experiencing new ways of being married can replace the built-in drudgery of static thought. Correction of the process can be seen as an alternative to divorce. We are the children of our metaphors. Static metaphors have wreaked ineffable harm on the gentle reality of marital friendship. Changing to a more processual understanding is not a threat but a blessed release.

On the Nature of Friendship

My second principle for the discussion of marital friendship is this: *friendship thrives when it promotes the growth possibilities of the friends.* I am not suggesting that friends exploit one another for the growth value obtainable in the relationship. This would be mercantile egoism, not friendship. Rather, friendship should contribute to the flowering of human life and not to its stunting. On that note I look to our basic personal needs to understand how these needs are met in a good marital friendship. I suggest that it is here, not in the analysis of sexual technique or the enumeration of orgasms, that marital possibilities and problems are best discussed. Indeed, the sexual is quite related to the full panoply of personal aliveness that I am discussing here. Bedroom problems, in other words, are not just bedroom problems, and the same may be said of bedroom success.

There is no little boldness in attempting to list the basic human needs that are joyfully met in friendship. Yet ethics and moral theology have always been preoccupied with doing just that. The age-old listing of the "virtues" was an effort to etch the lineaments of human life fully alive.

Marriage is enlivening or deadly. It is enlivening if it meets needs such as those I schematically list here. I note at the start that only one of the needs, the first, is listed in order of importance. The others need not be viewed ordinally or hierarchically. The first, however, I offer as supremely and unequivocally essential.[12]

Respect

Respect is the opposite of insult, and insult is the root of rebellion. Respect tells us that persons consider us to be fully enfranchised as human beings. The absence of it is unbearable. This is why sexism is cancer in a marriage. Sexism is the belief that women are inferior. If a husband believes that to any degree, friendship and maritality are maimed and incapacitated. Marriage involves the most intimate relating possible. It is the ultimate in mutuality. Superior/inferior status militates against mutuality. It is only compatible with dominance and oppression. The forms this takes in marriage will be myriad and often subtle, but always devastating. Thus, the rise of feminism is friendly to marriage. The fact that when some women become feminist, their marriages fail, does not indict the woman seeking mutuality, but the man denying it. The marriage had already failed. It is the repressive and strained accommodation that is ruptured and called divorce.

Esthetic

Persons need beauty as they need oxygen. Massive doses of beauty are essential to human life. The sharing of the beautiful is a bonding part of marriage. The blasé can never be fully friendly. The Philistine is no mate.

American culture is in default here and it affects our marriages. We buy beauty, visit it, and photograph it, but we rarely pause before it in ecstasy. Beauty merits the contemplative pause. A pragmatic, doing people are ill equipped for such sensitive inactivity. The result is a famishing of the spirit. Friendship grows in shared appreciation. Time for the sharing of beauty is not optional in a marriage, or in any friendship or community.

Intellectual

With confessed irony I would say that in spite of what we do in our educational institutions to make learning painful, the love of truth is never extinguished in the human mind. Friendship is, among so many other things, a shared quest for truth. Learning should end at death. If it is slowed earlier, elements of *rigor mortis* enter in. Growing in truth together is one of the friendliest things people can do. Its yield is discovery, enrichment, and joy—all very sociable experiences—and this sharing, like all wholesome sharing, is unifying.

Apollo and Dionysus

The ancient gods Apollo and Dionysus have grown, at the instigation of Nietzsche, into modern symbols of personality types. In this

adapted version of these gods, the contrasts are great. Apollo is a god
of order. His devotees are called to discipline, accuracy, and tight distinctions between mine and thine, between human and divine. The
Apollonian draws lines, build fences, and has everything in its place.
If you were going in for brain surgery, you would like a very Apollonian doctor.

Dionysus is another case. In Dionysian worship, the prime value is
not order but celebration. The Dionysian devotees are called to danc-
ing, drinking, and merriment. Lines between yours and mine, the human and the divine are blurred in this ecstatic cult. Dionysus is a
dancer, Apollo a martinet.[13]

Marriage, like life, needs an ecumenical blend of these two gods.
Much of American marital malaise traces to the victory of Apollo in
the dominant American culture. We sent the Maypole dancers back to
England in chains. We had natives to rout and a wilderness to clear.
There was no need for an "early American" dancer. And so our character was shaped. One need only fly over this land to see who reigns.
Every field is carved out and divided carefully. Chaos has been banished as far as possible from the landscape. The lines have been drawn;
discipline has triumphed. Clearly the results of this are generally good.
People would be hungry if Apollo had not been at his dutiful tilling.
But people are still hungry, since Apollo's head is tense and bowed at
his work. He does not see that, beyond his tidy field, the conditions
are desperate. As Sam Keen says: "When Dionysus is not given his
due, Apollo becomes a tyrant, a god to be killed."[14]

We invented the word "workaholic." It is the product of untem-
pered Apollonian zeal. Work is a marriageable entity, and many are
wed to it. Only with chemical assistance can many Americans relax.
Work is, of course, part of our God-like glory. We are made in the
image of a doing God. But work can also constitute infidelity to other
values and a defection from humane living. For marriage and health,
workaholism is fatal.

Unredeemed Apollonianism is also lethal for sex. In cultures where
Dionysus is managed but still dancingly alive, "sex clinics" where persons are taught how to "do it" are quite unimaginable.

Sexual

Marriage is sexual. The patterns of sexual exchange in marriages
are highly individualized and varied. Marriages ideally are based on
both admiration and passion. Admiration is respect at full term and it
brings the enthusiasm that the marital process needs. But marriage

should also be entered passionately. The form of this passion will change, as I have said. It may go from a "major" to a "minor," but it should never be dropped from the curriculum. Celibate moral theologians in the past warned against excessive sex in marriage. Father Benedictus Merkelbach says it is morally excessive if a spouse asks for sexual intercourse "three or four times in the same night."[15] The opposite is the danger. The married should have sex and prepare for it as often as they comfortably can. The sexual passion should be cultivated and nurtured.

Let me be concrete. Imagine a married couple with several children who have a leaky roof on the third floor and have just put enough money aside to fix it. Relatives arrive from Dubuque and tell them that they will baby-sit and let the two parents get away together for five days. In my judgment, the two have a moral obligation to carry buckets to the third floor and get out of town. They need this just as a monk needs a retreat to recapture the eros of his vocation. Pragma must not submerge romance. A leaky roof is less disastrous than the draining out of passion. Sex is unitive, and healthy.

But sex is also reproductive. An Appollonian Catholicism certainly made much too much of this. Vatican II was a corrective by teaching the positive value of sexual liturgy and the equally primary standing of the unitive ends of marriage. It failed, however, to clear up the moral status of the reproductive end of marriage.

It is one thing to say that sex is reproductive. The point could hardly be missed. None of us expects it to be replaced by cloning. However, the reproductive and unitive ends of marriage are not parallel lines. The reproductive line might never exist in some marriages and does not always exist in any. Our reproductivity has moral and physical limits. The species obviously needs reproduction. (It also needs control of reproduction.) But this species-need cannot be translated into an obligation binding every act of sexual exchange in every marriage. In fact, no one defends the position that sex is permitted only when fertilization is possible and likely.

The unitive and the reproductive do conjoin in one way. Reproduction can be the most unifying and maritalizing experience of a relationship. The ecstatic sharing in the miracle of birth and childhood may be the most unitive of experiences. Reproduction, however, is not necessary or feasible for every union, and it is not essential to every marriage. It is also not the grounds for ruling that every homosexual union is dehumanizing and immoral. The definition I give of marriage does not require heterosexual orientation. Homosexual marriages and childless marriages should also exemplify the unitive fidelity of love and thus be personally and socially fruitful and sacramental.[16]

Humorous

G. K. Chesterton wisely observed: "Life is serious all of the time, but living cannot be. You may have all the solemnity you wish in your neckties, but in anything important (such as sex, death, and religion), you must have mirth or you will have madness."[17] We are all a bit ridiculous, and when we live closely, we must admit and feast together on the appropriate laughter. Laughter purifies society. Marrying well means laughing well together.[18]

Sacred

Marriage without a sense of the sacred is impossible. If we have no gods, we deify ourselves, and you cannot marry a god. Shared commitment to sacred values, whether religiously identified or not, is essential to serious friendship. If we do not reach, we shrink. The religious impulse is natural to us. We are questers for the meaning that lies beyond the apparent. We are drawn to commitment to values that transcend us. Shared commitment to the sacred discovered in our midst is a most intimitizing communion.

Am I rehearsing here the past condemnation of "mixed marriages" which implied that different faith experiences do not mix well? No. As theologian Benjamin Hubbard says, spouses do not need the same religion (in the organized sense) but they do not need the same spirituality.[19] Sacred values are deeply held. Fateful collisions can result where some spiritual commonality is not present.

A Talent for Reconciliation

Marriage allows for little distance. Such closeness challenges patience. A wag put it on this way: "In marriage two become one. The battle is over *which* one." Differences can be harmonized in mutuality or repressed by domination. The latter route leads to battle. To be married long and well is to have excelled in the art of reconciling and forgiving.

Marriage is the most challenging of relationships. In marriage, two persons, unequally socialized in different family settings, merge. Mergers in any plane of life are never free of tension. To some degeree, every merger, however friendly, is a collision of unaccommodated interests and proclivities. Even the marital merger cannot be pure bliss. Upon dour reflection, it is no great wonder that the bedroom has been called the most murderous room in our society. Only the gentle can marry well. And reconciliation is the genius of the gentle.

A Capacity for Risk

To marry is to leave a harbor of apparent safety and set out on a voyage that cannot be charted in advance. In itself it is an act of courage, and it is a healthy expression of our native need to take risks. An overweaning yearning for security is as suffocating in the realm of love as it is in the realm of ideas. We have to escape the stranglehold of the *status quo*, and that takes risking. Foolhardiness is no virtue, but the effort to hermetically exclude risk arrests growth in or out of marriage.

Loving Beyond Reason

The French say that true love is always a bit mad. Real love is an adventure, not an investment. It is not based on the calculation of merit and of what is deserved. The Hebrew *hesed* and the Greek Christian *agape* capture this idea of love as grace gratuitously given, *gratia gratis data*. Marital love is trusting, not computing. You cannot deserve it. It is a risk one takes in another.

Space

True union, says Teilhard de Chardin, differentiates. It doesn't blur. It doesn't make you less of what you are, but allows you to express more fully your individuality and to become more fully what you are. True friends do not crowd one another out. Too much togetherness can smother. Thomas Aquinas saw this in writing about union as the first effect of love. Love tries to make one of two. *"ex ambobus fieri unum."* This rush to union, however, could overwhelm and corrupt one of the lovers or both. *"accideret aut ambo aut alterum corrumpi."*[20]

The crushing need for unity in all interests, all friends, and all activities is bred of insecurity and is not the mark of a daring and healthy love. A cloying need to banish all diversity and separation is self-defeating, producing the very separation it seeks to bar. It introduces control and breeds resentment.

Love does assimilate. An ancient saying had it this way: "Love either finds you alike, or makes you so." *Amor aut invenit aut facit pares.* But there are limits, and the union of true love brooks diversity, breadth, and freedom.

Diffusion

Love diffuses itself, *Amor diffusivus sui*. Marriage should not become a form of dualized egoism *(egoisme à deux)*. Early love may retreat from community in the rapture of new discovery and in the insecurity of early and precarious limerence.[12]

Enduring friendship, however, enriches more than the friends. Friendship is a social event. The friends, being ever more truly themselves, have more to give to the world. Ideally, marriage and the family are the workshops for social justice in a society. Within the matrix of committed love you can better see what human life deserves. The family, in some form, is normally the primary unit of socialization which creates positive or negative attitudes toward social and distributive justice. Good love is marked by outreach. A good family hungers and thirsts after justice.

Dreams

The marriage ceremony could take these words from Yeats:

I, being poor, have only my dreams;
I have spread my dreams under your feet;
Tread softly because you tread on my dreams.[22]

Dreams are a tender treasure. And we live on them. In marriage, dreams meet and new ones are begotten. We are born either to dream toward more or to atrophy. It is dreamers who wed, and they must not stop dreaming. Made in the image of the infinite, we are not content to pasture on the terrain of the given. The horizon beckons and so we dream. Reality disciplines our dreaming, but the talent for dreaming must repeatedly resurrect. And so it is for the married to dream and struggle and tread softly.

CHAPTER 8

The Morality of Homosexual Marriage

For a significant minority of persons in the human community, erotic desire is focused, primarily or exclusively, on persons of the same sex. Psychiatrists are divided on whether to label this *de facto* variation pathological or not. Similarly, moralists are divided as to whether this orientation is an inclination to moral perversion, or a simple variation in the human quest for intimacy. If it is pathology, medical science should look for a cure; if it is an ingrained tilt toward unconscionable behavior, ethicists must counsel its containment.

The psychiatric or ethical position that sees homosexuality as clinical or moral pathology is blessed with striking simplicity. Clearly, pathologies are not to be encouraged under the specious claim of freedom or self-fulfillment. We find in the human sexual lexicon such manifestly pathological conditions as zoophilia, pedophilia, necrophilia, fetishism, sadistic or masochistic sex, exhibitionism, voyeurism, and rape. If homosexuality fits somewhere in that listing, we need not labor long in discussing its moral or psychological status. We do not speak of a well-adjusted necrophiliac, nor do we consider necrophiliacs as having a moral and civil right to access to corpses. There is no cry for rapist or fetishist liberation. Some things are abnormal and harmful at least to the agent who acts out on them. Is this the case for homosexuality?

Those who say yes face two critical difficulties: (1) they must show that those who act in any way on their homosexual orientation victimize themselves or others and (2) they must show that celibacy is good for all nonheterosexual persons.

First, regarding the harm, it is empty nominalism to name something harmful in the absence of identifiable harm. It is illogical to speak of a moral or psychological cure for a harmful condition if we cannot show what harm the cure is to address. Illness is known by its symptoms. In the absence of symptoms, we assume persons are well. If psychiatry would label homosexuality a pathology or illness, it must show how it adversely affects persons who express their intimacy-needs homosexually. The delineations of these adverse effects must also show that these are due to the orientation itself and not to the sociocultural effects of seeing the condition as an illness. If a society falsely imputes negative meaning to a sexual orientation, this will adversely affect persons who act out on that orientation, though the fault would be with the social stigmatizing and not with the orientation itself.

Clearly, then, psychiatry and ethics must pass the "show-me" test when they speak of homosexuality as a malady in need of a remedy. The test is not met simply by stating that homosexuality is a "disorder" because it is a minority phenomenon or because anatomy and reproductive needs suggest male-female coitus as the unexceptionable norm. Minority status does not of itself mean objectionable deviance. Indeed, the presence of minority status is the spice of variety and thus of life. But is not anatomy destiny? The penis and the vagina do enjoy a congenial fit, and the species' need for reproduction relies on that. But sex rarely, in any lifetime, has to do with reproduction, and not even heterosexual persons are limited to coitus for sexual fulfillment. Also, the species' need for reproductive sex is being met and often overmet.

In ethics, the term *biologism* refers to the fallacious effort to wring a moral mandate out of raw biological facts. The male-female coital fit and its relationship to reproduction are basic biological facts. The biologistic error would leap from those facts to the moral imperative that all sexual exchange must be male-female coital in kind. The leap could only become likely if you reduce human sexuality to the biological simplicities of the stud farm. Given the infinity of meanings beyond baby-making involved in human eroticism and sexuality, such a leap is misdirected and, literally, unreal.

No. If homosexuality is an illness requiring a cure, if it is an orientation to sin, it is because it is harmful to persons. If that harm cannot be pinpointed, the charge of sin or illness must be reconsidered.

George Bernard Shaw reminded us that it is the way of barbarians to think of the customs of their tribe as the laws of nature. Is the homosexually oriented quest for intimacy contrary to the laws of nature or simply to the current customs of our tribe? That question is regularly sent to go a-begging. The discussion, however, depends on facing it squarely.

The second question confronting those who see homosexuality as pathology regards celibacy as the only moral option for nonheterosexuals. Moralists of this position say that the condition of being homosexually oriented is not evil in itself since it seems irreversible in many or most instances. (Some deviant Christian fundamentalists see homosexuality as a contumacious and wicked option that can be cast out by prayer and fasting. In the absence of *any* supportive data, we commend such a position to its own embarrassment.) The evil would be in acting out one's homosexual proclivities. The morally good homosexual, in this view, is the celibate homosexual. This position has inherent contradictions. Implicitly it is reducible to the position of the deviant Christian fundamentalists since it says: You may be homosexual but, with prayer and fasting, you will never have to express it. It insists that there is nothing wrong with being a homoseuxal as long as you do not act on it. That is too tidy. There is a lot wrong with being a homosexual if all the values that attach to sexual expression are denied you. Sex is more than orgasms; it is an important avenue to many personal values. If the sexual avenue is categorically closed off to gay persons, that is no slight impairment. It makes the condition itself an abridgment of personality.

This "be-but-don't-do" position rests on three errors: (1) a materialistic and narrow view of sex; (2) a stunted epistemology; and (3) a departure from biblical good sense.

First, then, it views sex narrowly and materialistically, missing its linkage to such deeply felt human needs as intimacy, trust, and friendship. It would be gratuitous to say that a celibate cannot meet those human needs—that sex is necessary for human fulfillment—but it is equally gratuitous to say that a whole class of persons involving as much as 4 or 5 percent of the human population can be barred morally from the only kind of access to sexuality that attracts them.

Erotic desire is deeply interwoven into the human desire and need for closeness and for trusting relationships. The desire for a significant other with whom we are uniquely conjoined is not a heterosexual but a basic human desire. The programmatic exclusion of gay persons from the multiple benefits of erotic attraction, which often opens the way to such a union, is arbitrary, harmful, cruel, and therefore sinful.

Again, I am not saying that marriage or sexual activity are necessary for human fulfillment or psychological normalcy. Voluntary and involuntary celibacy is more common than is generally noted in a time of sexual overemphasis. Celibacy, voluntary or not, does not exclude human fulfillment. Sexually unfulfilled persons may be very fulfilled humanly. However, I stress that the sweeping exclusion of all gay persons from this important access route to meeting intimacy needs could only be based on a narrow and, I must insist, macho-masculine conception of what sex is and how it functions in human personal development.[1]

This position also lumps together without distinction all manifestations of homosexuality. Basically, the position is anthropologically naive. Few areas of human life are as variegated as sexual activity. This holds also for homosexuality. Some manifestations of homosexuality are harmful to human personal and social good. A moral argument opposed to homosexual activity in those instances can be made. However, to claim to know, by some encyclopedic intuition, that only celibacy befits homosexuals in any culture, clime, or time is—to say the least—immodest. More accurately, it is epistemologically absurd. It involves a kind of *essentialist* approach to knowing. Thus, even before all the data is in on what homosexuality is, how it develops, what it means in persons and societies, how it interrelates with other aspects of human relating, etc.—before all of that is known, a formula-panacea has been found that exhausts the moral meaning of homosexuality by prescribing celibacy.

Such essentialist thinking in ethics has a poor track record. Once we thought we had intuited the nature of money so clearly that we could say that all interest taking was sinful regardless of circumstances. Once we thought that we had so intuited the nature of sex that we could know that all contraceptive sexual exchange was wrong. We also believed that we had so thoroughly plumbed the meaning of speech that even to prevent serious harm such as murder we could not speak untruth. All of these essentialist visions have been humbled. The road to truth is longer and more tortuous than we thought. But now, regarding homosexuality, we are again told that the nature of homosexuality can be so perfectly intuited (especially by heterosexuals) that we can, with majestic calm, make a transcultural judgment that any expression of it anywhere is wrong and dehumanizing. Such arrogance is not the hallmark of truth.

Any position about the complexities of human behavior and development that ignores the witness of experience is suspect. The position the asserts that homosexuality is all right as long as you do not act on it is innocent of and apparently unconcerned with the experience of homosexually oriented persons. The more one looks into that experience and hears sensitive witness from gay persons, the less comfortable one can be with the glib "be-but-don't-do" approach to this human mystery. This approach gratuitously and stubbornly assumes that homosexuality fits with such things as pedophilia and obsessive voyeurism. It assumes with signal cruelty that homoeroticism has no more humanizing possibilities than incest or zoophilia. In this view, homoeroticism is, like all of these demonstrably noxious realities, sick. Since the conclusion of this error is a prescription of universal celibacy for all gays, the burden is clearly upon those who would so prescribe. Instead we receive poor exegesis of religious texts, biologisms, and warmed-over biases in place of argument. Neither ethics nor persons are well served by such careless intuitionism and empirically bereft moralizing.

Jean-Paul Sartre has told us that the greatest evil of which persons are capable is to treat as abstract that which is concrete. That is precisely what the "be-but-don't-do" school does to homosexuality. It takes the infinitely diverse experiences of homosexual persons and classifies them without distinction as evil. Such a globular approach does not commend itself to intelligence.

The final error of the "be-but-don't-do" position relates particularly to Christians who should be nourished by the earthy wisdom of the Bible. Facile urgings of celibacy for persons who do not happen to be heterosexual fly in the face of biblical good sense. Saint Paul, in his celebrated First Letter to the Corinthians, talks about the possibility of celibacy. Even though he is writing in a state of high eschatological expectation, and with the expressed conviction that it is better not to have sex (1 Cor 7:1), he allows that sexual needs are such that it would be better to marry (7:12). He concedes that persons may lack self-control (7:15), and so even married persons would be better advised not to be sexually abstinent for long. He would prefer all to be celibate but notes that each one has his/her own gift from God (7:17), implying very clearly that not all have the gift of celibacy. Again, he would prefer the unmarried and widowed to stay celibate but, once more, allows for the possible lack of "self-control" and concludes that "it is better to marry than to burn" (7:19).

The "be-but-don't-do" position would certainly allow, with Paul, that it is better for heterosexuals to marry than to burn. But, apparently their message for our homosexual brothers and sisters is: "Burn, burn!" We should not be terribly surprised that gay persons do not see this as "the good news." They can point out that Paul in this passage is reflecting the good sense of Jesus, who also said of voluntary celibacy: "Let him accept it who can" (Mt 19:12). The Church itself, in the Second Vatican Council, has taken up this sensible idea, describing voluntary celibacy as "a precious gift," not as something indiscriminately given to whole classes of peoples.[2] The council points out that chastity will be very difficult, that it will face "very severe dangers" even for seminarians and religious with all the safeguards built into their life-style.[3] Those who would embark on a life of celibacy "should be very carefully trained for this state."[4] The council calls voluntary celibacy a "counsel," not a mandate, "a precious gift of divine grace which the Father gives to *some* persons," but not to all.[5] This gift of "total continence" is seen as worthy of special honor and as something "unique."[6] Celibate chastity "deserves to be esteemed as a surpassing gift of grace . . . which liberates the human heart in a unique way."[7] Persons entering religious orders should be warned in advance that celibacy, even in the sacred confines of religious life, is not easy. Involved in the celibate project are "the deeper inclinations of human nature." Candidates for a celibate religious life should have "a truly adequate testing period" to see if "they have the needed degree of psychological and emotional maturity." They should be warned of "the dangers confronting chastity."[8]

To all of which, our gay brothers and sisters might reply: "If total continence is so difficult for nuns and priests, why is it so easy for us? If it is a counsel for them, why is it a precept for us?" These are good questions. If celibacy is so difficult that only some heterosexuals can undertake it—and then with the most extraordinary systems of support—how can we say that all gays have this "unique" talent for self-containment? If celibacy is seen as it is in a religious context as a special charism, are all gays charismatically blessed with celibate graces? Is this not a radical theological restatement of the position that "gay is good?" It is a traditional axiom of Catholic moral theology that no one is held to the impossible (*nemo ad impossible tenetur*). Are gays, nevertheless, held to what is impossible for nongays? For nongays, in this view, celibacy is a gifted feat that symbolizes the special, generous presence of the power of God. For gays, it is just a way of life, and the least that they can do. There are problems here that even minimal insight and honesty could see and should admit. The pastoral position resulting from this contorted ethical position is equally strained. The only advice it leaves for gays is this: Pray and repress your erotic tendencies. God does not demand the impossible, and so God will give you the strength to do what moral theology, written by heterosexuals, has decided God wants you to do. If you fall from grace, appeal to God for forgiveness and your pastoral counselor will receive you with kindness and compassion.

Such pastoral advice embodies the theological error of "tempting God." It also harkens back to the medieval "ordeal," which contrived tests and put God on notice to come up with the response dictated by the test. If the fire burned you, you were evil. In this ordeal which we impose on gay persons, ethicists have boxed themselves into an arbitrary theological position which requires total celibacy from all gays and then leaves it up to God to pull off this implausible feat through prayer, sacraments, and pastoral counseling. Poor theology always puts God on the spot.

When we do theological ethics, we are painting a picture of our God. To say that something is good or bad is to say that it is in agreement or disagreement with the perceived will of God. In the position under discussion, we have God asking one thing from gays and considerably less from heterosexuals. If gay persons accept this particular ideological position on the ethics of homosexuality as the mind of God, *and* if they find it in contradiction to their own experience of reality, they have been pushed into the position of having to accept themselves *or* God. It is a position calculated to do precisely what pastoral theology should not do—alienate persons from the experience of God. Even at some risk to their professional situation, pastoral counselors are required not to offer either formal or material cooperation with a position that is so insensitive and religiously devastating.

Marriage as an Option for Homosexuals

Marriage is the highest form of interpersonal commitment and friendship achievable between sexually attracted persons. Nothing in that definition requires that the sexually attracted persons who are conjoined in committed, conjugal friendship must be heterosexual. Neither is the capacity for having children required. Reproductive fertility is not of the essence of genuine marriage. Even in the Roman Catholic tradition, sterile persons are permitted to marry, and, as a recent celebrated case in the Diocese of Joliet, Illinois, illustrated, even male impotence is no barrier to marriage. This means that the basic sense of the current Catholic position on the relationship of marriage and childbearing is this: If there are to be children, they should be born within the confines of marriage. Yet, even fertile heterosexual persons do not have an obligation to have children. As Pope Pius XII taught, there can be a variety of reasons—social, economic, and genetic—for excluding children from a marriage entirely. Marriage clearly has more goods than the "good of children," the *bonum prolis*. And those other goods, in themselves, are enough to constitute marriage as a fully "human reality and saving mystery."[9]

The Second Vatican Council produced a major statement on the dignity and value of married life. The council Fathers were, of course, speaking of marriage between heterosexual persons. In fact, however, aside from the "good of offspring," which they stress is not essential for a genuine marriage, the goods and values they attach to marriage are not exclusively heterosexual in kind. The needs that marriage fulfills are human needs. The values that marriage enhances are integral to humanity as such and not to humanity as heterosexual. In fact, the *indispensable* goods of marriage are those that do not relate intrinsically to heterosexuality. The *dispensable* good—offspring—is the only good that does relate to heterosexuality.

Let us look to the council's statement on marriage and see what "good news" we might find there for gay persons who seek a humanizing and holy expression of their God-given orientation.

The image that the council gives of marriage is, on the whole, very positive and sensitive to personal needs. Marriage is seen as "an unbreakable compact between persons" of the sort that must "grow and ripen."[10] "Marriage persists as a whole manner and communion of life, and maintains its value and indissolubility, even when offspring are lacking."[11] Married persons should "nourish and develop their wedlock by pure conjugal love and undivided affection."[12] The council continues in a decidedly personalist tone:

This love is an eminently human one since it is directed from one person to another through an affection of the will. It involves the good of the whole person. Therefore it can enrich the expressions of body and mind with a unique dignity, ennobling these expressions as special ingredients and signs of the friendship distinctive of marriage. This love the Lord has judged worthy of special gifts, healing, perfecting, and exalting gifts of grace and of charity.

Such love, merging the human with the divine, leads the spouses to a free and mutual gift of themselves, a gift proving itself by gentle affection by deed. Such love pervades the whole of their lives. Indeed, by its generous activity it grows better and grows greater. Therefore it far excels mere erotic inclination which, selfishly pursued, soon enough fades wretchedly away.[13]

To make married love prosper, the couple are urged to "painstakingly cultivate and pray for constancy of love, largeheartedness, and the spirit of sacrifice."[14] The married couple are to become no longer two, but one flesh by rendering "mutual help and service to each other through an intimate union of their persons and their actions. Through this union they experience the meaning of their oneness and attain to it with growing perfection day by day." The goal of marriage is "unbreakable oneness."[15] Such "multi-faceted love" mirrors the love of God for the world. It will be marked by "perpetual fidelity through mutual self-bestowal." It should lead to the "mutual sanctification" of the two parties and "hence contribute jointly to the glory of God."[16]

The council does not look on this love as angelic and asexual. In fact, it stresses that this mutually satisfying and sanctifying love "is uniquely expressed and perfected through the marital act."[17] Sexual expression is extolled: "The acts themselves which are proper to conjugal love and which are exercised in accord with genuine human dignity must be honored with great reverence."[18] Again, reflecting the biblical sense of the natural goodness of sexual liturgy and its importance to conjugal love, the council warns that "where the intimacy of married life is broken off, it is not rare for its faithfulness to be imperiled and its quality of fruitfulness ruined."[19] Abstinence from sex, therefore, is viewed cautiously.

All of these texts of the council show a keen sense of the kinds of needs that are met in marital love. Married love will not survive on the thrills of early eroticism. What persons seek in marriage is total acceptance of all aspects of the self, the corrigible and the incorrigible, the lovely and the unlovely, the strong and the weak. Married love is not a selfish investment but an adventure in self-sacrificing, creative love. It is a school of holiness where persons may grow closer to God as they grow closer to one another and where their conjugal love may fuel their passion for justice and love for all people.

By what reasoning should values such as these be reserved for the heterosexual majority and denied to our gay brothers and sisters? By what twisted logic could we assume that gay persons would not experience the advantage of a love that produced such an "unbreakable oneness?" Why would gay persons in love be forbidden to aspire to and pray for "constancy of love, largeheartedness, and the spirit of sacrifice" to sustain their love? If erotic love between heterosexuals "is uniquely expressed and perfected" through sexual language, why would homoerotic love be judged moral only if sexually mute?

Two Objections to Homosexual Marriage

Two immediate objections might be these: (1) gay persons do not display the psychological stability and strength necessary for lifelong commitment in marriage, and (2) the data indicate that gay persons prefer promiscuity to closed one-to-one relationships, showing that marriage is a heterosexual ideal being imperiously imposed on homosexuals.

How stable are gays psychologically? In an important study, Professors Alan Bell and Martin Weinberg bring extensive research to bear on the common stereotypes our society maintains regarding homosexual persons. At the heart of the stereotyping is the belief that homosexuals are "pretty much alike." Accordingly, it is significant that Bell and Weinberg entitle their study *Homosexualities: A Study of Diversity Among Men and Women*. According to the stereotype, the homogeneous homosexuals are marked by "irresponsible sexual conduct, a contribution to social decay, and, of course, psychological pain and maladjustment."[20] The study presents strong evidence that "relatively few homosexual men and women conform to the hideous stereotype most people have of them." The authors describe as their "least ambiguous finding" that "homosexuality is not necessarily related to pathology."[21]

Regarding the psychological adjustment of homosexual men, Bell and Weinberg discovered that only one or two of the homosexual subgroups compared adversely to heterosexual men as to psychological adjustment. "The remaining subgroups tended to appear as well adjusted as the heterosexuals or, occasionally, even more so."[22] One quasi-marital subgroup, which the study styles "close-coupled" fared more than well in comparison to heterosexuals. "They felt no more tense, and were even happier than the heterosexual men."[23] Lesbians differed even less than male homosexuals in measures of psychological adjustment. In fact, close-coupled lesbians came out better in some regards than comparably situated heterosexual women.[24]

These findings are remarkable when we consider the stresses gay persons are subjected to in an antihomosexual society. All adolescents are vulnerable in their self-image. They are normally moving out from the nurturing closeness of family life, where their value has been consistently and reliably affirmed. In coping with this the adolescent vacillates between shrillness and bombast and shyness and tears. If, in the delicate move from familial to somewhat broader social endorsement, the young persons discover that a profound aspect of their personality is loathsome to the dominant majority, a painful crisis ensues. The discovery that one is a "queer," a "faggot," and a "pervert" is terrifying news to the delicate emergent ego. The news is so frightening that some self-protectively blind themselves to their own sexual identity in an amazing feat of denial. Others cope, often alone, with little or no solace or support. Even those on whom they have most depended up till now are normally of no help. Parents and siblings usually give clear witness to their detestation of homosexuality. Sexual awareness, then, brings the homosexual adolescent into a terrible loneliness. That so many of them bear this solitary suffering so well and arrive at such high levels of psychological adjustment is a striking tribute to resilience of the human spirit. Heterosexual youths have their own tensions, but normally nothing comparable to the crushing rejection that greets the young gay person with the onset of puberty.

In view of all this, it is both arrogant and unjust for the heterosexual and dominant majority to perpetuate the myth that gay persons are psychologically unsound when these persons have passed more tests of psychological adjustment than many heterosexuals are ever required to do. There is simply no evidence that the psychological state of gays disqualifies them *as a class* from deeply committed and specifically conjugal relationships. The gratuitous assertion or assumption that they are lamed in this respect constitutes, in terms of traditional Catholic moral theology, a mortal sin of calumny. It is also a sin of injustice requiring restitution. Few of us heterosexuals are without sin in this regard, and so we are required by the virtues of justice and veracity to take the trouble to know better the actual situation of our gay brothers and sisters and to make appropriate reparatory responses to their needs.

The second objection to marital friendship for homosexual persons rests on their alleged preference for promiscuous sexual life-styles. Again, studies do not support these stereotypes. Lesbians are particularly prone to form lasting marriagelike relationships. Even among male homosexuals, where promiscuity is more common, prolonged "affairs" are common. The Bell-Weinberg study reaches this conclusion:

Our data indicate that a relatively steady relationship with a love partner is a very meaningful event in the life of a homosexual man or woman. From our respondents' descriptions, these affairs are apt to involve an emotional exchange and commitment similar to the kinds that heterosexuals experience, and most of the homosexual respondents thought that they and their partners had benefited personally from their involvement and were at least somewhat unhappy when it was over. The fact that they generally went on to a subsequent affair with another partner seems to suggest a parallel with heterosexuals' remarriage after divorce rather than any particular emotional immaturity or maladjustment. In any case, most of our homosexual respondents spoke of these special relationships in positive terms and clearly were not content to limit their sexual contacts to impersonal sex.[25]

There is, of course, evidence that homosexual men are more promiscuous than any other group. This fact, however, must be put in
context to be evaluated. A major factor is the high availability of sex
in the male homosexual world, and homosexual men are men. As the
psychologist, Dr. C. A. Tripp writes: "The variety of sex the heterosexual male usually longs for in fantasy is frequently realized in practice
by the homosexual. . . . There is no indication that homosexual promiscuity is any greater than its heterosexual equivalent would be in the
face of equal opportunity."[26] There are other reasons that account for
the promiscuous pattern among many male homosexuals. Two men do
not have the same social freedom to live together that women enjoy.
It often amounts to revelation of one's orientation with all the hazards
that entails in a biased society. The prejudice of the community and
of traditional Catholic moral theology discourages stable relationships
and indirectly opens the way to promiscuity. Homosexual unions also
usually lack children. As the Vatican Council noted, "children contribute in their own way to making their parents holy."[27] Part of that holiness is the holiness of fidelity and stable, enduring love. By excluding
any serious consideration of mature and stable gay couples adopting
children, or of lesbian couples having children by artifical insemination,
we block, without due ethical process, this inducement to healthy relationships among gays. Another factor that inclines to promiscuity
among gays is the fact that they are more likely to find partners that
are more culturally diverse, which makes for greater likelihood of incompatibility on the long haul.

Therefore, we may not simply look from a distance at the statistics
of greater male homosexual promiscuity without distinguishing the
various groupings of homosexuals and without recognizing the pressures against marital relationships in the life situation of many gays.

The Marriage Option and Solidly Probable Opinion

Within the confines of Roman Catholicism, there is division on the
ethics of homosexual behavior. A number of moralists hold the traditional "be-but-don't-do" position and a number of others are open to
humane expressions of gay sexual love. The hierarchical magisterium
seems firm on the "be-but-don't-do" position. The theological magisterium is divided. The hierarchical position is admittedly noninfallible
and is not an obstacle to open debate as long as there is due account
of and study of that position. What tools for such a pluralistic situation
did the Roman Catholic tradition provide? The answer is that the tra-

dition provided an excellent moral system known as probabilism for precisely such a situation. The system has been in a state of disuse, and this represents a major loss of a traditional Catholic treasure.

Probabilism, like all good things, was abused, but the theological achievement that it represents was significant and, until we see how it relates to the charismatic theology of Paul and John and to the concept of the moral inspiration of the Holy Spirit in Augustine and Saint Thomas Aquinas, it has not been given its theological due. Another reason for bringing probabilism down from the Catholic attic is that after Vatican II's recognition of the truly ecclesial quality of Protestant Christian churches, neoprobabilism could be the test of ecumenism. Is our ecumenism merely ceremonial or can we really begin to take Protestant moral views into account in discussing liceity in doubtful matters? The older probabilism did not even face such a question.

The triumph of probabilism in the Church was an achievement of many of our long-suffering theological forebears and we do well to harken back to their work. Let me briefly repeat what probabilism is all about. Probabilism arose, and finally gained prominence over competing systems, as a way of solving practical doubt about the liceity of some kind of behavior. In practice, it confronted a situation in which a rigorous consensus claiming the immorality of certain behavior was challenged. The question was: At what point does the liberty-favoring opinion attain such respectability in the forum of conscience that a person could follow it in good faith? Those who said that even frivolous reasons would justify departure from rigorous orthodoxy were condemned as laxists by Popes Innocent XI and Alexander VII. At the other extreme were the absolute tutiorists who taught that you could never follow the liberal opinion unless it was strictly certain. Even being most probable (*probabilissima*) was not enough. In graph form the situation was like this:

A	/ B

A represents the dominant rigorous opinion claiming that certain activity could never be moral. B represents the liberal dissent. Laxism claimed that the most tenuous B would override A. Absolute tutiorism claimed that until B replaced A and was beyond challenge, it could not be followed. The Jansenists found absolute tutiorism attractive, but Alexander VIII did not, and he condemned it on December 7, 1690. Thus between the two banned extremes of laxism and absolute tutiorism, the Catholic debate raged with probabilism gradually becoming dominant.

Probabilism proceeded from the twin insights that *a doubtful obligation does not bind as though it were certain,* and that *where there is doubt there is freedom.* It held that a solidly probable opinion could be followed even though more probable opinions existed. To be solidly probable, a liberal opinion had to rest upon cogent though not conclusive reasons (intrinsic probability) or upon reliable authority (extrinsic probability). As Tanquerey puts it in his manual of moral theology, to be probable, an opinion could not be opposed to a "definition of the Church" or to certain reason and should retain its probability when compared with opposing arguments.[28] Since there is no "definition of the Church" regarding homosexuality and since furthermore it is clear that the Church does not have the competence to define such issues infallibly,[29] that condition cannot stand in the way of using probabilism.

Intrinsic probability, where one followed one's own lights to a solidly probable opinion, was not stressed in the history of probabilism, but it was presented as a possibility. Stress fell upon extrinsic probability where one found "five or six" moralists known for their "authority, learning and prudence." Even one extraordinarily preeminent teacher alone could constitute probability. What this meant is that minority B on our graph became solidly probable through private insight or through the insight of five or six learned experts even though the enormous majority of theologians disagreed. Note well that the basis of probabilism is insight—one's own or that of reliable experts. Insight is an achievement of moral intelligence. It cannot be forbidden, neither does it await permission to appear.

Note also that probabilism does not require a consensus or certitude. As Father Henry Davis writes, "when I act on the strength of a probable opinion, I am always conscious that though I am morally right in so acting, since I act prudently, nevertheless, the opinion of others who do not agree with me may be the true view of the case."[30] Obviously, the perennial debate will be between those who argue that the defenders of probability in a particular case are actually crypto-laxists and those who argue that the deniers of probability are disguised absolute tutiorists.

Probabilism was a remarkable development, and represents a high point in Catholic moral thought. It recognized that the apparent safety of absolute tutiorism was only apparent. The acceptance of such a rigorous position, as Father Tanquerey explained, would impose an impossible burden on the faithful contrary to the mind of the Gospel, which promises that the yoke will be sweet and the burden light; it would thus increase sins, generate despair, and drive many from the practice of religion.[31] Those reasons and probabilism itself are still relevant today.

To dismiss probabilism as the legalistic bickerings of the sixteenth and seventeenth centuries, is theologically shortsighted. In the heyday of the debate, extravagant claims were made. Caramuel, who became known as the "prince of the laxists," taught that Adam and Eve used probabilism sucessfully to excuse themselves from many sins, until their wits and their probabilism failed them and they did fall. Vigorous efforts were made to trace the formal doctrine of probabilism to Augustine, Jerome, Ambrose, Gregory of Nazianzen, Basil, and Thomas Aquinas. One need not become party to such adventures to insist on and argue how compatible probabilism is with deep Christian traditions. The early Church was remarkably sanguine about the presence of the illumining Spirit in the hearts of the faithful. As Vatican II says:

The Spirit dwells in the Church and in the hearts of the faithful as in a temple (cf. 1 Cor 3:16; 6:19). In them He prays and bears witness to the fact that they are adopted sons (cf. Gal 4:6; Rom 8:15–16, 26). The Spirit guides the Church into the fullness of truth (cf. Jn 16:13) and gives her a unity of fellowship and service. He furnishes and directs her with various gifts, both hierarchical and charismatic, and adorns her with the fruits of His grace (cf. Eph 4:11–12; 1 Cor 12:4; Gal 5:22).[32]

The Church has shared the confidence of Saint Paul when he said that the spiritual person "is able to judge the value of everything."[33] Augustine and Thomas manifest in strong theological language this exuberant confidence in the presence in all Christians of the illumining Spirit of God. Augustine asked: "What are the laws of God in our hearts but the very presence of the Holy Spirit?"[34] And Thomas Aquinas, arguing that the new law is not anything written (including the New Testament), cites Jeremiah's promise that in the future testament God will put moral law into the minds of his people and inscribe it on their hearts. In its primary meaning, then, the new law for Thomas is not the writings of biblical authors, Church officers, or theologians, all of which are secondary, but the instructive grace of the Holy Spirit.[35]

This, admittedly, is a heady doctrine which called for and did historically elicit a theology of the discernment of the Spirit. One must test one's claimed inspiration against all the witnesses to truth within the community. And yet this heady doctrine, with all of its perils, is not a private preserve of the current charismatic movement in the Church, but is rather *bona fide* mainstream Catholic thought. It is also, I believe, eminently congenial with the spirit of the debate that led to the championing of probabilism. The debate on probabilism in many ways seems a curious and stilted period piece, but it would be ungrateful and unconservative of us to reject this achievement of the Catholic tradition. And reject it, in effect, we did. Of course, it maintained its presence in the manuals, but in practice it was rendered nugatory. This was done by simply ignoring the genuine possibility of intrinsic probability and by controlling the theological enterprise in such ways that any theologians favoring a liberal opinion that did not square with the contemporary Vatican view were quickly deemed neither learned nor prudent. Thus did extrinsic probability pass. And thus were the doors thrown open to a juridical positivism based on the hierarchical magisterium.

The neoprobabilism for which I call would have to be extended to include Protestant and other witnesses to moral truth. Vatican II said of Protestant Christians that "in some real way they are joined with us in the Holy Spirit, for to them also He gives his gifts and graces, and is thereby operative among them with His sanctifying power."[36] It becomes unthinkable, therefore, if these words mean anything, that we accept that solid probability could not also be achieved through the witness of Protestants and others who are also subjects of the "gifts and graces" of God. I submit that if that thought is unpalatable, our ecumenism is superficial and insincere.[37]

Obviously, within Protestant and Catholic Christianity, there is considerable support for the possibility of moral, humane, and humanizing sexual expression by gay persons. Extrinsic probability does obtain. Intrinsic probability is within the reach of mature persons. There is no reason why this traditional tool of Catholic thought should not be used by pastoral counselors. Obviously the acceptance of the ideal of marriage for gay persons is not something that could be celebrated with public liturgy at this point in the history of the Church since such a celebration would imply a general consensus that as yet does not exist. The celebration of private liturgies, however, to conjoin two gays in permanent and committed love would seem commendable, and well within the realm of the principles and spirit of probabilism. The marital good of exclusive, committed, enduring, generous, and faithful love is a human good. We have no moral right to declare it off limits to persons whom God has made gay.

Part 4

THE NEW MORALITY OF FEMINISM

The assault on sexism (the belief that women are inferior by reason of their gender) is an event in the histoy of ethics. Feminism *is* the assault on sexism. It seeks to recover the lost possibilities of a humanity splintered by sexism. It is not a womens' issue but a human issue. It is an effort to correct the skewed concept of humanity that has been polluting politics, institutions, and relationships through all of history.

Chapters Nine and Ten look to the reshaping of morality and religion in the healing perspectives of a new feminism. Chapter Eleven addresses the male monopoly on ministry and power in the Christian churches and argues that this exclusion is self defeating and unjust. These three chapters are part of an effort to rethink the basic categories by which we define our humanness. We are only at the beginnings here of a seismic revolution of moral consciousness.

CHAPTER 9

The Feminization of God and Ethics

On September 12, 1852, an editorial writer for the New York *Herald* penned the following words:

How did woman first become subject to man, as she now is all over the world? By her nature, her sex, just as the negro is and always will be to the end of time, inferior to the white race and, therefore doomed to subjection; but she is happier than she would be in any other condition, just because it is the law of her nature.[1]

That statement is a specimen of first level sexism—a robust and candid imputation of inferiority and subjection as natural to womanhood.

Almost a century after that editorial, George Kennan wrote, warning us against making "constant attempts at moral appraisal" in the analysis of international politics. "If," writes Kennan, "instead of making ourselves slaves of the concepts of international law and morality, we would confine these concepts to the unobtrusive, almost feminine, function of the gentle civilizer of national self-interest in which they find their true value," our efforts would be more fruitful.[2] This is second level sexism. The feminine is the unobtrusive, unquestioning civilizer of the masculine world of power. If the *feminine*, and the paralleled, feminized *moral*, know their place and stay there, their influence will be benign. The 1852 editorial put the feminine in the company of negritude, and distorted both. Kennan's statement (from which we may trust he has duly repented) puts the feminine in the company of morality and distorts both. Sexism contaminates all of its associates.

There is a third level of sexism, that can not be tied to a single quotation. It is a sexism from which, I submit, none of us has adequately repented. This sexism laughs at the 1852 editorial and explicitly repudiates imputations of inferiority. It blushes at second level sexism which consigns the feminine either to the pedestal or to the unobtrusive and benign backdrop of real life. The third level sexism eschews sexist language, accomodates to affirmative action, holds no meetings in states that have rejected the ERA. Yet, with all of this, like the rich young man who left Jesus sadly, this sexism avoids baptism by total immersion in feminine liberation. The third level sexist will often be a liberal and humane male who believes that feminine liberation is a cause to be struggled and suffered for—by women. It is their problem, and he wishes them well with it.

Third level sexism misses the fact that sexism is the elementary human sin. If the essential human molecule is dyadic, male/female, the perversion of one part of the dyad perverts the other. You cannot distort one-half of a correlative without distorting the other. But, to distort femininity *and* masculinity, the constitutive ingredients of humanity, is to distort humanity. Nothing will be spared the fallout from so radical a corruption. Here is *original* sin. Here is the fundamental lie which will have to mark all human ideas, customs, and institutions. The most fundamental form of otherness is male/female otherness. If this otherness is marked by opposition and disdain, it will be easier to oppose other others—be they black, Jewish, foreign, or poor. Third level sexism misses the fact that feminism is integral to any humanism and any ethics since it addresses the foundational crisis of the correlative perversion of the male/female human.

The title of my paper suggests a bias, and since the uncovering of biases is the beginning of wisdom, let me at once make my presuppositions overt. Something profound is going on, and feminization is its name. It is going on in the culture, shaking foundational categories of awareness, striking at long regnant myths and metaphors, affecting not just the splashing waves of issue-debates, but actually shifting the deep-running affective and symbolic tides that carry our thought in ways that argument often does not even know. The affective, subliminal, and genetic regions of understanding are being happily infiltrated with a fresh and integrative infusion of healing appreciation. And herein is my bias revealed. I welcome the incipient feminization of our culture. What we see at present are but the first auguries of what will be, if this still fledgling, but potentially epochal, reevaluation of human identity continues. Yet, even now, at this early time, there is much visible and beckoning our minds. The intellectual challenge here is not dull, since intellectuality is never more exciting than when it is engaged not in recording the past or analyzing the present, but in midwifing a new worldview. As Rosemary Ruether says, the feminist undertaking is nothing less than "an effort to reach behind the history of civilization to a lost alternative."[3] There is, then, no modesty to the enterprise at hand.

My approach to this massive subject will be this: first I will argue that the exclusion of women from most of the centers of power in most civilizations has impoverished the species because the experience of women has given them certain advantages in their moral perceptivity. Contrariwise, the experience of macho-masculine culture has in varying ways impeded male sensitivities, giving men (and women) who are significantly influenced by macho-masculinity, distinct debits in moral and religious knowing. I will then suggest how this has affected both ethics and the study of God. The moral and the sacred are the seedbeds of our most significant metaphors and symbols. Any shift here is seismic. My conclusion will not point to the triumph of femininity over masculinity, but to an emerging humanity which banishes stunted femininity and macho-masculinity and blends the masculine and the feminine into ever more genuine modalities of the species human.

There is an obvious danger in this subject. To speak of feminism and feminization implies that there is a corresponding masculinism out there that is under assault. There are combative implications in talk of feminization. There is also the immanent danger of distortional stereotyping or the fateful acceptance of anatomy as destiny. When we contrast masculinity to feminity, when we seek to feminize the patriarchal symbols and structures of our culture, we seem to be awash in amorphous generalizations.

Ungrounded generalization is, indeed, the root of much error. It represents the mind in flight from patient empirical analysis, and it does lead to fudgy stereotypes that blur differences in favor of a cozy generality. But generalization can also be grounded in the discovery of trends and patterns that appear in the historical unfolding of life. The mind, disciplined by empirical analysis is not limited to empirical analysis. We can also discern patternings amid the mass of images that present themselves. If we remain aware of the limits of these patternings we may avail ourselves of their strengths.

Applied to femininity and masculinity, our generalizations are not cut loose from the moorings of the real. These are meaningful terms, first of all, because there is some difference between boys and girls. The eyeball itself can spot them. But beyond the externally apparent we do know that even at the chromosomal level, boys and girls are different. Some studies indicate that the brains of males and females develop differently as a result of endocrine influences, and that there are differences in the central nervous systems of males and females which correlate with differences in behavior.[4] There are also dramatic differences in reproductive biology that must make for important personal differences. Unless we turn to cloning or artificial wombs, there is a basic difference between the woman's experience of reproduction and that of the inseminator. If, as Teilhard de Chardin has said, nothing is intelligible outside of its history, male and female histories are at variance. Role assignation was different. Also, from the dawn of history woman has experienced a seemingly invincible ostracism and subordination, and this would clearly make a difference. Some of the psychological differences resulting from all of this are now being charted by psychologists like Carol Gilligan, who shows the ways in which women organize data and evaluate differently than men. With the arrival of women into the academic disciplines—that is, women who do not ape men as the price of their academic success—new insights are shaking patriarchal thrones. For example, women scholars in the Hebrew and Christian scriptures are demonstrating that these influential books had always been read through male eyes with results that not surprisingly shored up patriarchal assumptions about power and life. So biology, history, psychology, sociology, anthropology and theology all give us grounds for saying that we are not adrift if we use terms like femininity and masculinity. We are touching life and we are staking out distinctions that correspond to real differences. Biologically and historico-culturally, men and women differ. If our bodies and our stories are different, we are, in some ways, different. Noting those differences, and their limits, is not distortional stereotyping. Denying them reflects a belief that sameness is the basis of human dignity. We may think God that is not so.

Feminine Advantages

There are notable advantages in feminine experience and in the moral evaluative capacities of women. Feminization which incorporates these advantages in ethics and in the study of religion is therefore progress. Again, I do not say that this advantageous femininity is only in women or in all women, or that the macho-masculinity I will describe is only in men or in all men to the same degree. I also do not deny that the history of women could not but damage them *and* that certain capacities in the masculine branch of humanity can be gainfully emulated by women. As should be obvious, I do not suggest that sin is a masculine prerogative. Still, it is my thesis that the moral sensitivity of women is generally enhanced and therefore better in at least four basic ways. The four ways are these: (1) Women are less alienated from bodily existence and are thus less seducible by abstractions; (2) the affective component of moral judgment is less suppressed in women; (3) women have historically had more opportunity to "go to school" on children and thus to be more identified with the moral rhythms of minimally corrupted human life; (4) women enjoy the wisdom that accrues to the alienated.

(1) *Women's at-home-ness with bodily existence.* However well metaphysical abstractions serve us, moral values ultimately reside in the concrete order of flesh and soil and rock. Biology and history have seen to it that women are more attuned to values in the concrete. This does not mean that women are less intellectual, but just that their intellectuality is more wholesomely rooted in the terrestrial order where persons dwell and where reality is experienced. To be specific, only a man could have stood in the ashes of the totally destroyed village of Ben Tre during the war in Vietnam and announce as one colonel did: "We had to destroy this village in order to save it." Womanly experience does not fit women to miss the disconnection between ashen destruction and *saving*. Helium-filled abstractions like "national security," "national interest," "nuclear superiority," can mesmerize the male mind, to the undoing of all concrete "security," "interest," and "superiority." Male economists speak easily of "economic success" *and* "acceptable levels of unemployment." Such abstraction comes harder for woman. She is closer to the flesh and to the earth in which all value resides.

In the sexual encounter, man can inseminate and ride off dreamfully into the sunset, but for woman a biological drama of symbiosis may begin which, through pregnancy and nursing, will tie her to the moment for many months. Indeed, by historical role assignment, it may link her there for a good chunk of a century, immersed in child care and "homemaking." Woman's body gives her menstrual reminders that life is not lived only from the neck up. Male imposed standards of pulchritude also have pressed women to bodily attentiveness. If it is true that, at birth, society looks at our crotches and then appoints us to one of two available cultures, the feminine or the masculine, the feminine culture that even childless women are placed in is filled with the memories and symbols of earthy service of the body and its actual environment. The feminine symbolic matrix is mind-enriching, leaving women less likely to do what Sartre called the greatest evil in the human repertoire, to treat as abstract that which is concrete. Clearly that is an advantage.

(2) *Women's integration of affect in moral judgment.* All moral experience is grounded in affectivity.[5] Affection is the animating mold of all moral knowing. Unlike technological knowledge, moral knowledge proceeds from an affective, indeed, at root, a mystical knowledge of the value of persons and their environing earth.

In woman, affect is less blunted than in men. The roles assigned to women by nature and in history nourished affect and indeed required it. It is not surprising then to read in psychological studies today that the moral judgments of women differ from those of men in that they are more closely tied to "feelings of empathy and compassion and are concerned more with the resolution of 'real-life' as opposed to hypothetical dilemmas."[6] Of course, in the present and in the past, this has been looked on by male researchers as an imperfection. If we are to judge by Kohlberg's all-male study (!) that has enjoyed such incredible currency, women are deficient. They do not achieve in the way that men do that progressive freeing of thought from contextual and affective "constraints" that supposedly mark the bloom of thought. If one's bias is that males are the paradigm, women will come off as deviant or deficient. And so it has been judged.

If, however, affectivity is indeed the enlivening mold of moral judgment, and if moral judgment is the basis of civilization, those in whom affect is less suppressed are more integral and more reliable in moral judgment. In fact, those who have freed their thought from psychological and historical restraints (mature men, in Kohlberg's vision) would actually seem dangerous. The colonel at Ben Tre is brother to the tearless politicians who have prepared for us the end of the world and stored it in their silos, all in the name of security.[7] The question is not whether *women* could function in intrinsically moral enterprises such as politics. The burden of proof has been classically misplaced.

(3) *Association with children.* One of the elements of the Christian scriptures that seems a triumph of insight is the recognition that unless one becomes like a child, he/she will never understand what God is attempting to do on this earth.[8] It was Jesus' teaching that God reveals to children what is hidden from wise and prudent adults.[9] It is a lost insight of Christian theology that it is not children who need cleansing from "original sin" but rather adults who have the infection and will spread it to the little ones. In the veins of our children, the gentlest rhythms of our humanity flow—trust, celebration, love. Indeed, if

those gentle rhythms do not prevail, our future is in terminal peril. Children have the appropriate horror of non-flourishing human life. Adults learn to live with conditions where many and sometimes most cannot survive, much less thrive a little. They come to accept misery as normatively normal and joy as only a fortuitous exception. Happily, there is a minority report, filed by children, which asserts and insists that ecstasy is our destiny. The normative primacy of joy is a childhood conviction. And it is replete with ethical import. Women have historically been graced with closeness to the repositories of such convictions. The male, out to encounter the hostile life, fell under less benign, more corrupted influences. He is the poorer, she the richer for this.

(4) *Alienation.* If you draw a circle and cut me out of it, I will become acutely aware of what is going on inside that circle. Alienation, in a painful and perverse way, lends light. The alienated must needs be defensive, and the defensive have big eyes. Thus, even disadvantages may be food for growth, as the history of women shows.

With all of this it should be stressed that women could not go through what they have without enduring wounds. Capacities for self-confidence and initiative, for independence and the avoidance of unnecessary leaning, are often diminished in women. Also, feminine advantages do not imply immaculate conception. Our sisters are not without sin. Indeed, even some fervidly feminist women rival macho men in the violence-sowing sins of separatism and hubris. Also, men with their masculinity have not just done ill. They have not simply ravaged the earth. They have also aggressively sought out cures and possibilities for humane living, and, in some instances, men have embodied in their persons the best of both the masculine and the feminine. And yet, turn we must next to their failings.

The Perils of Macho-Masculinity

It is a blunt historical fact, involving only aberrant exceptions here and there, that men have been the warriors of the race. They left the nursing woman in the cave and, in facing the resistent world without, they struggled against nature and their own kind. The struggle shaped them and gave them their cosmologies and their worldviews. It left them and all of us creatures of earth with some pervasive pathologies. Male-dominated institutions, cultures, and disciplines could not be entirely impervious to the influence of this deviant masculinity. The principal liabilities of the macho-masculine blight would seem to be these: (1) a proneness to violent modes of power; (2) an anti-communitarian, hierarchical proclivity; (3) a disabling abstractionism; (4) a consequentialist bias; (5) a culturally devastating and widely manifested hatred of women. Not every male in every culture has all of these debits; indeed, not any man in any culture has them in all their vigor. But history is not so irrelevant to historical beings that the millennia of male domination could have left no discernible impact on the realization of masculine identity.

(1) *Violence.* The Amazons are creatures of myth; war is a male preserve. The courage that was held through much of male history in such high esteem was mainly the courage of the warrior. Even gentle early Christianity, which saw itself as the vanguard of *Shalom,* had little enduring success in taming male bellicosity. For three hundred years Christian literature was pacifistic. Practice followed theory as Christian men were disposed to beat the sword into a plowshare. As late as the year 240, Origen conceded to the critic Celsus that Christians were pacifists. And yet when the Constantinian sword proved friendly, Christian men began to rejoin their brothers in arms. *By the year 416, you had to be a Christian to get into the army of Rome.* After only a brief demurrer, this heroic effort for a new, non-macho style of life collapsed.

Warriors, fortunately, do not always find wars. But the military mindset can translate into non-warring forms of aggression. The macho-masculine approach to life tends to be aggressive, not caring, engendering, or relational. Look at our own male-dominated culture, and hear the tale told by our metaphors. Problems are *assaulted,* not solved; diseases are *defeated,* not cured. A *killing* is made in the market. The Christian cross becomes a *triumph,* and God a *mighty fortress.* The system is to be *beaten,* and the frontiers of knowledge *pushed back.* Even poetry is called a *raid* on the inarticulate. A good personality is a *winning* personality. An ancient axiom says that it is at play that we most reveal our moral orientation. (*Inter ludendum mores se detegunt.*) A look at a National Football League game, and at the names of the teams competing in that league, gives a grim portrait of the American male at play. Aggression, not harmony, is supreme. The impact of this, in a male-dominated world, on religion, mores, and learning is not slight. The infection goes to the roots and affects in some way all the issues we ethicists address.

When the warrior male goes into business, business becomes war. Competition takes on a ruthless ferocity. Some businessmen can speak admiringly of one another as sharks. Business is aggression in the United States. In the language of the hunt, you must "corner the market," "wipe out" the competition, and see that the bull displaces the bear. Small businesses are swallowed up by bigger ones, willing or no. The shark, after all, does not invite you to dinner. The inefficient or aged are fired. Growing old, in fact, is not tolerated. Aged warriors we do not need. The marketplace is a heartless zone.

Macho America is belatedly taking notice of Japanese business. The culture that bred the Samurai is, of course, not free of macho-masculinity. Neither could any one rubric analysis do justice to the social and even feudal complexities of Japan. Still, holding fast to these provisos, one can dare to suggest that the business world of Japan follows more of a feminine model. Japanese workers, even those who prove less efficient, are tenured and retrained. (A mother would not throw a child out for inefficiency in the home.) Labor, government, and management work together in what has been called a "corporate" model of nationhood. Accommodation and patience mark their dealings. There is no effort to get one "off the back" of the other in the controversy model of American life. Japan, with half of our population, has some eleven thousand lawyers while we have over 500,000. Conflict resolution is more sophisticated and does not regularly descend to the war of litigation, as is done with knee-jerk regularity in this country. It is redemptive for the American male to be finally noticing that this more feminine model is also more productive.

(2) The second macho-masculine debit flows from the first. It is *the hierarchical instinct*. Violence and aggression seek not cooperation, but dominance. Dominance, of course, is the antithesis of friendship and of community, both of which are based on mutuality and harmony. Hence, the macho-male tendency in state, church, corporation, and family is hierarchy and control, rather than communion.

Hierarchy is also essentially divisive. Subordination separates. We see this in the male-dominated academe. Is it too harsh to say that not truth, but triumph, is paramount there? A combative spirit prevails among us scholars. The clubbing (or pack instinct) pits group against group. Appreciation is grudging and creative achievement, a threat. (In the macho-masculine academe do we not often show more excitement about miscarriages than live births?) The various disciplines become beleaguered and fortified enclaves. The disciplines should realize their common goal. Ecumenism and sharing is natural to them, but in their actual state they are hostile units, with guards posted, sealed off from one another by passwords of jargon that the stranger does not know.

The same spirit spreads to male-dominated Christian churches which multiply and divide. Efforts at ecumenism are tentative, hedged, and most often merely liturgical. Again, separateness, defensiveness, and implicit hostility are the rule, even though there is no theological grounding for structural division at all.

All of these sins of division cannot be ascribed simply to "macho-masculinity." Simplicity is always suspect in complex human affairs. However, the behavior involved here is congenial to the macho-masculine mode of addressing life, and the signal influence of this dominant cultural force could be with difficulty denied.

(3) Pernicious *abstractionism* also attaches to the militarism of the macho-masculine mode. Violence requires abstracting. If we do not abstract in anger from the humanity, vulnerability, kinship, and similar weaknesses and strengths of our enemy, our zeal for battle evanesces. Needed, in J. Glenn Gray's phrase, is an "image of the enemy" to hate. This image is not the enemy, but a mythic, abstract creation. Only a mind beguiled by abstractions can sustain a violent, non-relational mode of addressing reality. The advantages of women in this regard have been noted above.

The abstractionist tendencies of the male make it possible for him to lose contact with the present tense. To be task-oriented is to be future-oriented. The prize of the struggle is not yet. Thus a hard working man could sacrifice any real contact or friendship with his children because he is working so hard to make their futures secure. This devastates the man himself. He loses the present to an abstract future.

The past illumines; the future beckons; but the present is. The workaholic who is consumed by his goals plans to live later. He has no time for ecstasy or delight, which are present-tense phenomena. The result is gray men, with ink and oil in their veins, who are financially successful but are human failures. And they die. It is estimated that a majority of all the persons in the United States who own ten million dollars or more are women who did not earn that money outside the home. The "successful" men who made them rich have followed the logic of their vision to the grave. To "make it" in a world of warriors is dangerous to one's health. Statistics on longevity show this. It is the masculine, more than the feminine, that needs liberation, but it is machomasculine men who are in control.

(4) *The bias for consequentialist thinking.* Consequentialism is a strain of thought in ethics which tends to posit that *that is good which produces good effects.* In business jargon, it is "bottom line" thinking. The assets measured on the bottom line are of prime importance. How you got to the bottom line is of diminished interest.

The consequentialist is an engineer—not to say that licensed en-

gineers are necessarily lacking in moral sensitivity—but rather, symbolically, that the consequentialist is intoxicated with results. The end
is more important than the means or the style. The collateral damage
is less important than the triumph of the completed work. In this sense,
John W. Dixon is on to something when he writes in his article on "The
Erotics of Knowing," "Engineering may be the model for the masculine
as biology is the model for the feminine."[10]

(5) *Hatred of women.* Hatred is, admittedly, a strong word. Too emotive, perhaps? An unhelpful rhetorical indulgence? No. Hatred is,
sadly, the perfect word for the macho attitude toward women. But how
does one go about hating those whom we put on pedestals and cen-
terfolds and with whom we share both bed and board? The answer is:
complicatedly.

Hatred is sustained anger and disdain. If anger is a transient emotion, hatred is tenured anger. It is marked by aversion and degradation.
One mark of operative hatred is exclusion. The form that sustained
exclusion takes is monopoly. Look to the United States. For 200 years,
we have operated on a rigid quota system that insisted on and got a
90 to 100 percent monopoly for white males in all the principal centers
of power in government, business, church, and the professions, and
in the competition for desirable jobs at every level.[11] The success of
this monopolistic venture could be due to only one of two things: either
the males deserve this status and have, like cream, risen to the top,
or an effective, multi-leveled monopoly has banished women from
many desirable areas of life, relegating them to more menial and subservient positions. Male ego might prefer the first option, but it has
little going for it.

A monopoly is hostile and egoistic. It implies the superiority of the
monopolizers and the inferiority of the excluded. The more comfortable
the monopolizers are with the monopolistic arrangement, the more
deep-seated is their disdain. If they were uneasy with the privileges
they have arrogated to themselves, it would imply some recognition
of unduly excluded value in the outgrouped persons. The American
monopoly is comfortably in place and even slight efforts to ease it, like
the Equal Rights Amendment and affirmative action programs, are
being successfully resisted. Hatred is a fair name for all of this.

The E.R.A. and affirmative action refer to politics and business, but
the hatred is not limited to these orders. It is virulently present in
religion as well. Let me look to the Catholicism that gave me religious
birth. What attitude toward women do I find there? Again, hatred is
the appropriate response. First of all, Catholicism accepts the maleness

of God, and the singular divinity of the male figure, Jesus. Chalcedonic Christology is not the only explanation of how God was in Christ Jesus, but it has official standing in Catholicism and in much of Christianity. It remains for feminist theologians, male and female, to explore the exclusivist patriarchal assumptions of that particular Christology.

Beyond that, Catholicism has insisted on an all-male clergy. This is again powerfully symbolic. Whoever would stand at the holy place of the masculine God must also be masculine. The priest must be a man. This is a deeper level of sexist religion. And there is a third. If the priest is, in effect, contaminated by matrimonial contact with a woman, he is disqualified to preside at Catholic worship. The mandatory celibacy of the male priesthood, however rationalized, looms symbolically as an institutionalized aversion to woman. Could this aversion be fairly called by so virulent a term as hatred? Recent church history suggests that it could.

Pope Pius XII entered into a concordat with Nazi Germany which permitted the church to keep functioning under Nazi rule. It also apparently inhibited the church's prophetic resistance to the holocaust of the Jews. Catholic theologian John Pawlikowski puts it this way: "[The ecclesiology of Pius XII] was one that largely defined the church in its essence as the institution through which the vital ingredients for human salvation—Mass and the sacraments—are made available to the human community. Since the continued existence of the church was of the very highest priority the goal had to be to keep the church alive no matter what the cost in non-Catholic lives."[12] To keep the sacramental system of the church going, the Jews had to be viewed, in professor Nora Levin's term, as "unfortunate expendables."[13]

Yet today, with thousands of priests leaving the ministry, and with seminaries closing, the sacramental system is being shut down in many mission areas of the church for long periods of time. These very areas have trained catechists, married men and women, who could be ordained to sacramental ministry, were it not for the policy excluding women, and men married to them, from priesthood. Yet in this context the church does not relent on its mandatory celibacy requirement, and permits non-sacramental worship to go on for long periods, or in situations such as places in Latin America, almost indefinitely. Criticism of the holocaust could be muted in favor of the sacramental system, but the exclusion of women cannot be eased in the same cause. Implications of indentured hatred here are difficult to escape. Hatred of women also shows up in bold relief on the radical "Christian" right. Much can be said of their unsubtle misogyny, but is it enough, by way of single vignette, to note that they want to eliminate all federal support for centers for battered wives?

Conclusions for Religion and Ethics

Many conclusions are already implicit in what has been said. Beyond that, permit me to suggest that Christian ethics has largely been a white male club. The effects of that could not be wholesome. Mary Daly may be too harsh when she indicts our "dreary ethical texts" and when she dismisses all our efforts at metaethics as "male-authored and male-identified theory about theory" which amounts to little more than "masturbatory meditations by ethicists upon their own emissions."[14] And yet the unduly harsh is not always unduly inaccurate. Mary Daly might have been watching our curious and unfruitful obsession with the naturalistic fallacy, and wondering why we wouldn't call a moratorium on that. She also may have been watching with some wonder C. D. Broad's teleology/deontology dichotomy that replaced Sidgwick's confusing trichotomy of intuitionism, egoism, and utilitarianism, with no notable improvement. She may have worried, too, about our Rawls-mania and wondered why Christian ethicists would not fuel their theories of justice more with the neglected richness of the Hebrew and Christian Scriptures. She might have pondered too why so many of us seem more interested in life in a petri dish than in life in a ghetto or barrio, or in the current scuttling of the second brief Civil Rights Movement in the history of the United States. She may have been piqued because we, the inseminators, write about abortion with insufficient sensitivity to the rights of the bearers. But our troubles predate Mary Daly's criticisms.

A crucial failure of our discipline might be entitled the intellectualistic fallacy.[15] Macho-masculine abstractionism, which disenfranchises the affective component of moral knowing has wreaked no little evil upon our endeavors. The intellectualistic fallacy is an epistemological error that confuses moral knowing with other kinds of cognition. If I tell you that water boils at a certain temperature, you may go to the kitchen and verify it. Again, if I tell you that water freezes at a certain temperature and that metal expands when heated, you may again repair to the kitchen and verify both assertions. But if I tell you that promises should be kept even when the promisee is now dead (to refer to W. D. Ross's famous example), or that persons are worth sacrificing for and even dying for, another trip to the kitchen will not be helpful, for you have entered a whole new genre of knowing, moral knowing.

In this kind of knowing, *caring* is intrinsic. The affective experience of the worth of persons and their environing world that undergirds the knowledge of moral *oughts* and moral *mights* specifies moral knowing. Although ethics proceeds to logical and metaphysical debate, it emanates from awe and is rooted in the affective and indeed mystical bases of our being. Moral knowing is also an exercise in faith. And therein lies the mischief of the intellectualistic fallacy. Affect, mystical perception, and faith are all slighted or disowned. We have striven for a mathematics of ethics, a science of ethics, or an ethics conflated with linguistics. Each is epistemologically absurd. Moral knowing is a different breed. It is embodied in a unique way in caring, feeling flesh. Beverly Harrison complains that "in the dominant ethical tradition, moral rationality is *disembodied* rationality."[16] It is to that disembodiment that I speak.

In what sense is moral knowledge affective, mystical, faith knowledge? "Mystical" is a bruised word. The media regularly referred to the Ayatollah Khomeini as "the mystical leader of Iran." That did not help. St. John of Alcantara, who practiced such "custody of the eyes" that he could not find his way around the monastery and often bumped into walls and doors—and who obviously needed counselling—is a textbook "mystic." Modern studies of mysticism treat the phenomenon as rare and reserved to specialists. The normalcy of the mystical is therefore lost.

I look to the medieval Thomistic tradition. There "mystical" meant affectivity at its profoundest depths. As such it is both normal and normalizing. Indeed, if moral knowing is not rooted at mystical levels of appreciation of persons and their environment, it will pass like the morning's mist. We do not look for the mystical dimension of our moral knowing, and so it escapes us. We do not know how deeply moral knowledge grips us.

Let me give an example with which we may easily identify. Sartre once spoke of the experience of holding an infant in his arms. He was suddenly struck with the appreciation that if all of his life's work were put on a value scale, balanced against that child, it would weigh as nothing compared to the gentle preciousness he held in his arms. That was a mystical moment. In our appreciation of children, uncompetitive and delightful, we can best sense our mystical depths. But also, it is only a mystic who could know with Socrates that it is better to suffer injustice than to inflict it, or with Jesus that greater love cannot be found than is found in the ability to lay down one's life for the brother or the sister.

Sometimes it is only in what I call "the sense of profanation," when life is broken, that we sense the mystical depths of our evaluation. Is there one of us who forgets the photograph of the naked and screaming little Vietnamese Kim whose back was ablaze with napalm—a picture which may as much as anything have communicated the immorality of the debacle in Vietnam. Such experiences signal the depths of affective moral knowledge. Moral knowledge is not peripheral but mystical in its reach.

But what of moral knowledge and faith? Faith is a child of affection. The certitudes of faith, in Aquinas' phrase, exist "in the genre of affection." Says Thomas: "The knowledge of faith proceeds from the will."[17] Faith is, in a little noticed phrase from the Thomistic school, "affective knowledge."[18] It is the wisdom of the heart, and the moral knower lives by faith. Sartre could not see or prove the value of the infant in his arms, but he knew it believingly. We cannot see or prove that persons deserve self-sacrificing and sharing love, but civilization and all of ethics rests entirely upon that belief.

The denigration of affect and faith devastates ethics. It drives us to inappropriate paradigms of knowledge. It wreaks reductionism on ethics, disembodies our rationality, and makes us less real. The acknowledgment that mind and knowledge involves affect and faith as well as syllogism and principle is no threat to intellectual vigor, any more than flesh is threat to bone or blood to artery. The intellectualistic fallacy sins by partiality, and then by irrelevance, and then by boredom. It leaves us standing amid the tedious ashes of our discipline saying with the Colonel, "we had to destroy this enterprise in order to save it." It also leaves us Christian ethicists writing, for the most part, like high-minded philosophers or social theorists, embarrassed and therefore unfed by the vibrant pieties that bred us as a Christianly creedal people. Christian faith is the shape that believing takes in Christian ethics. It should be more visible in our work. Ethics, then, has been hurt by banishing woman and all that is associated with her. That includes affectivity and affectivity's daughters.

But since we are involved in religious ethics, what of our macho-masculine God? We have, in fact, accepted the maleness of God and the singular divinity of the male Jesus. The male God is a legacy from patriarchal Judaism. (Again, Mary Daly in her radically critical book *Gyn/Ecology: The Metaethics of Radical Feminism*, refers to Judaism and Christianity as "Yahweh and Son" religion.) This maleness of God, of course, is a gratuitous assumption. God-talk arises when persons look at themselves and the world around them. They see the bird in flight, the rose in bloom, and the infant blessing us with smiles, and they utter the primal expression of religious consciousness: "there is more to this than meets the eye." The religious inference is that deep down in things there is a creative presence, a directing force, that underlies the complexities and the beauties of our setting. This presence is then called God. To infer to the reality of this presence and then go on to say it must be male, is a baffling step. Sexually identifying the presence might have some symbolic helpfulness, but clearly exclusionary maleness is utterly arbitrary. The fruitful maternal womb, in fact, seemed to almost all early religions a more promising image of the divinity. Yet even there, there are limits to this imagery. God is always beyond our symbols.

When you say that God, the source of all being, is male, you have adopted both an ontology and a cosmology of masculinity. Your male chauvinism is absolute, since it conditions all that is. All that is, is made in the image of the masculine.

A feminized God would be drawn from a different experience. She would not need to be almighty. As Marjorie Reiley Maguire says: impotence, even relative impotence, is less threatening to a woman than to a man. Could a macho God be other than almighty?[19]

If Jean Piaget can use his children in his work, let me as theologian use mine. Our six-year-old son, Tommy, has thus far been raised almost free of religious education. We did not want to bring him answers before he had questions. He did come up with both questions and answers, but did not come up with a macho-masculine God. His first question was about gender. He found our reply that God could be both male and female unlikely, because he had heard the male pronoun applied. His conclusion: "I think God must have a sister." Later he accepted the idea that an invisible person could be both man and woman, but he added a Trinitarian idea of his own by saying: "God is a man and a lady and also a kid." "Why?" we asked. "Because," he said with some impatience, "the kid God makes kids." (How else in the image and likeness?) When Tommy saw his first tree split and killed by lightning, he immediately decided that God was good and playful, but not almighty, and, indeed, a little inept. God sent the lightning to play with the tree, but obviously God could not always get the lightning straight. God did the best that God could, which was not always enough. God also, in the gospel according to Tommy, resides in the earth, not in the skies. This yields a more nourishing, embracing God than the hierarchical God who rules from on high. Tommy's God is more feminine than macho-masculine.

A feminized God can love without limit and yet be limited. The macho-masculine God is, to steal a phrase from Robert Browning, "faultless to a fault." The macho-masculine God, to be lovable, must be perfect. That is a cruel view and does not fit womanly experience. Maternal love extends even to the guilty child. Our God, we ought to admit, has a lot to answer for. Earthquakes kill and volcanoes destroy and children are born with broken brains. There is a realism that is congenial to womanhood in the rabbis in Auschwitz, who put God on trial, reached a guilty verdict, and then repaired to worship their Guilty God. That may offend Spartan logic and theological schemata, but it squares with life where life is lived, where paradox does not always succumb to reason.

In fine, when we reach the moral and the religious, we are in the seedbed of our most important symbols and metaphors. Changes here are epochal. Feminization has entered these realms with exquisite promise. When a healed masculine and feminine blend into a more genuine humanity, we will be different, and we will be better. Our pale discipline of ethics will grow more aware of the pluriform riches of human consciousness. It will also grow more beautiful and more holy. When we press to the depths of the good we must remove our sandals and confess that this is a Holy Place. The good and the holy are inseparable siblings. To say religious ethics is to utter a tautology. In no other discipline is the imprint of the divine more palpable. Indeed, in no other discipline does research issue more naturally into worship.

CHAPTER 10

The Feminist Turn in Ethics

Anyone who plies the noble art-science of social ethics (moral theology, Christian ethics), while taking no account of the feminist turn of consciousness, is open to charges of professional irresponsibility and incompetence. No. That is not an overstatement or an overblown rhetorical lead-in. The history of ethics is turning an epochal corner. To miss the turn is to be lost and useless.

Feminism is concerned with the shift in roles and the question of the rights that have been unjustly denied women. But all of that, however important and even essential, is secondary. The main event is epistemological. Changes in *what* we know are normal; changes in *how* we know are revolutionary. Feminism is a challenge to the way we have gone about *knowing*. The epistemological *terra firma* of the recent past is rocking, and, as the event develops, it promises to change the face of the earth.

The main impact of feminism will be felt in the area of moral knowledge. That, of course, is broader than ethics since all of the social sciences are heavy with moral assumptions and evaluations. Economics, politics (simplistically called political science), education, journalism, business administration, engineering, *et al.* are all intra-familial siblings of social ethics, although educational systems have treated them as separable strangers. (This mischievous separation, indeed, is a natural target of the emerging feminist consciousness.)

Feminism, however, addresses itself most directly to social ethics. Every category and tool of this discipline is touched by this new awareness. Before I argue and try to show that this is the case, an obstacle is present and should be faced.[1]

Conversion and In-Depth Knowing

The new feminine consciousness reaches the affective depths of moral knowledge. *Learning* about it is not like learning about a new medical procedure or a new approach to mathematics. It involves conversion and a shift of horizons that can bring considerable pain and threat. Here is where insight involves investment, and where knowing and vocation unite. To call someone to feminist reappraisal we would be well advised to mimic the fair warnings of the Gospels in announcing their new and good news. *Metanoiete* is the first cry of Mark's Gospel. It is often translated "repent," but that misses the challenge. It is a call for a new *nous*, a radically new mind and outlook that is not simply achieved. To achieve it it would be necessary to raise up all the valleys of the mind and to level all our mountainous presuppositions. The axe must go to the roots of our old views, so that a new heaven and a new earth will present themselves to our consciences. Indeed, the shift is such that it can be compared to reentering one's mother's womb and being born again. With some persons, it indeed might seem hopeless. One can be tempted to say that we might as well leave the dead to bury the dead. The impossible is impossible. You can't get a camel through the eye of a needle. But, yet, with God, all things are possible. And so the feminist challenge must be issued.

I once heard Gabriel Marcel, the French existentialist philosopher, speaking at the University of Pennsylvania. In his youth, Marcel had had great antipathy toward religion. Later religion was to become a major concern in his work. Someone asked him how such a dramatic shift had come to be. His answer was dogmatically existentialist: "Through personal encounters. Nothing else ever changes anyone in any important way." The change from sexist-patriarchical to feminist and eventually inclusively humanistic thinking is massive. No simple argument will achieve it. An old saying from Latin Christianity comes relevantly to mind: "It is not through logic that God's salvation reaches us." *(Non in dialectica complacuit Deo salvum facere populum suum.)* Personal, grace-filled encounters must play their crucial role. We must be open to the *kairos*, the moment of opportunity.

Geoffrey Wood once compared a *kairos* to a log jam. All kinds of logs coming from all kinds of places suddenly come together. When they are together like this they will support your weight. No single one of them would do so. The *kairos* is the moment when many influences coalesce into a saving unity and new bouyancy. To switch metaphors, it affords a new horizon by reason of which nothing ever looks the same again. In simple language, something clicks, and we are "a new creature."

The conversion may be dramatic or it may be subtle like the slow light-growth of early dawn. In the latter case, we may not be quite able to say at which moment it became day. The conversion experience is needed not just by men, since women too have drunk the social poisons of sexism and come to believe in their own inferiority. Elsewise they could not be so tolerant of their banishment from the mainstreams of power and life.

It will not be amiss for me to recount here the conversion experience of one woman which came about with dramatic suddenness. The woman is my conjugal colleague and the story (given with permission) is this: some years ago, Margie was not a feminist. When asked if she were a feminist, she would reply: "No. Dan is!" Then two popes died in quick succession and the stage for conversion was interestingly set. Our television was filled with *papalia*. Two elaborate funerals and two prolonged installations. Our two-year-old son, Tommy, resented our absorption in the papal events since even Sesame Street was proscribed during those hours. But he joined us and caught the spirit of the moment. At one point, he left us, went to the kitchen, got his red Cheerios bowl, plopped it upon his little head, and announced: "I a pope!"

How lovely it is when grace comes in merry moments. Margie was struck by Tommy's endearingly immodest ambition. It was so normal and so refreshing. Childhood requires no limits to the imagination. The whole world must be the child's imaginative oyster. He/she must think they can be anything. As the richness of reality unfolds to them, they must feel that they can have a go at all of it. The limits will eventually be felt, but in that early budding of consciousness, all doors must be seen as open to the hopeful imaging of the child. At that point Tommy had a moral right to hear that indeed he might be pope, or Easter Bunny, or snowplow driver or any of his already announced ambitions. But it struck Margie with lightning strength and suddenness that, if Tommy were a girl, he would have to hear sooner or later that he could not be pope or many other things—merely because of being a girl. The world would not be as open to him. Then Margie looked to the television set and saw the scene there in a new light. Only men were at the throne of God. Masculinity was the sacrament of encounter with a God who was also conceived as male. Actual barriers had been constructed for the occasion to separate women from the holy place. It struck her that there was a message on that screen about her mother and her three sisters and about the daughter she hoped she would one day have and about herself. A feminist was born!

The story illustrates many things (not the least of which is that popes do not die in vain). No new information was available to Margie at that moment. She had heard it all. She had read feminist literature. But she had been inured, and now she was receptive. "Whereas I was blind, now I see" (John 9:25). The mystical core of her being, where moral knowledge is born in an affective appreciation of personal and terrestrial life, had been reached. Indentured rationalizations had been pierced, and she was now free to hurt for herself and for her sisters and to rise from that hurt to new life. And it all began with a Cheerios bowl on a delightful little head.

Conversion is a process that does not end. He/she who claims to be a feminist and without sin in the area of sexism is a liar. (The same is true of racism and class elitism.) To dare to teach ethics is to accept a professional commitment to ongoing conversion. We can't just "bone up" on feminist thought; we have to "heart in" on it. "I believe, Lord: help my unbelief" is the posture of an honest searcher in the field of ethics.[2] Teilhard was right when he said that all research is worship. Ethical research is manifestly such. Macho-masculine scholarship needs to learn that. It was too smug and cocksure of itself, too abstracted and too tut-tuttingly tolerant of the male-made problems we study in the world and in the church. Feminism is *the* major event in ethical theory of our day. Macho-masculine scholarship must come here, not as to a well-intentioned and laudable side-show, but as to the major revolution on the theological and ethical scene today. No ethics will be profound or holy that does not join this revolution.

The Epistemological Revolution

The subtlest form of sexism, as I have said, is to see feminism as a woman's issue. It is a human issue of first-order importance for social ethics. Feminism represents a reappraisal of (1) the nature of nature; (2) the nature of person; (3) the linkage of private and public morality; (4) the plight of technologized rationality, which has humanity at the brink of disaster; and (5) the sources of theological ethics.

(1) *Nature.* Feminism calls us from a two-nature to a one-nature ethics. As Beverly Harrison writes: "Thomas Aquinas argued, following Aristotle, that male and female 'nature' differed because biological structure differed. This two-nature idea runs deep in Christian theol-

ogy."[3] The heresy here is one of division. Male and female were we made; in God's image, that is, were we made. Macho-masculine scholarship split the human molecule, degrading the feminine component and perverting the masculine into a dominator. As I said in the previous chapter, "If the essential human molecule is dyadic, male/female, the perversion of one part of the dyad perverts the other. And, to distort femininity *and* masculinity, the constitutive ingredients of humanity, is to distort humanity itself; nothing will be spared the fallout from so radical a corruption. Here is *original* sin. Here is the fundamental lie that will have to mark all human ideas, customs, and institutions."[4] From disarmament to abortion, there is no moral problem that presents itself to "the valuing animal," as Nietzsche called us, that does not bear the mark of this sexist perversion of nature.[5]

(2) *Person.* Person as such does not exist. Only boys and girls, men and women exist. Person, unsexed, is a figment of the imagination. Yet person is a key term of modern moral discourse. A two-natures ethics, however, could not bring clarity to the term. Such an ethics could only offer an isolationist concept of person, lacking in the relational and sharing aspects of a more realistic personology. Harsh individualism results. God becomes "wholly other", and human persons become autonomous and self-possessed by definition. Again Beverly Harrison with a feminist correction: "The ecologists have recently reminded us of what nurturers always knew—that we are part of a *web of life* so intricate as to be beyond our comprehension."[6]

(See Margaret Farley's radically suggestive essay, "New Patterns of Relationship: Beginnings of a Moral Revolution." Sister Margaret is a member of the Sisters of Mercy, an order of women that has suffered much of late from macho-Vatican oppression. Think of that as you read her and pray for "clicks" of conversion in high places. See also, by that convert to feminism, Marjorie Reiley Maguire, "Personhood, Covenant, and Abortion," for a bold and original new view of personhood. The discussion is illustrated by reference to the abortion question, but its meaning goes beyond.[7])

(3) *Linkage of private and public morality.* When we split the human molecule and relegated women to truncated personhood, we also ghettoed the qualities associated with woman. (A pedestal is a clean ghetto.) Trust, affectivity, caring, nurturing, identification with children and their needs were deemed party to the frailty of woman. Then we handed politics over to those whose socialization disparaged those "womanly" qualities. The result is a planet in terminal peril, with

"third" and "fourth" worlds full of hunger, and more than a million dollars every thirty seconds spent on military fantasies and plans. By the fruits of macho-masculine politics we shall know macho-masculine men. Men are the warriors of the species—the Amazons are but a myth—and war is not the extension of statecraft but its collapse. There have been 150 wars since World War II, and 4,000,000 men are involved in battle throughout the world at this writing, according to the Center for Defense Information. Macho-masculine politics stands embarrassed.

So too, macho-economics. Unfortunately, a dehumanized masculinity has been the seed bed of our controlling metaphors and symbols in economics, in political theory, and in social ethics. The fact that politics and economics are servants for the *nurturing* of life—that they are by nature *caring* enterprises, has been missed. (The arms race and Reaganomics are the natural issue of such deviance.)

When a healed masculine and feminine blend into a fruitfully inclusive humanism, all the disciplines and professions that deal with the polity will be unified around a theory of justice. Macho-masculine social science has excommunicated as femininely tainted many of the qualities of a *just* society. Ironically, a truly and excitingly humanistic theory of justice has lain all too fallow in the pages of the Jewish and Christian scriptures. (Toward a recovery of biblical justice, read Stephen Charles Mott's *Biblical Ethics and Social Change*, particularly chapters four and five.)[8]

(4) *Technologized rationality.* One terrible story symbolizes the problem here. In the Christmas season of 1983, we stationed our Cruise and Pershing II missiles in Europe. The Cruise, if it works as designed, will skip ingeniously over mountains, hovering close to the earth below the scanning eyes of radar. The Pershing II can strike its Russian targets some six minutes after launch. With their installation, the "hot line" becomes irrelevant. Launch on Warning, or automated reaction, becomes the new command system of Soviet warcraft. Moral choice is abdicated to the machine. In this case, that means the Soviet electronic machine, which is less sophisticated (as men say) than ours. Rationality yields to a second-rate technology. Specifically human wisdom, which by its nature cannot be machinized or computerized, is undone. Politics moves to second place and the world teeters on the brink of the computer error that can end the world.

Let me underline the inherent madness of this parable of technologized rationality. We hide our computer secrets from the Soviets for reasons of alleged security. But if we insist on these unstoppable missiles, we will have to start a massive lend-lease program to give all our technical knowledge to the Soviets so their inferior equipment will not mistakenly signal an attack and launch the salvoes that end the world. The so-called "Star Wars" project is but another example of frantic faith in a technological fix for a moral problem.

In symbol form we have here the eschaton of technologized rationality. If human intelligence is patterned on machination, then machination in some form may replace human intelligence. So it has happened. (The computer was, after all, *Time*'s Man of the Year.) We are empowered by our personhood to choose life or to choose death. That power is passing to the mechanical Man of the Year. The reductionistic technologizing of rationality is complete.

Feminism is curative for this kind of mind-default. It brings on an wholistic epistemology. It eschews "the intellectualistic fallacy"[9] and takes account of affectivity as the animating core of moral knowing. It leads to embodied rationality which shrinks from the sacrifice of flesh to abstraction.

(5) *The theological sources.* Human knowing is an event in which the knower both receives and gives. To know is to interpret, a word that comes from the Latin *interpres*. An *interpres* is a broker, a negotiator, an agent who arranges a bargain between two parties. The *interpres* in Christian exegesis and historical studies has been a male, and usually a subtly or bluntly sexist male. The bargains struck by such brokers are up for reevaluation. Clearly, not all exegesis done by men is suspect, but the healing supplement to male labors in this field is now arriving. Insightful scholars like Elisabeth Schüssler Fiorenza, Phyllis Trible, Sandra Schneiders, Elaine Pagels, to mention only a few, are bringing new grace and perspective to the study of the *sacra pagina*. Read them with good appetite.

Conclusion

Every man and woman doing feminist studies is contributing to social ethics. Our discipline is affected every time they lift a pen or offer a challenge, whether they are working in scripture, history, systematic theology, or social science. Feminist retooling by all social ethicists is simply mandatory. If there is a burden here, it is sweet and rewarding. Let what Madonna Kolbenschlag says in her *Kiss Sleeping Beauty Good-Bye* be our last word: "The faith that is expressed here, and that is asked of women and men who would be truly free, is not backward-looking or nostalgic; nor is it blindly iconoclastic and memoryless. It nurtures the seed of our future becoming in the revelation of the present, in a tradition that remains faithful to itself by transcending itself."[10]

CHAPTER 11

The Exclusion of Women from Orders: A Moral Evaluation

Concerning a deaconess, I Bartholomew make this constitution: O bishop, thou shalt lay thy hands upon her in the presence of the presbytery, and of the deacons and deaconesses, and shalt say:

O Eternal God, the Father of our Lord Jesus Christ, the Creator of man and of woman, who didst replenish with the Spirit Miriam, and Deborah, and Anna, and Huldah: who didst not disdain that Thy only begotten Son should be born of a woman; who also in the tabernacle of the testimony, and in the temple, didst ordain women to be keepers of Thy holy gates, do Thou now also look down upon this Thy servant, who is to be ordained to the office of a deaconess, and grant her Thy Holy Spirit, and cleanse her uncleanliness of flesh and spirit, that she may worthily discharge the work which is committed to her to Thy glory, and the praise of Thy Christ, with whom glory and adoration be to Thee and the Holy Spirit for ever. Amen.

Apostolic Constitutions, VIII, 19–20

The question of the ordination of women has moved from sacramental to moral theology. Church history shows that women were ordained as deaconesses over a considerable period of time. Biblical exegesis, patrology, and theology are showing that there are no grounds prohibiting the ordination of women even to priesthood. Scholarship is recovering the egalitarian, "feminist" nature of the Jesus movement in its origins. In a word, a strong and broadly based theological consensus favors the ordination of women. Still, Church management adamantly forbids women access to orders. The issue then is squarely put to moral theology: is the current exclusion of women from orders morally defensible?

This article argues that the current ban on the ordination of women is immoral on these counts:

(1) It is a sin of injustice in three ways:
    (a) It is unjust to women who wish to serve the Church and the world through ordained ministry.
    (b) It is unjust to those Christians who desire a sacramental ministry tied to orders.
    (c) This increasingly conspicuous and arbitrary exclusiveness manifests sexism and further confirms the Church and the rest of society in its sexism.

The specific sins of injustice, then, are distributive and social injustice within the church, and scandal, within and without the Church.

(2) The exlusion of women from orders is a sin against the Church because it denies the Church this distinctive service of women and it damages the credibility of the Church in other areas, thus impeding its mission as a witness to the possibilities of the Reign of God on this earth.
(3) The exclusion of women from orders is a sin of sacrilege, because the male monopoly on orders is presented as the will of God.

The Theological State of the Question

Theology has been markedly sensitive to the desire of many women to be ordained priests. Scholars have zealously joined the issue and the literature is abundant. The evidence for women priests in the past is scant. As patrologist Jean LaPorte writes: "In Christian history women have never been ordained as priests, except for rare cases in marginal groups."[1] For those who ply a "the-past-is-destiny" ecclesiology, the case for women priests might thus seem weak. Since, however, church history shows a lot of creative change and adaptation, as well as retrenchment and retreat, respect for our past does not translate into paralysis. To be true to the past is to accept a vocation of creative adaptation in the service of the Reign of God. We are not mortgaged to all that is past, since it is clear that sin too became tenured and traditional.

What scholarship does show is that the exclusion and alienation of women was not always a fact of ecclesial life. Christianity began on an egalitarian note. As Professor Carolyn Osiek writes: "Characteristic of new religious movements is an initial burst of energy that often abolishes customary social barriers and creates instead a community of radical egalitarianism. Such is the vision of Galatians 3:28—Jew and Greek, slave and free, male and female are all one in Christ Jesus."[2] A new religious and moral vision, however, faces a recalcitrant culture, and accommodation occurs. Says Osiek: "Early Christianity in this regard is no different from any other new religious beginning."[3]

Jesus, for starters, appears as a revolutionary feminist in his behavior and teaching. As Leonard Swidler writes: "The model of how to live an authentically human life that Jesus of the Gospels presents . . . is an egalitarian model." What Jesus taught "in his words and dealings with women, namely egalitarianism between women and men, was also taught by his own androgynous life-style."[4] All four Gospels show women as prominent in the public life of Jesus. Matthew, Mark, and Luke describe the activity of the group of women followers of Jesus as "ministering" (diakonia).[5]

Jesus' dealings with the Samaritan woman in John's Gospel are actually stunning.[6] First of all, he violated the indentured code by speaking to her—a code that was twice as binding on a rabbi. He shocked his male followers by even taking a drink from her, since Samaritan women were considered ritually unclean and menstruant from the cradle on. On top of all this, Jesus is said to give his first unequivocal revelation in John's Gospel of his Messiahship: "I who speak to you am he." (John 4:26) Then, even while taking note of her striking matrimonial record, Jesus goes on to commission her as an apostle to her village. Just as the other apostles left their nets and professional apparatus, she left her water pot and preached and "through her word" they came to believe. The text puts this woman into the same witnessing role as the disciples at the Last Supper. As Raymond E. Brown writes, "The Evangelist can describe both a woman and the (presumably male) disciples at the Last Supper as bearing witness to Jesus through preaching and thus bringing people to believe in him on the strength of their word."[7] One must question Brown's "presumably male" since an all-male company at the Last Supper may not be safely presumed—Italian art to the contrary notwithstanding. Indeed, Quentin Quesnell argues convincingly that the whole community, women included, were present at the Supper in Luke. (In *Political Issues in Luke-Acts*, editors R. Cassidy and P. Scharper, Orbis, New York, 1983, pp. 59 to 79)

The four Gospels also unanimously testify to the presence of women at the tomb as the first witnesses of the Resurrection. Of course, retrenchment had set in by the time of the writing of Acts and the twelve men had become the official witnesses. (Acts 1:22) Only men could be public witnesses in Judaism, and so the women were excluded for cultural reasons. Subsequent tradition, however, did not overlook the apostolic role of Mary Magdalene, "the apostle to the apostles," whose "I have seen the Lord," was formal apostolic language. (John 20:18; see 1 Cor. 9:1) Women were immersed in the ministries that later were tied to "priesthood." Tabitha in Acts 9:36 is called a disciple, and Phoebe is the first of the deacons. (Rom. 16:1–2) Junias, who probably was a woman, is called an "apostle" by Paul. (Rom. 16:7)[8] The Christian scriptures, of course, are not free of ambivalent and negative attitudes toward women in the community. The culture was fighting back against the egalitarian revolution started by Jesus, and it made inroads.[9] The primeval egalitarianism, however, did not disappear.

As Elisabeth Schüssler Fiorenza writes: "While—for apologetic reasons—the post-Pauline and post-Petrine writers seek to limit women's leadership roles in the Christian community to roles which are culturally and religiously acceptable, the evangelists called Mark and John highlight the alternative character of the Christian community, and therefore accord women apostolic and ministerial leadership."[10] Most of the Christian scriptures were written during the last third of the first century while the Christian communities were experiencing persecution from both Gentiles and Jews. The post-Pauline literature attempts to lessen these tensions by accommodating to the patriarchal and sexist structures of the Greco-Roman society. Historically, the accommodationists succeeded. But as Schüssler Fiorenza writes: "This 'success' can not be justified theologically, since it cannot claim the authority of Jesus for its own Christian praxis."[11]

The biblical testimony gives no comfort to those who would now exclude women from orders on the basis of the Christian scriptures. As Professor Sandra Schneiders of the Jesuit School of Theology at Berkeley puts it: "Suffice it to say that there is wide consensus among reputable New Testament scholars that there were no Christian priests in New Testament times and therefore certainly none ordained or appointed by Jesus. The Priesthood does not emerge in the early Church until the end of the first century at the earliest and, even at that relatively late date, the evidence is scanty and unclear."[12] That there should be "priests" at all is unsettled in Scripture. That there must be priests and that priests must be male are assertions that can find no biblical warranty.

Efforts to prove that Jesus insisted on male priests because the

Twelve were all males are both fatuous and anachronistic. Functions that we call priestly were never limited to the Twelve and there is no evidence that the Eucharistic function was ever performed by the Twelve. Again, Professor Schneiders: "The Twelve are immortalized as the foundation of the Church. As such they have no successors. And as disciples, apostles, teachers, early Church leaders, etc., in which capacities they do have successors, they are members of a wider group which was never all male."[13] What is clear about the biblical testimony is the free adaptiveness of the early Christian community in the creation of offices and ministries. We find apostles, prophets, evangelists, teachers, pastors, overseers, deacons, presbyters, leaders, presidents, stewards, administrations, and more. These ministries were never presented as a divinely made grid into which Church life must be pressed, but emerge rather as creative responses to needs within the Christian life of service and worship. The lists of ministries (1 Cor. 12:28–31; Rom. 12:6–8; Eph. 4:11) vary without apology. One individual might claim several ministries. There is no indication of a fixed set of "offices" destined for all time. In Acts, we see the apostles giving up service at table to have more time for preaching. So they "created" deacons for the table work. (Acts 6:2–3) Yet, lo and behold, before long the deacons too opted for preaching over serving at tables so that in our own day the diaconate symbolizes the office of preaching (Acts 6:8–15). (May we assume the women were left with the job of waiting on tables?) John R. Donahue, S. J., states the theological principle: "From its very beginning the Church embodies a principle of sacramental adaptation."[14]

In conclusion, on the basis of the Christian scriptures, the ordainability of women, even to the priesthood, is as clear as any issue of sacramental life in the Church and clearer than most. The January 27, 1977, Declaration on the Question of the Admission of Women to the Ministerial Priesthood issued by The Sacred Congregation for the Doctrine of the Faith rejected this ordainability and became the most quickly repudiated Vatican document of modern times.[15] The glaring errors of this document in scriptural exegesis did not even take account of the Vatican's own official Pontifical Biblical Commission. In their April 1976 meeting on the subject of the ordainability of women, the seventeen commission members had voted 17 to 0 that the New Testament does not settle in a clear way and once and for all whether women can be ordained priests. The Commission also voted 12–5 that Christ's plan would not be transgressed by permitting the ordination of women.[16] The members of the commission are chosen by Vatican authorities as models of orthodoxy. One might assume that their positions would not be unduly adventurous. Ignoring even their reflections on the state of the question obviously relates to the ethics of maintaining the current male monopoly on orders.

The Post-biblical Witness

In post-biblical Christianity, the egalitarian spirit of Jesus receded further, and much raw sexism thrives in the Christian literature. In spite of this, widows and virgins predominated in the contemplative ranks of the early church. The importance of this should not be missed since "the contemplative life was considered to be the height and end of Christian life."[17] For a long time women functioned as lectresses and cantors.[18] Most significantly, women were ordained formally and with the imposition of hands to the rank of deaconess.

In his book *The Ministry of Women in the Early Church* Roger Gryson says of the ordination of the deaconesses that "it was a sacramental ordination." He observes that it was "not a marginal fact or a fantasy rejected by legitimate authority, but on the contrary, an institution peacefully accepted by a large part of Christianity for several centuries."[19]

The creations of the deaconesses is another manifestation of "the principle of sacramental adapation." The author of *Didascalia Apostolorum* in writing about the deaconesses is clearly at pains to justify what was a novelty. S/he cites the fittingness of having women anoint women at baptism and visit sick women, so as to avoid any appearances of indecency or indelicacy.[20]

In fact, it was this spirit of adaptiveness that functioned negatively in the exclusion of women from priesthood. The early Christians were proud to proclaim that they did not have an altar but a table and that all the Christians were the priests making their own offerings.[21] However, they then proceeded to accommodate to the mores of the synagogue. This leads Jean LaPorte to conclude his study with this judgment: "The ultimate reason for the absence of women from the Christian priesthood is found in their absence from the Elders of the Synagogue. The Christian churches inherited their structure from that of the synagogue."[22]

Interestingly, this conservative adaptationism also supports the ordination of women today. If the sex of the elders of the ancient synagogue is normative for Christians today, why not their cultic need for circumcision? Adaptation is adapatation, whether it reverts to older forms or creates new ones. Adaptation or accommodation to the synagogue was not the only possibility for Christians historically, nor is it now. In conclusion, we can say that it is not the will of Christ, but the will of the ancient synagogue that the male monopolists of orders are imposing on the Church today. If some theologians feel we must follow the customs of the synagogue, let us follow the example of the modern synagogue which is accepting women as rabbis.

But, after all, Jesus was a man . . .

Let this summary of the theological state of the question end with the lightest of the objections to the ordination of women. The objection states that Jesus' gender is normative for priesthood. How could a woman "represent" a man? How could a woman be an "alter Christus" or an *eikon* of Christ?

First of all, it has been pointed out by a number of writers that if Jesus' sex is crucial for priesthood, why not his Jewishness or his blood type? Of all the particularities of Jesus, why pick on his gender as essential to his mission? Indeed, focusing on Jesus' Jewishness and insisting that all priests be Jewish men might make more sense, since Jesus' Jewishness clearly was crucial to his religious vision. The Jesus movement was a renewal movement within Judaism.[23]

Secondly, insistence on the maleness of Jesus as the grounds for male priests is a *novelty* presented as *tradition*. Professor R. A. Norris, in a too little noticed article, writes that the present form of the argument is "virtually unprecedented."[24] The idea that Jesus' maleness is "one of the crucial things about him which ecclesial priesthoods must image" is new.[25] The church has not believed that the maleness of Jesus is salvific. Again Norris: "The Church is interested in Jesus as the Christ—christologically. . . . To put the matter simply, the Church, unlike the historian, the would-be portraitist, the biographer, or the psychiatrist, is not interested as such in Jesu-ology, but in Christology, in Jesus as the bearer of God's salvation. . . . The maleness of Jesus is of no christological interest in patristic tradition."[26] The patristic principle was that Jesus must be the same sort of being as those he saves. "What is not assumed is not healed," was Gregory Nazianzen's classic assertion against the heresy of Apollinarius.[27] Person, not gender, is of the essence in this Christology. The introduction of gender as a Christological principle infringes on the universality of redemption. In the classical Christology, women are baptized "in Christ" and "represent" and "image" Christ in whom there is neither "male nor female." (Gal. 3:28)

The theology of baptism long since decided that women could "represent" and "image" Christ to the world.

Any position so beset by bad arguments, poor exegesis, uninformed scholarship, and strident appeals to undefined authority is in need of humble reassessment. And so this brings us to the formal moral assessment of the institutional exclusion of women from orders.

The Ethics of the Male Monopoly on Orders

At the outset it should be noted that not all theologians who are sensitive to feminism argue for the ordination of women. The priesthood as we know it was not an original mark of the Christian communities. And while the ordination of ministers through the imposition of hands has had a long and distinguished history, it has also introduced clericalism and hierarchicalism into the Church. Many writers suggest that this is the last structure women should seek to join. However, I would agree with Sister Sandra Schneiders who writes: "I regard the exclusion of women from ordination as the symbol of (the) domination of women by men. The exclusion of women from Orders both expresses and realizes the assumed right of men to determine the nature and identity as well as to limit the role and functions of women in the Church."[28] In agreement with Dr. Schneiders is Professor Mary Buckley of St. John's University in New York: "That women cannot be ordained as priests means, in effect, that women have no decision-making power in the Roman Catholic Church."[29] The issue, then, is not just one of sacramental theology—is Christian worship best served by an ordained clergy? It also involves the use of power in the church to maintain a theologically gratuitous monopoly. The ordination issue raises the issue of *sexism* and the *just* use of power in the Church.

The Injustice of the Male Monopoly on Orders

I have said that the exclusion of women from orders constitutes the sin of injustice in three distinct ways: it is unjust to the women who wish to serve the Church this way; it is unjust to the Church members who are thus not served by these women; and finally, it constitutes the sin of scandal, a species of injustice that does spiritual and moral harm to persons. The obligation of reparation obtains when the harm done can be identified.

The core belief underlying Christian liturgy is that wherever two or three are gathered in God's name, there God is in the midst of them.

(See Matt. 18:20.) In the Christian theology of worship, we come together in faith—reaching for the God who is reaching for us in this
sacramental moment. Liturgy lives in the faith of "God with us." Worship is born of this confidence in God's readiness to nourish us with
his/her healing presence. It belittles this faith to say that it would be
short-circuited if a woman were to preside or preach. "There am I in
the midst of you as long as males dominate the assembly!" The insult
inflicted here on our mothers, sisters, daughters, and wives is supreme. Masculinity becomes the sacrament of the encounter with God.
Femininity becomes the impediment which, if it were not kept unobtrusive and veiled, would desecrate the holy times and places. There
is not a scintilla of evidence that this situation represents the mind of
Jesus Christ or of the God who shone forth in the life and vision of
Jesus.

Many women around the world wish to serve the Church in priestly
ministry. Many women have pursued this desire by enrolling in our
seminaries, in some instances keeping those seminaries financially
afloat. It is unjust to them to frustrate their legitimate and reasonable
desires in this fashion.

Injustice, remember, is the fundamental sin. We can do better than
justice; we can love. But justice is the minimal essential due to each
person. To deny person justice is to deny their elementary human
worth. It is to undervalue their humanity.[30]

This is what the arbitary exclusion of women from orders does. At
the heart of injustice of any kind is hatred. In this case, the form of
hatred operative is sexism. Sexism is the disparagement of women's
humanity. Another common word for it is misogyny, the hatred of
women. The exclusion of women from orders manifests the sin of sexism, the hatred of women.

Liturgy without lived commitment to justice is not worship. If ritual
today is tied to unjust structures of exclusionism and unfounded monopoly, questions beyond the tidy category of validity are raised. If
prayers arise from male altars marred by injustice to women, how are
they received by the God who is a lover of justice (Ps. 99:4), whose
delight is in justice (Jer. 9:23), whose holiness in manifested in the
sacrament of justice (Isa. 5:16)?

So here we see the first two forms of injustice in the male monopoly
on orders. It insults women by treating them as a sacramental obstacle
and by arbitarily frustrating their spiritual desires for ordained ministry. Furthermore, it denies ordained ministry to increasing numbers of
Christians who desire ordained ministry and do not have it, even

though women and men married to women are ready and able to assume this service. Note again: even marriage to a woman has the effect of disqualifying men for ordained ministry. Again, hatred of women is a fair term.

Finally, there is the injustice of scandal. In traditional Catholic moral theology scandal was a sin of providing the occasion for moral and religious harm to others.[31] Confirming Catholics and those outside Catholicism in their sexism is scandal in this sense. The Church is a powerful teacher, not just in her words, but in her symbolic structures and liturgies. There, male gender is given sacramental status, with the implied disparagement of women. The message is transverbal and subliminal. Women are out of place in the holy of holies. This comforts in a scandalous way a society which also excludes women from top positions in government, business, the professions, and even the arts. The Church's exclusivism gives wordless blessing to the multiple exclusions that pervade our sexist societies.

Sins of injustice impose a burden of reparation. Church management, therefore, bears a heavy moral burden. It must work to undo the exclusionary messages of sexism in its worship structures. If the forthcoming pastoral letter of the American bishops or women does not address this scandal in all of its implications, it would be better unwritten. If the bishops cannot bring themselves to criticize Vatican policy here, their silence would endorse it. A call for more study would be a failure of nerve. The theological groundwork has been done. (It has been suggested that what the Church needs is for women to write a pastoral letter on bishops.)

The other two sins follow all too easily from the above. The exclusion of women is a sin against the Church and a sacrilege. The human molecule is a dyad. Male and female, in the image of God were we made. The distinctive human experience of women has been bracketed out of ministry. Male and female, in the image of God, our ministry has not been. Humanity becomes whole when a healed masculine and a healed feminine blend into a humaneness not yet experienced on this earth. The Church should be the exemplary workshop for this process, starting at the altar where all of our symbols meet.

The ordination of women is not an internal matter. It has caught the attention of sensitive people across the spectrum of faiths and value systems. The Church appears not only unable to lead, but even unable to follow, in doing justice to women. Defending masculine monopolies in an age when all monopolies are suspect is historically akin to defending feudalism and the divine right of kings when these conceptions had already been successfully challenged. On the feminist issue, the Church appears wed to archaism, and this hurts its mission elsewhere. Its important messages of justice and peace are less credible when it cannot even do justice and make peace at the altar.

And, finally, we must speak of sacrilege. The Vatican's 1976 Declaration on the Question of the Admission of Women to the Ministerial Priesthood has no hesitations about the grounds for the exclusion of women from orders. It says it is God's idea. It appeals to "the light of Revelation."[32] The discipline, as it is, is "God's choice."[33] "It is the Holy Spirit, given by ordination, who grants participation in the ruling power of the Supreme Pastor, Christ."[34] "Christ chose 'those he wanted' " (3:13). The buck stops with Christ. The Church is simply "bound by Christ's manner of acting."[35] This exclusion is necessary "to confirm to Gods' plan for his Church."[36] In what is perhaps the most insulting line of the Declaration, it is said that the exclusion of women is necessary "in order to proclaim better the mystery of Christ and to safeguard and manifest the whole of its rich content."[37] Here the inherent sexism of the document is most manifest. Women, half the human race, are a threat to *safeguarding* and *manifesting* the *whole* of the rich content of the mystery of Christ. The content apparently would be polluted if the "men only" policy were ended. (The "whole" in Vatican geometry is somehow independent of the half.)

God is tragically dependent upon theology, for theology images God to the world. Bad theology, therefore, bears the mark of sacrilege. Tying ordination to masculinity is bad theology. Enforcement of bad theology by the officers of the Church is unworthy of the Church and must be called by its name. Its name is injustice. It's name is sacrilege. Those who are committed to the renewal of the Church's worshipful mission must resist the male monopoly on orders and work for the wedding of liturgy and justice. We must leave our gift at the altar, and go to be reconciled with our sisters. (Matt. 5:22–24) The time for this reconcilation is past due.

Part 5

MEDICINE AND MORALS

Medicine, like much of science, dreamed that it was value free, that it could do its work in a moral vacuum. Belatedly, it has discovered that this is not so. Every new technical achievement makes new moral questions. Medicine is neck high in ethics, and it has no choice but to learn to do ethics well. In response to this realization, a whole new field of bioethics has appeared, generating some 1,500 articles and numerous books every year. Chapter Twelve looks at the moral revolution in health care. Chapter Thirteen describes the experience of abortion through the eyes of a male Catholic moral theologian. Chapter Fourteen raises the question of the extent of our moral freedom over the dying process. May we take positive steps to hasten the dying process when death appears to be the best that life offers?

CHAPTER 12

The Moral Revolution in Health Care

Death consciousness has been rising steadily in the last decade. Much scholarly writing and journalism reflect this by focusing on particular death issues such as abortion and mercy death. Such fixations could easily miss the deeper epistemological event that is upon us, an event that may implicate epochally the whole of our self understanding.

We are the only animal blessed with reflective mortality consciousness. Any serious reappraisal of our mortality is a reappraisal of life for we can only view the death that we have not yet experienced in terms of the life we know. A shift in death consciousness is a shift in life consciousness.

Furthermore, since death is the ultimate challenge to our being and meaning, a reassessment of death shakes the foundations of our thought. Everything from God to economics, from ethics to health care, from sociology to politics, will show the effects of so basic a move. Clearly this broadens our agenda beyond the debates, however significant, on the liceity of abortion and of mercy death. It is to the breadth and the depth of this ongoing revolution that I now attend.

First, the revolution is felt in the area where death occurs, in the *health care field* whre the principal agents and agencies are all undergoing radical reappraisal. Next, heightened death consciousness touches on our viewing of the rapidly growing minority of the *aged*. The basic human problem with *suffering* is also appearing in new light. A *new pluralism* has arisen on issues involving the right to impose or to yield to death leading to changes in the doing of ethics. Finally, the notions of *immortality* and of *God* are affected by the revolutionary impetus of the new mortality consciousness.

In recent years in the United States, death has become more and more professionalized. This is signaled by the theater to which it is assigned. Increasingly we allow death to happen only in an institutional setting. In 1937, 37 percent of Americans died in institutions; by 1949, the figure was close to 50 percent, and in some areas it had climbed to over 70 percent by the late 1960's.[1] What has happened in recent years is that as we rethink death, we have been rethinking its institutional setting and all that this setting involves. The myths surrounding the roles of doctor, nurse, patient, and hospital are all being challenged. Such a challenge merits critical and creative ethical response.

First, the doctor. Traditionally, the doctor's person has been draped in myth. Hippocrates tried to rip the physician from the tangled web of superstitious religiosity. He failed. The aura of sacrality persists, and understandably so. Hues of the religio-sacred naturally attach to ultimate experiences such as birth and death. And it is over both that the doctor presides. The doctor ministers to the deeply felt needs of survival and well being and to the fear of death, and around such needs and fears the gods always hover. The doctor is priest, and the health care scene, the altar. Titles, and vestments, privilege and deference all reveal the clerical status of the doctor. When our culture was successfully denying death, the sacrality of the doctor was enhanced. He got the credit for the containment and receding power of death, and much of this credit was truly earned by the remarkable genius of recent medical science.

But now death awareness is demythologizing the priests of healing. In the name of malpractice, we are suing our gods. The limits of the medical art-science are being discovered and the faithful feel betrayed. While this is uncomfortable for doctors, it is also progress. Unrealistic myths advantage no one. The opportunity of the moment is to rethink the role of the doctor.

Up to now, the priesthood of the doctor was paternalistic and ordination was limited almost exclusively to men. The dominant metaphor of the doctor-patient relationship was that of authoritarian father to child. The authoritarian father divulges little, subordinates, and anticipates humble obedience. He speaks to you familiarly—if sternly—but requires his title in return.

The present *kairos* permits the introduction of a new metaphor. In place of father-child we could turn to the metaphor of *trained expert* to *amateur expert*. The shift would be from hierarchy to collaboration. The adult patient should be an amateur expert.

Strangely, our educational system tried to make us amateur experts in arcane species of mathematics that we will never use and in languages we may never speak. Yet we are graduated as medical illiterates. Every profession, George Bernard Shaw warned us, is a conspiracy against the laity. Keeping the laity in darkness supported the medical hierarchy's control. This should change. Titles should disappear. The English language should be adopted by medical experts. Hepatosplenomegaly can be called enlarged liver and spleen, with no loss except to Greek persons. Photophobia can be called sensitivity to light with an actual gain in medical precision, since the patient who is unduly sensitive to light is not afraid of it as *phobia* suggests. (*Pruritus ani* might be retained out of delicacy.) Parents, having heard the doctor out, might still insist on an antibiotic for their child without insult to the trained expert or detriment to science. Hospitalization and surgery would be less frequently prescribed because of the shift in decision-making. And so forth.

As we focus on death and its customary setting, the role of nurse is also being reviewed. Traditionally the nurse has been a *woman* who attends the altar of the high priest and fulfills the menial tasks of caring that did not befit the hierarchy. As with the witches of old, her skill was deprecated by the hierarchy in the profession. Regardless of her training and experience, she could prescribe nothing. She was not seen to be what she is, a physician. Terms like nurse-physician and doctor-physician can be used. As hierarchial symbols decline, the roles of nurse-physician and doctor-physician should grow together into ever more fruitful collaborative patterns.

The patient, in this new model of health care will be removed from tutelage and puerility and become a full, adult participant in the community of discernment that the medical "team" will become.

The victory of the hospice concept most clearly signals the power of the new view of death. Since hospitals, especially in a death-denying culture, are committed to graduating patients into health, the dying patient became an anomaly. Euphemisms surrounded his/her plight. These translated into rationalized neglect. Hospital personnel gave no serious consideration of where and how a person should die. A paralysis of imagination suppressed questions that are now beginning to be seen as obvious: why should someone die in a hospital where almost everyone else is busily getting better? How many forms of illness would permit persons to die at home? Why not stress pain control research for situations where pain is defeatable though the disease is not? Why are dying persons allowed no contact and conversation with other dying persons? Why are medical students and students of pastoral ministry so unsophisticated in aiding the dying and the bereaved? Happily, and revolutionarily, as these questions are asked, paralysis is yielding to creative life.

Religiously affiliated hospitals are also coming due for serious re-examination. These medical ministries began when many of the poor could get no medical help. Religiously motivated humanitarians literally lifted poor sick persons off the streets and brought them to whatever place they could find for care. These care centers institutionalized and grew and are today fixtures throughout the medical landscape. The questions they must face in today's new light are these: are these institutions here because of the momentum of history or do they do something specifically religious that would not be done in a private or governmental hospital? Are religious persons and monies being tied up for purposes that are no longer missionary? Monks in the past used to help in extinguishing fires in the community when no civic program was available. They moved on when other agencies appropriately took over; hence we have no Christian firehouses. Are the Christian hospitals Christian firehouses? Can they meet the demands of "sunset" evaluation?

Catholic hospitals especially face questions. Beyond the questions already stated, what harm may a Catholic hospital do in an area where it is the only health care center within a reasonable distance? The possibility of licit contraceptive sterilization is a solidly probable opinion in Catholic moral theology today. If a Catholic hospital forbids it not only to Catholics but to a whole pluralistic community, how can they justify this sectarian intrusion into the public domain?

In all of this, we have a perfect pattern of the evolution of moral consciousness. In all of this, we are in debt to death. A shift in awareness of a fundamental phenomenon—in this case, death—leads to a more searching understanding of the focus of all that surrounds newly appreciated reality. It is a moment of high promise for ethical inquiry.

Living While Aging

Not surprisingly, while death-denial in the culture was in full sway, we indulged in the glorification of youth and in the depersonalization of the aged. We did our best to hide from the mortal implications of that vital process that early on is called growth and later, aging. In a variety of subtle and not so subtle ways, we excommunicated the aged. They were driven into physically comfortable isolation in the case of the well-off and into destitution and premature death in the case of the poor. Aging is the disease we cannot cure and is therefore the ultimate threat to an adolescent culture. If we would hide from death we must hide from those who are seen to be in death's antechamber. The aged embarrass our delusions of non-mortality. But as we face up to death as destiny we begin to face up to that condition from which we would all prefer to die, old age. Here again opportunities for moral gain beckon.

It is indeed high time for us to attend to the aged. We are witnesses to the birth of gerontology. It is estimated that 25 percent of the persons who ever reach 65 years of age are alive today. Immortality eludes our grasp, but not longevity. Medical science, as well as politics, has been forced to look toward this new and burgeoning minority of aging persons. What we find there are persons with special needs, special possibilities, who are also the victims of special prejudices.

Ancient and medieval art reveal the inability of our forebears to appreciate the uniqueness of childhood. Children were painted in art (and clearly thought of) as small adults. Work laws and customs reflected this. Gradually the special claims of gentle childhood impressed themselves upon us. Child labor laws, schools, pastoral care, and, eventually, family life began to reflect this, and childhood was enfranchised. Something akin to this is now commencing regarding old persons. The problem is complex. We had come to look on them either as disabled, obsolescent adults, or as children. In neither case did we accept them for what they are.

One clear signal of all of this was our systematic desexualization of the elderly. The term "dirty old man" is a vulgar vehicle of this dehumanizing prejudice. But the prejudice is ensconced in our folkways and even our architecture. Homes for the aged (a cruel concept, at best) reflect an in-structured assumption of celibacy. Some few are changing and providing "petting rooms" for privacy. Shock in response to this idea must be examined.

Since sexuality pertains to humanity, programmatic desexualization is dehumanizing. This is not to say that sexual expression is essential to normalcy or that celibacy is toxic. Celibacy, chosen or not, is the lot of most persons at most times. The dehumanization enters in, however, with the programmatic exclusion of a class of persons from possible sexual expression. It shows in the resistance of grown sons and daughters to the marriage or dating of older widowed parents. Such resistance is often not traceable to the sexual abstemiousness of these sons and daughters, but to bias against commingling sex and old age. Medical science in the recent past has encouraged this by exaggerating claims of senile impotence and vaginal tissue sensitivities in older women. Corrective medical data are now happily forthcoming.

By excommunicating the aged, we impoverished ourselves. In many cultures, the older a person was, the more esteemed he or she was. The aged had tasted more of life and its surprises and were deemed wiser for that. This has not been the attitude in the United States. To carve out this nation from the wilderness, youth and physical strength were prime credentials. The prerogatives of age fell into understandable, but not forgiveable, neglect. By isolating the aged, we deny them and us their contribution to the celebration and development of life. A culture where the "elders of the land" are made mute, is condemned to shallowness. Cleverness will reign over wisdom. The quick and the slick will win undue esteem.

Time is the richness of the old. They have had more of it, and, by the assignment of roles, they will have more of it now. They have time for children (whose needs for attention are literally infinite) and the old should not be banished from contact with them into "Golden Age" prisons. They have time for contemplation of the true and the good, the beautiful and the holy. Old age is an acquisition, not a blight, and those who achieve it are a resource to all. If our new mortality-consciousness opens us to this appreciation, it again can be seen as salvation.

Suffering

To know that you will die is to suffer, for our consciousness abhors death as nature abhors a vacuum. A death-denying culture could never be profound in its assessment of the human predicament of suffering, for suffering is mortality's sibling. If we deny one, we shy from the other. Coming to grips with inevitability of suffering is the mark of maturity in a person and in a culture. The revolution in death-consciousness is an invitation to maturity in meeting life and its intrinsic pain.

Our cultural assessment of suffering is doubly lamed. It proceeds from deficient mortality consciousness, as I have said, and secondly it is infected by a sado-masochistic poison with historical Christian roots. Now is the acceptable time for reappraisal.

Suffering is not of itself a good. It is a physical and mental evil to be eased whenever possible. To say this is not to negate the possibility of a healthy "theology of the cross." Human life has the alchemic potential to transform negative experiences into human good. Helen Keller left a legacy of hope for all of us. If personal life could emerge and flower from the desolate debits of deafness and blindness, persons with even lesser afflictions may all take heart. Helen Keller's victory is in-spiriting to us all. We do not therefore glorify deafness or blindness. Neither do we practice crucifixion because of the value we attach to the crucified Jesus. The value is not in the suffering, but in what the sufferer may bring to tragedy. Sado-masochism misses this essential point and much of Christian asceticism tumbled into this error.

The history of Christian asceticism shows this in full expression. Saint John of the Cross spoke for the tradition when he urged pious souls not to seek what is easy but what is hardest, not to please our tastes, but to seek what is distasteful and disgusting, to despise one's self, to seek to be despised, and to renounce everything in the world.[2] Many took to this negativity with gusto. We read of hair shirts and iron chains, of whips and leather undergarments with nails affixed and turned toward the flesh, the glorification of lice which came to be seen as "celestial pearls," the cultivation of sleeplessness, hunger, thirst, filth, and the deliberate exposure to disease. The suffering was seen to have sacramental value. Of one holy woman it was written:

Her love of pain and suffering was insatiable. . . . She said that she could cheerfully live till the day of judgment, provided she might always have matter for suffering for God; but that to live a single day without suffering would be intolerable. She said again that she was devoured with two unassuageable fevers, one for the holy communion, the other for suffering, humiliation, and annihilation. "Nothing but pain," she continually said in her letters, "makes my life supportable."[3]

In that quote we see sacramental communion and suffering on a par, along with a twisted delight in pain that is characteristic of sado-masochistic deviations. Whence this sickness in a religious tradition which was born in the belief that human life should thrive and rejoice and that not misery but ecstasy is our destiny?

Any such deviational development is complex but some things even in this brief format can be said. Early Christianity was faced with a problem. Its religious leader suffered ignominious crucifixion. Christians did not rush to make crucifixes at that point in history but they did search for images in their religious tradition that would make sense of the gory violence that was visited upon their mentor.

At hand were the images of sacrifice and holocaust. *Homo religiosus* seeks to give something to the God who seems possessed of all. "What do you give to the God who has everything?" is the prime problem of generous piety. In sacrifice the pious took what was good, the fairest lamb in the flock, the best wine, or foods, and with holy violence, destroyed them, returning them to nature and nature's God. Only thus could you give to the Giver. Within this symbolic context, therefore Jesus became the sacrificed "lamb of God." Poured out like wine and burnt like a holocaust, the violence done Jesus took on some categorial sense.

There was ingenuity in this theology, but there was also danger. It played into the hands of the blood vengeance instinct, one of the most persistent instincts of the species. It also saddled Christianity with redemption brought about through human sacrifice, and put God in a most sadistic pose. (Bad theology embarrasses both the theologian and the theologian's God.) Eye for eye, and tooth for tooth vindictiveness and a positive *per se* value of suffering were built into this theology. As theologian Piet Fransen wrote, influenced by the "thought and customs about the freeing of serfs and slaves and about the blood money one tribe paid another in the case of manslaughter, the theology of the early Middle Ages built up a theory of redemption which has weighed heavily upon our spirituality to this day."[4] All of this translated into the sacralizing of suffering and the excesses of asceticism alluded to above.

When this poison arrived into modern medicine, it could not support a healthy concept of suffering. Some years ago, I was present at a discussion of a gravely brain-damaged child who had no remaining powers of recognition but who was still, of course, sentient. The child began to beat himself and so had to be tied in his bed. Still the doctors treated each onset of pneumonia or other illness and the child lived on. Everyone in the group seemed to be convinced that the child should have been allowed to die as he would have long since if the doctors had permitted. One woman, however, rose, to urge that the child should have been kept alive because "suffering has a purpose." The audience gasped, not knowing whence the lady came. She was, of course, a victim of the sado-masochistic poison that has been long tenured in much Christian piety and theology. Persons possessed by such a view are not thereby sadists, but they are convinced of a sadistic religious error. In the awesome realm of religion, one's natural critical talents may be unduly subdued. Persons may cling to noxious errors that would in other contexts repel them. As we take a new look at death and suffering this old poisoning is ripe for therapeutic evacuation.

A genuine Christian viewpoint would recognize that, of itself, suffering is a physical evil, a manifestation of the incompleteness of creation. Those scientists who work to control it are doing God's work. Fabry's disease, which afflicts children, involves what some physicians call the worst pain known to medicine. It involves an enzyme deficiency. Recently a cure has been developed to treat that disease by introducing the missing enzyme into the child's system. Screams turn to smiles and peace. The scientists who pioneered in this effort were, in religious terms, cocreators with God as well as coredeemers.

When suffering cannot be relieved it may at times be transcended through the human good of the sufferer, not through the inherent value of the suffering itself. Not all suffering works unto good. Some tragedy is unmitigated and not a blessing in disguise. A healthy Christianity must know and confess that tragedy is real but that it is not the name of our God. Those who work against it are helping to improve God's tender grip upon this nascent universe. In the current atmosphere of reexamination, this is more easily appreciated. And that, again, is gain.

Death and A Rebirth of Ethics

Our new awareness of death goes to the depths of ethics. No questions are more basic than those that address our moral dominion over dying. Life is a shared and precious glory and any decision to cut others out of it is supremely serious. Such decisions today are undergoing dramatic reevaluation.

We are beginning to appreciate that traditional moral theology was overly generous in blessing killing to promote social discipline and to effect social change, but was inconsistently uncontextual about imposing death in private contexts such as abortion or mercy death. The same tradition which found categories to countenance military slaughter could not "kill the baby to save the mother." A sequestered Catholicism was unembarrassed by the disagreement with this theory entertained by most persons of good will on planet earth. Changes within Roman Catholicism and the new focus on death questions have opened previously closed questions and forced Catholicism to come to grips, as it did artfully in the past, with ethical pluralism.

On the issue of abortion, the Absolute Tutiorist position banning all direct abortion, is not representative of the subtleties of the tradition. The Christian tradition distinguished between the animated and the unanimated fetus, and at least by the Middle Ages only abortion of the formed fetus was deemed homicide in the calculation of sacramental penances. Some Catholic theologians in the mid-nineteenth century defended abortion to save the life of the mother but Holy Office and papal interventions stifled the Catholic theological magisterium on this issue. The state of the question has, however, changed. In Vatican Council II, enclave Catholicism officially yielded to the recognition of the true ecclesial status of Protestant Churches. Catholic moral theology entered the ecumenical age and the current abortion debate reflects that.

Catholic and Protestant positions on abortion now range from absolute prohibition to more moderate and nuanced openness. Charles E. Curran gives a mainstream Christian position when he writes: "In conflict situations I would allow abortion to save human life or for other values that are commensurate with human life. This would obviously include grave but real threats to the psychological health of the woman and could also include other values of a socio-economic nature in extreme situations."[5] Ecumenical moral theology is also more open on questions of mercy death in extreme situations.[6]

What Catholic moral theology has done here, without always taking note of it, is to rediscover its own indigenous theory of moral pluralism known as Probabilism. (See Chapter Eight.) Probabilism, which became ensconced by the end of the seventeenth century, was based on twin insights: *a doubtful moral obligation does not oblige as though it were certain,* and, *where there is doubt, there is freedom.* Probabilism taught that in respectably debated moral matters one might follow a "solidly probable opinion" even though other opinions were entertained by experts and Church officers, and sustained by some plausible reasoning. Solid probability rested on insight, not on permission. One's own insight carefully and prayerfully refined, gave warranty for action in good conscience without any support from authorities. This was called "intrinsic probability." The insight of several reliable experts in moral theology constituted "extrinsic probability." The rigorous view (Absolute Tutiorism)), which is unfortunately still in some vogue, held that the most restrictive position had to be followed until all doubt was dissipated. On December 7, 1690 Pope Alexander VIII condemned this extremism. It is also condemned by common sense.[7]

In life/death debates today on such issues as abortion and mercy death, the wisdom of Probabilism has revived. Catholic moralists are no longer locked into the older stance of undue situational permissiveness on issues of war and capital punishment, and unsubtle absolutism on issues such as abortion, mercy death, contraception, sterilization, etc. This could only enhance Catholic contributions to on-going life/death debates.

There is a growing consensus, gradually being reflected in state laws, on the traditional Catholic teaching of "ordinary and extraordinary means." This tradition hosted the good sense that "enough is enough." The tradition knew, in the Irishism transmitted to me by my mother, that "there are worse things than dying." When living does become worse than dying, death may be allowed to claim its due. In the time of death denial, death had no due. All forces, ordinary and extraordinary, were to be mounted toward its defeat. In the new mood, the wisdom of the "ordinary/extraordinary means" rubric is welcome. The distinction was based on the notion of appropriate care. (Natural Death Acts would be better called Appropriate Care Acts.) All persons, ill or not, deserve appropriate care. Since the Neanderthal period, we have recognized that even corpses merit appropriate care; we do not simply discard them. However, what is appropriate early on in an illness, and what, later, may change. In early illness, when there is hope of returning a patient to conscious health, the most dramatic interventions may be appropriate. Heart bypass, neurosurgical interventions, respirators and the like may help the healers ply their art. Later in the same illness, however, when best efforts have failed, the only appropriate care may be the fluffing of a pillow, the washing of a brow, and the murmuring of familiar prayers. No one should be prosecuted for abandoning tactics that would no longer be motivated by reasonable hope. It is unfortunate that this good sense is not legal in all states. It is broadly resisted by so called "right to life" tabooists who see it as somehow logically linked to abortion and mercy death. Making distinctions where there are differences is antidotal to this simplism, but distinction-making is never the forte of absolutist positions in intricate debates.

The current revolution in death consciousness is also witnessing a shift from micro-ethics to macro-ethics. The perennial temptation of privatistic individualism presses the mind to issues of interpersonal morality to the neglect of social and political ethics. We find a caricature of all of us in those German chaplains who accompanied the *Wehrmacht* in its ruthless invasion of the Netherlands, zealously warning the troops against the Dutch prostitutes. In their micro-ethical fervor they seem to have overlooked much of the Second World War and the ho-locaust of Jews, Poles, Gypsies, and handicapped persons. Contemporary bioethics has shown an overconcern with micro-ethical issues, even in the area of death. In the light of new death consciousness, this too is changing.

Our age is marked by death awareness of a planetary kind. In nuclear weaponry we have conquered the power of the sun and made elaborate preparations for turning that power loose upon earth. The realization has dawned that we have created the end of the earth and stored it in our weapons and missile silos. Each day new nuclear weapons are added to our already super-abundant capacity to destroy this earth. The peoples of the earth spend more than one million dollars a minute on armaments. Here is the ultimate threat to the right to life. Here is the primary medical crisis of humankind.

Though the hour is late, it is heartening to see groups like Physicians for Social Responsibility appearing and growing so rapidly. An international peace movement is arising. Its power is not yet adequate to the threat but it augurs incipient human awareness of our terminal peril. The revolution in death consciousness leading to a revolution of critical moral consciousness is nowhere more needed than here. Politics is the art of social power. Our ability to end all power and life on earth is the reason for reshaping international politics in our time. This is a moment of unlimited promise and unlimited threat. Our powers to choose death or choose life are historically unprecedented.

Life and Afterlife

There was a time when theologians spoke of afterlife and tabloids wrote of sex. The situation has reversed itself. Afterlife has become a popular modern obsession. Understandably so. When death denial is in charge in a culture, there is no need for after-death consideration. But when a people begin to look, however squintingly, into the sun of death, they reflexively try to look beyond. It is natural to wonder what dreams we will dream in this sleep of death. Our imaginations cannot image nothingness or descent into nothingness. Beyond that, the impressiveness of personal life intimates a sequel to death. "The soul survives the body," (*anima corpori superstes*), the ancients said, and the human imagination has agreed with insistent regularity. Our relatively recent disinterest in afterlife is historically atypical. But now, from the movie *Star Wars* to talk show discussions of "out of body" experiences, afterlife has returned to center stage of the contemporary imagination.

Christian theology, with its foundational teaching that resurrection and not death is the end of life, should find this new development of interest. So far it has scarcely stirred. The reason is clear. Christian theology, on a wide scale, had begun to ape the surrounding culture regarding afterlife. For many theologians, it is an embarrassing Cinderella, and they ignore it. Others explicitly deny it. Krister Stendahl says that belief in God does not entail belief in afterlife. "The issue is not what happens to me but what happens to God's fight for his creation."[8] Schubert Ogden sees belief in immortality as positively un-Christian. It is the original sin of wanting to be like God.[9] James Gustafson also joins in the explicit denial of immortality, seeing it as a product of egocentric imagination.[10] In the face of this, Marjorie Suchocki observes: "For New Testament writers subjective immortality was an integral component in God's victory over evil."[11] This leads to Marjorie Reiley Maguire's telling question for this time of reappraisal, can any sort of a "Christian" ethics "survive in theory or in practice if the link between immortality and ethics" be further ignored or denied?[12] Christianity's God is a "God of hope" (Romans 15:13). If hope is evacuated, Christian proclamation verges on vacuity. The questions facing Christian theologians are these: is hope inexorably linked to immortality? If not, what is the impact on the rest of the *kerygma*, on piety, and on the motivation for social justice? More answers than one are already forthcoming to these questions. By way of rare treat for lonely theology, broad public interest in this debate will not be lacking.

And what of God in all of this? Afterlife questions are God questions, for afterlife imports power beyond us. Death ends our initiatives; survival of death speaks of absolute dependence. Facing death is our most religious or anti-religious attitude. Here as nowhere else we must answer *yea* or *nay* to the possibility of an active and undergirding Power. There may be atheists in foxholes, but, given time for reflection, there are no religiously disinterested occupants there. Death reappraisal is God-talk time. The ultimacy of death takes us to the ultimate questions of source and meaning. Not surprisingly, religious imagination is quickening. Old gods are dying and replacements are in the wings. Traditional and rationalized modes of religiosity are on trial, and forms closer to living experience, however chaotic, are rising in preference. Custodians of older orthodoxies, which spoke successfully to past experiences, cry heresy, but their impotency is apparent. A new consciousness has spawned new questions. Perry's ships have entered our Yedo Bay with cargoes of questions that will leave us no foreseeable theological peace. And that is good. The ultimate religious question is again unleashed: what, if anything, is God? Is God's goodness more

impressive than God's power? Is God like the masculine or the feminine, or both, or neither? Are churches friends and shrines of God, or
are they idols and rivals? How could God do as well as God has done,
and why has God not done better? Since God is beyond our God-talk,
is such talk futile, or the supreme challenge to human appreciative
intelligence? These are some of the questions of the new catechism.

The most important theology today has not been written. It is as
yet only felt, sometimes in fear, and sometimes in exhilaration. This
time of theological opportunity merits humility and excitement.

Death consciousness is not immune to evil. Necrophilia has not
gone the way of smallpox and never will. It permanently tempts our
spirit. We live in the bloodiest of centuries. Our governmental budgets
reveal our mortal bias. And yet the death turn in these times of the
mind is a harbinger of good. It puts our superficiality on notice, and
it opens our ears.

CHAPTER 13

Visit to an Abortion Clinic

I should not have been nervous the first day I drove to the "abortion clinic." After all, I wasn't pregnant. And yet tremors from a Catholic boyhood wrenched my usually imperturbable stomach, producing gas pains. The route I took was the one I usually take to school, but now I was filled with a morbid sense of dread and foreboding. There would be no abortions done this day. I would see no patients and no pickets. I was simply going to meet the staff and see the clinic. And I was scared. I remember thinking as I turned onto State Street: "How would I feel if I were a Catholic woman, pregnant and scared and on the way to an abortion!" Half the women who come to this clinic are Catholics, and I had now experienced a new and unnerving kind of empathy for them. Looking back, I would label that the firstfruits of my project.

I pulled into the clinic drive, parked, and found myself looking around anxiously, wondering if anyone would see me as I entered this forbidden place. I had expected none of these emotions, but I am instructed by them yet. For when I met the outraged and self-righteous pickets some days later, I realized that they and I had some common origins.

So what was it that brought this Philadelphia Irish Catholic male moral theologian to the clinic door? Abortion has not been my academic obsession. As of two years ago I could say that not one of my some one hundred articles was on that subject. Only a quarter of a chapter in two of my four books treated abortion at any length—and one got an *imprimatur*, unsolicited by me, in its Spanish translation. My wife and I have had no personal experience with abortion, although it once loomed as a possible choice in our lives. Our first son, Danny, was diagnosed as terminally ill with Hunter's syndrome when Margie was three months pregnant. Amniocentesis revealed that the fetus, now

Tommy, had slipped through the genetic dragnet and was spared the drastic course that awaited Danny.

I can trace the immediate stimulus for my going to a clinic to the woman who visited with Margie and me in our home several days before her abortion at this same clinic. She agonized with us over the decision she had rather conclusively made, and asked us, as ethicists, to ponder with her all the pros and cons. She was almost six weeks pregnant. Her life situation was seriously incompatible with parenting, and she could not bear the thought of adoption. After her abortion, she told us she felt she had made the right decision, but she paid a price in tears and soul trauma. I remember her piercing words about the rosary-saying pickets: "They were taking a precious symbol of my faith and turning it into a weapon against me."

More generally, I was drawn to this uneasy experience by women. I have discussed abortion more often with women in recent years, and I found how differently they viewed it. I experienced their resentment at the treatment of the subject by the male club of moral theologians. One woman, author and professor at a Chicago seminary, wrote me after my first article on abortion ("Abortion: A Question of Catholic Honesty." *The Christian Century*, Sept. 14, 1983), thanking me and surprising me. She said she found it difficult to use the American bishops pastoral letter on nuclear war because these *men* could agonize so long over the problems of *men* who might decide to end the world, but had not a sympathetic minute for the moral concerns of a woman who judges she cannot bring her pregnancy to term.

I knew that my visits would not give me a woman's understanding of the abortion decision, but I hoped they might empty me a bit of my incultured masculine insensibility. My hope was that it might assist me, in the phrase of French novelist, Jean Sulivan, to "lie less" when I write about this subject and to offend less those women who come this way in pain. If experience is the plasma of theory, this experience obtained in a clinic three blocks from the Marquette library where I have done research on abortion, could only enhance my theological ministry. Those who write on liberation theology go to Latin America to learn; those who write on abortion stay at their desks. Until recently, all churchly writing on abortion was done by desk-bound celibate males. It is past time to hear from the women who make these decisions.

Meeting the Clinic Staff

One day last May, I called the Milwaukee Women's Health Organization (the clinic) and spoke to its director, Elinor Yeo, an ordained minister of the United Church of Christ. I was afraid she would find my request to spend time at the clinic unseemly and out of order. She said she would call back when she finished an interview with a patient and spoke with her staff. She called later to tell me that the staff were enthusiastic about my prospective visits.

The clinic door still had traces of red paint from a recent attack. The door was buzzed open only after I was identified. I realized that these people live and work in fear of "pro-life" violence. In the last seven months there had been twenty-five reported incidents of criminal violence at clinics, including bombing, arson, shootings, and vandalism. A sign inside the front door read: PLEASE HELP OUR GUARD. WE MAY NEED WITNESSES IF THE PICKETS GET OUT OF CONTROL. YOU CAN HELP BY OBSERVING AND LETTING HIM/HER KNOW IF YOU SEE TROUBLE.

Elinor Yeo sat with me for more than an hour describing the clinic's activities. Half their patients are teenagers; half, Catholics, and 20 percent, black. In a single day of the previous week, out of fourteen patients, one was thirteen, one fourteen, and one fifteen. Nationally, most abortions are within eight weeks, at which point the *conceptum* is still properly called an embryo, and 91 percent are within twelve weeks. At this clinic, too, most abortions were early, "in the first two months." Most of the patients are poor; the clinic is busiest at the time when welfare checks come in. The normal cost for an abortion here is $185. For those with a Medical Assistance Card, it is $100. I asked Elinor about the "right-to-lifers" claim that most women having abortions are rich. She replied: "The average age of an abortion patient is nineteen years. In what sense is a nineteen-year-old woman with an unwanted pregnancy rich?" I saw no rich women at this clinic.

I asked about the charge that doing abortions makes doctors rich. She assured me that, given their budget, all the doctors who work for them would make more back in their offices. These doctors are also sometimes subject to picketing at their homes. Their care of patients is excellent, and they often end up delivering babies for these same women later.

Each patient is given private counseling. About half want their male partners with them for these sessions. If there is any indication that the man is more anxious for the abortion than the woman, private counseling is carefully arranged. Every woman is offered the opportunity to see charts on embryonic and fetal development and is informed on alternatives to abortion. The consent form to be signed at the end of the interview and counseling sessions reads: "I have been informed of agencies and services available to assist me to carry my pregnancy to term should I desire. . . . The nature and purposes of an abortion, the alternatives to pregnancy termination, the risks involved, and the possibility of complications have been fully explained to me."

All counseling stresses reproductive responsibility. Two of the women counselors have worked with Elinor for fourteen years. One is the mother of five children, the other of three. Free follow-up advice on contraception is made available. It is the explicit goal of the counselors not to have the women return for another abortion. Those most likely to have repeat abortions are the ones who reject contraceptive information and say they will never have sex again until they are married. It became ironically clear to me that these women working in the abortion clinic prevent more abortions than the zealous pickets demonstrating outside.

Only 5 percent of the patients have ever considered adoption as an alternative. *Abortion* or *keeping* are the two options considered by these young women. (Ninety percent of teenagers who deliver babies keep them, according to Ms. Yeo.)

Adoption is, of course, facilely recommended at the bumper-sticker level of this debate. One patient I spoke to at a subsequent visit to the clinic told me how unbearable the prospect was of going to term and then giving up the born baby. For impressive reasons she found herself in no condition to have a baby. Yet even at five weeks she had begun to take vitamins to nourish the embryo in case she changed her mind. "If I continued this nurture for nine months, how could I hand over to someone else what would then be my baby?" It struck me forcefully how aloof and misogynist it is not to see that the adoption path is *supererogatory*. Here is one more instance of male moralists prescribing the heroic for women as though it was simply normal and mandatory.

The surgery lasts some five to ten minutes. General anesthesia is not needed in these early abortions. Most women are in and out of the clinic in two and one-half hours. They return in two weeks for a check-up. These early abortions are done by suction. I was shown the suction tube and was surprised to find it only about twice the width of a straw. This was early empirical information for me as to *what* it is that is aborted at this stage.

All patients are warned about pregnancy aftermath groups who advertise and offer support but actually attempt to play on guilt to recruit these women in their campaign to outlaw all abortions, even those performed for reasons of health. One fundamentalist Protestant group in Milwaukee advertises for pregnancy testing. When the woman arrives, they immediately subject her to a grizzly film on abortions of six-month-old fetuses. They take the woman's address and phone number and tell her they will contact her in two weeks "at home." The effects of this are intimidating and violative of privacy and often lead to delayed abortions of more developed fetuses.

Meeting the Women

My second visit to the clinic was on a Saturday when the clinic was busy. I arrived at 8:30 in the morning. The pickets were already there, all men, except for one woman with a ten-year-old boy. A patient was in the waiting room, alone. We greeted one another and I sat down and busied myself with some papers, wondering what was going on in the mind of this woman. I was later to learn that she was five to six weeks pregnant. She was under psychiatric care for manic-depression, and only lithium was keeping her from serious mental disturbance. In heavy doses, lithium may disrupt the formation of organs in embryos and early fetuses.

Pro-life? Pro-choice? How vacuous the slogans seemed in the face of this living dilemma! What life options were open to this woman? Only through her loss of sanity could a reasonably formed fetus come to term. This woman had driven a long distance that morning alone to get to this clinic, and she would have to return home afterwards alone. She had to walk through the pickets showing her pictures of fully formed fetuses and begging her: "Don't kill your baby! Don't do it." Well-intentioned those pickets may have been, but in what meaningful moral sense were they in this instance pro-life?

As I watched this woman I thought of my colleague Richard McCormick's recent confident assertion that there could be no plausible reason for abortion except to save the physical life of the woman or if the fetus was anencephalic. This woman's physical life was not at risk, and the embryo would develop a brain. How is it that in speaking of women we so easily reduce human life to physical life? Saving *life* involves more than cardiopulmonary continuity. Whence the certitudes that undergird McCormick's parsimony in allowing only two marginal reasons to justify abortion? Whence the Vatican's comparable sureness that while there may be *just* wars with incredible slaughter, there can be no *just* abortions? Both need to listen to the woman on lithium as she testifies that life does not always confine itself within the ridges of our immodest theories.

With permission I sat in on some of the initial interviews with patients. The first two were poor teenagers, each with an infant at home, and each trying to finish high school. One was out of work. Elinor Yeo let her know that they were now hiring at Wendy's. I was impressed that the full human plight of the patients was of constant concern to the staff. The other young woman had just gotten a job after two years and would lose it through a pregnancy. One woman counted out her $100 and said: "I hate to give that up; I need it so much."

The staff spoke to me about the various causes of unwanted pregnancies. One staff member said that it would seem that 90 percent of the men have "scorn for condoms." "Making love" does not describe those sexual invasions. For these hostile inseminators nothing should interfere with their pleasure. A few women concede they were "testing the relationship." Often there is contraceptive failure. One recent case involved a failed vasectomy. Sometimes conception is admittedly alcohol- and drug-related. Often it is a case of a broken relationship where the woman, suddenly alone, feels unable to bring up a child. Economic causes were most common. Lack of job, lack of insurance, a desire to stay in school and break out of poverty.

I wondered how many "pro-lifers" voted for Reagan because of his anti-abortion noises, even though Reaganomics decreased the income of the lowest fifth of society 8 percent while increasing the income of the rich. More of this could only be more poverty, more ruin, more social chaos, more unwanted pregnancies, and more women at clinic doors. Fixation, as ever, is blinding.

Meeting the Pickets

The pickets are a scary lot. Because of them a guard has to be on duty to escort the patients from their cars. Before the clinic leased the adjacent parking lot—making it their private property—some pickets used to go up to the cars of the women, screaming and shaking the car. The guard told me he was once knocked down by a picket. Without the guard, some of them surround an unescorted woman and force her to see and hear their message of condemnation.

There are, of course, passive pickets who simply carry placards and pray. One day, twenty boys from Libertyville, Illinois, were bused in to picket. They were not passive. They had been taught to shout at the women as they arrived. One staff member commented: "Statistically, one-quarter to one-third of these boys will face abortion situations in their lives. I wonder how this experience will serve them then."

A reporter from the *Milwaukee Journal* came when I was there, and

I followed her when she went out to interview the pickets. Two of the pickets immediately recognized me. Since I have been quoted in the press in ways that did not please, I am *persona non grata*. I was given a chance to experience what the women patients endure. "You're in the right place, Maguire. In there where they murder the babies." I decided they were not ripe for dialogue, so I remained silent and listened in on the interview.

I learned that some of these men had been coming every Saturday for eight years. Their language was filled with allusions to the Nazi Holocaust. Clearly, they imagine themselves at the ovens of Auschwitz, standing in noble protest as innocent *persons* are led to their death. There could hardly be any higher drama in their lives. They seem not to know that the Nazis were anti-abortion, too, for Aryans. They miss too the anti-Semitism and insult in this use of Holocaust imagery. The six million Jews and two to three million Poles, Gypsies, and homosexuals killed were actual, not potential persons. Comparing their human dignity to that of pre-personal embryos is no tribute to the Holocaust dead. Jews and other survivors of victims are not flattered.

Sexism too is in bold relief among the pickets. The references to "these women" coming here to "kill their babies" are dripping with hatred. It struck me that for all their avowed commitment to life, these are the successors of the witch hunters. As much as I would want to help the women I met, not to have to return to an abortion clinic, I am sickened by those who see them as witches or wound them as these pickets do.

Meeting the Embryos

On my third visit to the clinic, I made bold to ask to see the products of some abortions. I asked in such a way as to make refusal easy, but my request was granted. The aborted matter is placed in small cloth bags and put in jars awaiting disposal. I asked to see the contents of one of the bags of a typical abortion—a six-to-seven-week pregnancy— and it was opened and placed into a metal cup for examination. I held the cup in my hands and saw a small amount of unidentifiable fleshly matter in the bottom of the cup. The quantity was so little that I could have hidden it if I had taken it into my hand and made a fist.

It was impressive to realize that I was holding and looking at the aborted remains of what many people think to be the legal and moral peer of a woman, if not, indeed, her superior. I thought too of the

Human Life Amendment that would describe what I was seeing as having been a citizen of the United States with rights of preservation that would contermand the good of the woman bearer. I have held babies in my hands, and now I held this aborted embryo. I know the difference. This had not been a person or a candidate for baptism.

I thought of the statement of Carol Tauer in her 1984 lead article in *Theological Studies*: "Both theological and magisterial opinion, up until the nineteenth century, were open to the view that the ensoulment of the early embryo is highly improbable, if not impossible." I thought too of the *Catechism of the Council of Trent* which said the supposed rational ensoulment of Jesus at the moment of conception was clearly a miracle since "in the natural order, no body can be informed by a human soul except after the prescribed space of time." I came to admire anew the core sense of that tradition and to wish it were better known by those—hierarchy and lay—who presume to talk for the Church. Until the nineteenth century, this teaching of "delayed animation" was the common and traditional teaching of the church.

Conclusions

1. My four visits to the clinic made me more anxious to maintain the legality of abortions for women who judge they need them. There are no moral grounds for political consensus against this freedom on an issue where good experts and good people disagree. It also made me anxious to work to reduce the need for abortion by fighting the causes of unwanted pregnancies: the sexism, enforced by the institutions of church, synagogue, and state which diminish a woman's sense of autonomy; the poverty induced by skewed budgets; our anti-sexual bias that leads to eruptive sex; and the other *macro* causes of these *micro* tragedies.

2. I came to experience that abortion can be the least violent option facing a woman. In a utopian world, Beverly Harrison writes "it probably would be possible to adhere to an ethic which affirmed that abortions should be resorted to only *in extremis*, to save a mother's life." It is brutally insensitive to pretend that women who resort to abortion do so in utopia or that death is the only extremity they face. More often than we male theologians have dreamed, abortion is the best a woman can do in a world of diversified extremities.

3. I came away from the clinic with a new longing for a moratorium

on self-righteous and sanctimonious utterances from Catholic bishops on the subject of abortion. An adequate Catholic theology of abortion has not been written, and yet the bishops sally forth as though this complex topic were sealed in a simple negative. Bishops like New York's John O'Connor and Boston's Bernard Law, who use tradition as though it were an oracle instead of an unfinished challenge and task, are not helping at all. A position like O'Connor's has two evil yields: (1) it insults the Catholic intellectual tradition by making it look simplistic, and (2) it makes the bishops the allies of a right wing which has been using their new found love of embryos as an ideological shield for a mean-spirited social agenda. Antiabortionism, which seems so pure, has become a hideaway for many who resist the bishops' call for peace and social justice.

4. I come from the abortion clinic with an appeal to my colleagues in Catholic moral theology. Many Catholic moralists would now agree with Carol Tauer's modest conclusion that "when there are compelling, or even adequate, reasons for terminating an embryonic life, the application of probabilistic methods would permit some early abortions." But, overall, Catholic moral theology is in grave default on this issue, to the embarrassment and peril of some of our most justice-minded Catholic political leaders.

Many theologians (especially clerics) avoid this issue or behave weirdly or skittishly when they touch it. How do Catholic theologians justify their grand silence when they are allowing physicalism, crude historical distortions, and fundamentalistic notions of "Church teaching" to parade as "the Catholic position"? Why are ecclesiological and ethical errors, thoroughly lambasted in the birth control debate, so timidly tolerated when the topic is abortion? Geraldine Ferraro and Mario Cuomo took the heat and tried to do the theology on this subject. Their debts to American Catholic theologians are minuscule. What service do we Church teachers give when errors, already corrected in theology, are allowed to roam unchallenged in the pastoral and polictical spheres? Why are non-experts, hierarchy or not, allowed to set the *theological* terms of *this* debate? What service is it to ecumenism to refuse serious dialogue not only with women but with mainline Jewish and Protestant theologians on this issue? Vatican II said "ecumenical dialogue could start with discussions concerning the application of the gospel to moral questions." That dialogue has not happened on abortion, and our brothers and sisters from other communions are waiting for it.

I realize, as do my colleagues in Catholic ethics, that abortion is not a pleasant topic. At its best, abortion is a negative value, unlike the positive values of feeding the poor and working for civil rights. On top of that, it has become the litmus test of orthodoxy, and that spells danger in the Catholic academe. But, beyond all this, we in the Catholic family have been conditioned against an objective and empathic understanding of abortion. Affectivity is the matrix of all moral knowing. On this issue our affectivity is warped. We were more sensitized to embryos than to the women who bear them.

On my second trip to the clinic, my gas pains left me, in spite of meeting patients, and pickets, and listening, as I spoke with staff, to the suction machinery in the adjacent rooms. New emotions succeeded as this account shows. But I judge that my first visit brought reaction to my past conditioning on abortion; my others, to realities I had not well appreciated. I claim no infallibility on this subject, but I do insist that until we open our affections to enlightenment here, we will none of us be wise.

5. Finally, I am convinced that the subject of abortion in the Catholic communion involves much more than the moral value of embryos. The abortion issue is ecclesiologically freighted and sociologically complex. Sadly, it seems, a Catholic theologian could deny the biblical notion of God's option for the poor and not be considered unorthodox. Those arguing for a continued increase in nuclear arms are not drummed out of the faith. As one Catholic woman professor at a large eastern Catholic university said: "I could announce that I had become a communist without causing a stir, but if I defended Roe v. Wade [the 1973 Supreme Court decision legalizing abortion in the United States], I would not get tenure." If someone defends the morality of some abortions in tragic conflict situations, the wrath of the Catholic brotherhood descends. Why?

Partly, of course, as I have said, it is because Catholic manmade theology has not sufficiently incorporated the experience of women on abortion—and the abortion decision is ultimately that of a woman. It is not noted that the prejudicial expression "abortion on demand" leaves out the fact that it is a woman who is demanding and does not ask why she must "demand." But, beyond that, involved in this issue is the problem of the role sexuality and reproductive ethics play in Catholic self-identification.

Professor Samuel Laeuchli, in his book *Power and Sexuality: The Emergence of Canon Law at the Synod of Elvira* proposes a thesis on the role of sexuality in Catholic ecclesiology. His thesis is also applicable to reproductive ethics and abortion. He writes of the Second Vatican Council: "The council vaunted its dialogue with the modern world; yet in the most pressing of modern matters, sexuality, despite a few attempts, it failed." He cites "the abortiveness of the vatican synod's confrontation with the issue of sexuality." He offers reasons for this failure:

Despite some attempts, Vatican II did not come to terms with the contemporary sexual revolution because the issue was too dangerous. For the Church to change its position on sexual behavior and ideals weakens traditional authority, and such a transformation would have immense economic as well as psychological implications.

Laeuchli came to this dire judgment at the end of a study of the Synod of Elvira. That synod, held in the year 309, was defining Church identity at the dawning of the age of Constantine. As the church moved from a prophetic sect toward establishment status, it turned to sexuality to define itself. Almost half of the canons of the synod were related to sex. The real issue, however, was not sex, but power. What happened at Elvira was that "the Christian elite sought to carve out a clerical image" of the church, and sexual control was a tool in that project. The sexual obsession served two related synodal purposes: "the establishment of social coherence in the church's search for identity, and the creation of a clerical image which was to strengthen the clerical hold on the faithful."

This council, that was to be paradigmatic for much subsequent conciliar activity, brought sex into the ecclesiastical power equation. It is Laeuchli's well-argued contention that it is still there. It is an old hierarchical tradition, stretching back to Elvira to stake out sexuality (and reproductive ethics) as a prime zone for orthodoxy testing. If we believe with Teilhard de Chardin that nothing is intelligible outside of its history, then it would be unwise to separate the power question from any ecclesiastical treatment of sex or reproductive ethics. The fact that contraception was banned from conciliar treatment in Vatican II, while matters such as nuclear war, atheism, world community and government, and relations with other major religions were left open to free debate, signals again that the contraception issue was weighted beyond its own intrinsic merits.

True light will not shine upon the abortion debate within Catholicism until there is an honest admission of just what the discussion itself involves and conceals. Something unhealthy is afoot when an issue that is one of the most intensely debated issues in church and society cannot even be openly and freely discussed at most Catholic universities and colleges.

The issue will not be solved under a pro-choice or pro-life banner. It will be resolved through complexity consciousness— through a recognition that this issue is not simple and that the repetition of simple negatives will not do it justice. The issue will not be wisely handled until the experience of women is accorded paramount status in the Catholic ethics of abortion. Given the institutional stakes that have been attached to the abortion issue, the advent of free and ecumenical discussion in a Catholic setting is not yet in the offing.

CHAPTER 14

The Freedom to Die

Of old when men lay sick and sorely tried,
The doctor gave them physic, and they died.
But here's a happier age, for now we know
Both how to make men sick and keep them so.
Hilaire Belloc

We humans are the only animals who know we are going to die, and we have borne this privileged information with uneven grace. On the one hand poets and philosophers have gazed at death and proclaimed the significance of death-consciousness. Hegel saw the awareness of mortality as such as stimulus to human achievement that he could define history as "what man does with death." Schopenhauer called death "the muse of philosophy" and Camus saw our capacity for suicide as evoking the most fundamental philosophical questions. Poets have called death such things as "gentle night," "untimely frost," or "the great destroyer."

The average person, however, would rather forget it. This is especially true if the average person is an American since in this happiness-oriented land, death (outside of a military context) is seen as something of an un-American activity. It happens, of course, but it is disguised and *sub rosa*, like sex in Victorian England. Most Americans now die in hospitals. And they die without the benefit of the liturgies of dying that attend this natural event in cultures which accept death as a fact of human life. The dying process is marked by deceit where everything except the most important fact of impending death can be addressed. When the unmentionable happens, the deceit goes on as the embalmers embark on their *post mortem* cosmetics to make the dead person look alive. Mourners, chemically fortified against tears that would betray the farce, recite their lines about how well the dead man looks when, in point of fact, he is not well and does not look it.

All of this does not supply the atmosphere in which our moral right to die with dignity can receive its needed re-evaluation. Nevertheless, the re-evaluation must go on. Technology has already moved ahead of both ethics and law. As Johns Hopkins professor Diana Crane notes, "the nature of dying has changed qualitatively in recent years because of advances in medical knowledge and technology." These qualitative changes have dissipated older definitions of death, given greater power to doctors over life and death, shaken the never too fine art of prognosis, and presented all us mortals with options that old law and ethical theory did not contemplate . . . which options offer frontal challenges to some long-tenured traditions and taboos.

As if this were not complicated enough, the technological revolution has also caused a notable shift in our moral universe. The interplay between technology and morality is, of course, as old as the first primitive tool. With technological advance comes power and with power, responsibility, and the question of whether this power can be used without intrusion into the realm of the gods. Prometheus, the philanthropic god who stole fire, was judged by Zeus to have gone too far. Bellerophon in the Iliad came to a sorry end for trying to ride to the Olympus of the gods and for thinking "thoughts too great for humans." And Icarus, exulting in the technology of human-made wings, flew too close to the sun and perished. These myths, like the myths of Babel and Adam's sin, are relevant to the moral dilemma of the creative animal. What thoughts and what initiatives are too great for humans? Where are the sacred borders between the *can do* and the *may do*? Where does presumption enter into the knowledge of good and evil?

Medical ethics has long known the strain of this dilemma. We tend to consider the physical and biological to be ethically normative and inviolable. Blood transfusions were resisted by many on these grounds. Birth control was also, for a very long time, impeded by the physicalist ethic that left moral beings at the mercy of their biology. We had no choice but to conform to the rhythms of our physical nature and to accept its determinations obediently. Only gradually did we technological beings discover that we are morally free to intervene creatively and to achieve birth control by choice.

Can We Intervene?

The question now arising is whether, in certain circumstances, we may intervene creatively to achieve death by choice or whether we mortals must in all cases await the good pleasure of biochemical and organic factors and allow these to determine the time and the manner of our demise. In more religious language, can the will of God regarding a person's death be manifested only through the collapse of sick or wounded organs or could it also be discovered through the sensitivities and reasonings of moral persons? Could there be circumstances when it would be acutely reasonable (and therefore moral if one uses "reason" in a Thomistic sense) to terminate life through either positive action or calculated benign neglect rather than to await in awe the dispositions of organic tissue?

The discussion should proceed in the realization that the simpler days are past in which the ethics of dying was simple. Most importantly, the definition of death was no problem until recently. When the heart stopped beating and a person stopped breathing, the person was dead. (Interestingly, the old theology manuals were not too sure of this since they advised that the sacrament of final anointing could be administered conditionally up to about two hours after "death.") Medical technology has changed all of that. It is now commonplace to restore palpitation to a heart that has fully stopped beating. Even when the natural capacity for cardiopulmonary activity is lost, these systems can be kept functioning through the aid of supplementary machinery. Heartbeat and breathing can be artificially maintained in a person whose brain is crushed or even deteriorated to the point of liquefaction. Heartbeat is no longer a safe criterion of human life!

This has turned medical people to the concept of "brain death." Indeed, Dr. Robert Glaser, the Dean of Stanford's School of Medicine says: "Insofar as it involves organ donors and their rights, the technical question of death has been resolved, by popular consensus, in the recognition that the brain and not the heart is the seat of human life." Brain death, however, is not an answer without problems. A person with a hopelessly damaged brain could still have spontaneous heartbeat and respiration. Harvard's Dr. Henry Beecher asks the inevitable question here: "Would you bury such a man whose heart was beating?" And lawyers will be quick to tell you that the removal of vital organs from a body that has a dead brain but a live heart would raise the specter of legal liability.

All of this illumines the unsettling fact that death admits of degrees. Some organs and cells die before others. As Paul Ramsey observes, "the 'moment' of death is only a useful fiction." It may however be more fiction than useful if it leaves us hoping for a definition of death that will make it unnecessary for us to judge that a particular "life" may now be completely terminated by a positive act of omission or commission. Science will not give us a litmus test for death that will relieve us of all need for moral judgment and action. That day has passed and that is what makes for the qualitative change in dying and the ethics thereof.

It seems well to pursue this issue by considering four different dying situations: (1) the case of the irreversibly comatose patient whose life is sustained by artificial means; (2) the conscious patient whose life is supported artificially by such means as dialysis (for kidney patients) or iron lung; (3) the conscious patient who is dying of a terminal illness whose life is supported by natural means; (4) the case of self-killing in a non-medical context.

First, then, to the case of the irreversibly comatose, artificially sustained patient. It is a useful beginning here to look at the remarkable address of Pius XII on the prolongation of life, given in 1957. In this talk, the Pope stated that the definition of death is an open question to which "the answer cannot be deduced from any religious and moral principle. . . ." He allows that in hopelessly unconscious patients on respirators "the soul may already have left the body" and he refers to such patients by the ambiguous but interesting term "virtually dead." The Pope points out that only ordinary means need be used to preserve life and he supplies a broad definition of this slippery term saying that ordinary means are "means that do not involve any grave burden for oneself or another." The Pope is dealing with the unconscious patient of whom it can be said that "only automatic artificial respiration is keeping him alive." In these hopeless cases, the Pope concludes that after several days of unsuccessful attempts, there is no moral obligation to keep the respirator going.

The respirator is, of course, an extraordinary means especially when it is used on the irreversibly unconscious. For years now theologians have also argued that even intravenous feeding in this type of case is extraordinary and may be discontinued. (Law lags behind ethics on this.) I would argue further that in such a case where the personality is permanently extinguished, one needs a justifying cause to continue artificial, supportive measures. To maintain bodily life extensively at a vegetative level with extraordinary means is irrational, immoral and a violation of the dignity of human life. It is a burden on the family; also, there may be need to allocate these medical resources to curable awaiting patients. It is, moreover, macabre, irreverent and crudely materialistic to preserve by medical pyrotechnics the hopeless presence of what could best be described as a breathing corpse. Of these cases, when the patient is "irretrievably inaccessible to human care," Paul

Ramsey says (a bit too quickly, I judge) that it is "a matter of complete indifference whether death gains the victory over the patient in such impenetrable solitude by direct or indirect action."

One reason that clearly justifies maintaining this kind of life is to make possible the donation of organs since the human body thus sustained is considered to be the best possible tissue bank. Death, however, should first be declared and the law should be pushed to update itself to allow for this. Probably our society is not prepared to grant that the organs in such instances should, by eminent domain, be allocated to those who need them. Through cultural conditioning and taboo we are still disposed to prefer the "rights" of the dead to the needs of the living in this regard, and few people even carry donor cards now legal and available in all states. Thus the immoral waste of tissue that could be "a gift of life."

Our second case concerns the conscious patient whose life is artificially supported. This is a broad category and could be stretched to include those who attribute their perdurance to superabundant dosages of Vitamin C and E. We are thinking, rather, of those who are alive thanks to dialysis or an iron lung. As medicine advances this category will expand.

In assessing the moral right of such patients to die, one might be tempted to repair to the facile distinction between ordinary and extraordinary means. By the papal definition of ordinary means ("grave burden for oneself or another") both dialysis and the iron lung are extraordinary. Thus the patients involved would appear to be under no obligation to continue in this kind of therapy and would seem free to discontinue the treatment and die.

We must, however, avoid the simplistic allurements of a one-rubric ethics. There is more involved here than the patient and the extraordinary means. We must (as does the papal teaching cited) speak also of the patient's obligations of social justice and charity, remembering that an individualistic, asocial ethics has also infected medical morality.

We have all heard much of the redemptive power of suffering. Unfortunately, the pieties of the past often interpreted this in accord with primitive myths of vindication which implied that pain and bloodshed of themselves had an atoning power. These myths, replete as they may be with sado-masochistic elements, have had an enormous influence both on Christology and Christian asceticism, attributing a positive *per se* value to suffering. Such a value suffering does not have, but rather assumes its meaning, value, or disvalue from the concrete circumstances of the sufferer.

In this sense there *can* be a redemptive value to suffering. Take the example of a kidney patient who has not had a successful transplant. Could she not see her plight as a vocation? Her disease can become a rostrum and she could become part of something that is needed . . . a lobby of the dying and the gravely ill. To be more specific, this nation which has borne her is also ill. Its priorities are out of joint. It has, by morbid selection, chosen for itself what Richard Barnet calls "an economy of death." Its heart is so askew that only if disease could be shown to have *military* significance would it receive the government and private funding it desperately needs. Many illnesses could now be contained if the nation had given the zeal and the budget to life that it now gives to death.

The gravely ill with their unique credentials could do more here than they realize. By working creatively with politicians, national health organizations, medical and legal societies, news media, writers, etc.—and in ways as yet unthought of which their healthy imaginations will bring forth—the lobby of the dying and the gravely ill could become a healing force in society. Human nature is still so barbarous that the well attend more to the well than to the sick. Great obligations, therefore, devolve upon the sick. The well need the sick more than the well know.

Still, concerning persons in the category here discussed, if their artificially supported life becomes unbearable, they have a right to discontinue treatment and we owe them in justice and in charity the direct or indirect means to leave this life with the dignity, comfort and speed which they desire. (For a fuller argument of this, see my book, *Death By Choice*, 2nd ed. Garden City: Doubleday, Image, 1984).

What then of the conscious, terminal patient whose life systems are functioning naturally? May such a patient in any circumstance take direct, positive action to shorten the dying trajectory or is the natural course of the disease ethically normative in an absolute sense? Those who would deny the moral right to direct acceleration of the death process will adduce an "absolute" principle such as the unconditional inviolability of innocent human life. This is taken to mean that innocent life may in no circumstance be terminated by direct, positive action.

John Milhaven, in an important 1966 *Theological Studies* article, notes the tendency simply to proclaim this inviolability principle and work from there in right-to-death cases. He cites the failure of those who do this to indicate "the reasons that prove there is an absolute inviolability, holding under all circumstances." And he asks the fair and telling question: "How do we know this?" In point of fact, I submit that we do not know this because it is not knowable.

Those who use the principle accept no burden of proof and offer only a fideistic assertion. They present the principle without proof, as self-evident. In ethics, however, only the most generic propositions are self-evident, such as "do good and avoid evil"; "to each his/her own." The *evidence* emerges from the mere understanding of the terms. Such statements are universally true because they lack particularizing and complicating content.

Practical principles such as the one on direct termination of innocent life must be proved and the proof must come from wherever moral meaning is found. That is, it must come from a knowledge of the morally significant empirical data, the consequences, the existent alternatives, the unique circumstances of person, place, and time, etc. Moral meaning is found not just in principles but in all the concrete circumstances that constitute the reality of a person's situation, and the principles themselves are rooted in empirical experience and must at times be rewashed in an empirical bath to check their abiding validity.

To say that something is morally right or wrong in all possible circumstances implies a divine knowledge of all possible circumstances and their moral meaning. To say that something is universally good or bad regardless of circumstances is non-sense, for it is to say that something is *really* good or bad regardless of the *reality-constituting* circumstances.

An attempt can be made to base the "no direct killing of innocent life principle" on the reality of expected intolerable consequences. This is the cracked dike argument. *Après moi le déluge!* If X is allowed, then Y and Z and everything else will be allowed. This is a kind of ethical domino theory which has the deficiencies of any domino theory. It ignores the real meaning of the real differences between X, Y and Z. Good ethics is based on reality and makes real distinctions where there are real differences. It is, futhermore, fallacious to say that if an exception is allowed, it will be difficult to draw the line and therefore no exception should be allowed. It has been said quite rightly that ethics like art is precisely a matter of knowing where to draw lines.

Therefore, with regard to the principle in question, we can say that its absoluteness is, at the very least, doubtful. And then in accord with the hallowed moral axiom *ubi dubium ibi libertas* (where there is doubt there is liberty) we can begin to argue moral freedom to terminate life directly in certain cases. It would perhaps be better to put it in terms of Aristotelian-Thomistic moral theory. This principle, like every practical moral principle, is valid most of the time (*in pluribus*) but in a particular instance (*in aliquo particulari*) it may not be applicable.

To apply this whole discussion to the case of conscious terminal patients, it can be said that in certain cases, direct positive intervention to bring on death may be morally permissible. The decision, of course, should not ignore issues of social responsibility and opportunity alluded to in the preceding case. The patient must consider also the cultural and legal context, the mind-set of insurance companies, and the ability of others to cope with the voluntary aspects of this kind of death. The patient must also beware lest s/he is yielding to societal pressures to measure human dignity in terms of utility or to create the illusion that sickness and death are unreal.

Finally, to self-killing in a non-medical context. It is estimated that more than eighty Americans a day kill themselves. Jacques Choron calculates that between six and seven million living Americans have attempted suicide and that 25 percent of these will try again and many will succeed. From a moral viewpoint it may be said that an enormous majority of these cases represent unmitigated tragedy. Most suicides flow from a loss of the vital ingredients of human life, hope and a supportive loving community. Studies show the suicide as a lonely, desperate person. The act is *The Cry for Help*, the title of a book on attempted suicide by Farberow and Schneidman. Eighty percent of all suicides signal their intentions in advance, apparently by way of final, desperate pleading. Contrary to the rationalizing myth, most suicides are not psychotic. Alcoholism and drug use are, of course, not unrelated to the suicidal syndrome.

The incidence of suicide in certain groups is revealing. Suicide rates among blacks and Indians in this nation have reached epidemic proportions. Two to three times more women than men attempt suicide. Suicide increases in socially disorganized communities and the rate of successful suicide among divorced persons is remarkably high. There can be no doubt that most suicides are an indictment of the surviving community which failed to give the possibility of life to their suicidal victims.

The prime moral reaction to suicide should be to attack the causes that yield such bitter fruit. Those of Christian persuasion should be in the forefront here. For Christians, to contribute to the loss of hope in others is the elementary sin. Dietrich Bonhoeffer judged suicide severely from the perspective of Christian faith: "It is because there is a living God that suicide is wrongful as a sin of lack of faith." He did, however, realize that suicide is not univocal. Though usually akin to murder, "it would be very short-sighted simply to equate every form of self-killing with murder." Some suicides could be highly motivated and Bonhoeffer was inclined to suspend judgment with regard to these because "here we have reached the limits of human knowledge." Unless we do ethics by taboo, however, we must do more than supend judgment. We must also discuss the possibility of objectively moral suicide. The discussion here relies on the points argued in the preceding cases.

Some moralists have not suspended favorable judgment on all suicides. Some medievals, weighing the suicides of such as Samson and virgin saints who killed themselves to avoid violation, concluded that the Holy Spirit had inspired their actions. (This, of course, implied the unraised question of whether the Holy Spirit could inspire other suicides.) Henry Davis, in his *Moral and Pastoral Theology*, leaned on the abused distinction between direct and indirect and concluded that a sexaully threatened maiden "may leap from a great height to certain death, for her act has two effects, the first of which is to escape from violation, the second, her death, which is not directly wished but only permitted. The distinction between the jump and the fall is obvious. In the case, the maid wishes the jump and puts up with the fall." Davis' distinction is not obvious to today's moralists who would find the maiden's ability to dissect her intentionality remarkable.

Some modern moralists have defended the suicide of a spy who, when captured, could be induced by chemicals or by torture to reveal damaging data. Less attended to are the social witness type suicides related, for example, to the early phase of the Vietnam war. In assessing the objective morality of the suicide of Roger LaPorte which first signaled to many in Communist China and Indochina the depth of anti-war feeling in America, our judgment should *at the least* show the kind of reserve that Bonhoeffer brings to limit situations. Of the possibility of other moral suicides it must be said that there are strong presumptions against them, arising from the experience of grounded hope, from the number of alternatives open to persons in community and from the effects on the bereaved. However, no one is wise enough to say that those presumptions could not be overridden unless, of course, that someone is privy to knowledge of all possible circumstances. Realistic ethics requires more modesty than that. Thus, the possibility of objectively moral self-killing is an open question, and it may not be excluded that direct self-killing may be a good moral action, in spite of the strong presumptions against it.

In sum, then, death has lost its medical and moral simplicity. We know it now as a process, not a moment, and we have the means to extend or shorten that process. In the older ethics of dying, begged questions reigned unchallenged. The ordinary/extraordinary means rubric is still useful, but not self-sufficient. The borders between ordinary and extraordinary blur and shift, and years ago moralist Gerald Kelly, S. J., pointed out that even ordinary means are not always obligatory. The contention that life could be terminated indirectly and by omission but never directly by commission, was not proved—and that is a serious omission.

As Stanford law school Dean, Bayless Manning, has said: "The topic as a whole is still subterranean, and decisions are predominantly being made by thousands of doctors in millions of different situations and by undefined, particularized, *ad hoc* criteria." One partial solution to this would be a happily financed, well managed, hard-working, yearly study-meeting which would bring together doctors, lawyers, moralists of every stripe, insurance experts, nurses, social workers, morticians, sociologists, gravely ill persons, clergymen, journalists, etc., to discuss the current state of dying. The results each year should be energetically publicized in learned journals and in all news media, since death education is needed at every level. (Perhaps some mortal and affluent readers will let their treasures be where their hearts are in this regard.)

Hopefully, a healthier attitude toward death will emerge in our culture. We all could learn from a Donegal Irishman whose death a few years ago was a testimonial to wisdom. While on his deathbed, he was visited by friends who knew, as did he, that this would be their final visit. The dying man ordered his son to bring whisky for the guests. With this done, the son asked his father if he, too, would indulge. "Oh, no," replied the father with a gentle frown, "I don't want to be meeting the Lord with the smell of the drink on my breath." A few hours later, he died. If we were as at home with death as he, our deliberations on the subject might be more wise.

Part 6

FREEDOM OF CONSCIENCE AND CHURCH AUTHORITY

As the religious impulse becomes institutionalized, authority structures form to meet the needs for unity and coherence. Authority, in any dress, is tempted to excessive dominance. In sacral dress, it would seem, the temptation is even more compelling. Authority, of course, can and should function properly and creatively. Indeed, without authority, institutions perish.

Chapter Fifteen examines the slow demise of autocratic authority forms in Roman Catholic Christianity. What shape will teaching take in a post-infallibilist Catholicism? A humbler and more prophetic model is suggested here.

Though the Catholic struggles focused on here have some distinctive qualities, the authority problem affects all religions. When one moves from the authority problems in one church to those of another, the sense of *déjà vu* is always in attendance.

Catholic Ethics in the Post-Infallible Church

History does not commend a simple view of the magisterium. The magisterium may, with some adequacy, be described as the Church's active competence to teach and bear witness to the nature and consequences of God's revelation in Christ. This competence has been in the Church from the beginning. The object of this competence, however, as well as its subject and manner of realization, show the creative and passive-reactive shifts and changes that mark the history of humankind.

The magisterium appears in varied ways in history, depending on the prevailing ecclesiology, the status of communications, and the cultural views of authority and truth. Jesus could not concede to the Church a disincarnate immunity to the exigencies of essential human historicity. This does not say that the Church has been buffeted and shaped helplessly by "the forces of history"; it says merely that redemption is being achieved in time.

"Teaching" is not a univocal term. History shows a variety of teaching forms. It shows us the Sophists and Socrates and Aristotle; it shows us Jesus and Druids and the medieval university lectures; it shows us ecumenical councils, tribal elders, Montessori schools, and Marshall McLuhan. A teacher can be anything from an authority figure who imposes information on his subjects to a prodding stimulator of thought. Lessons good and bad are taught also by our actions. Thus it must be remembered that the Church acting is also the Church teaching.

From the beginning, liturgy was a primary means of teaching the good news. Important sections of the inspired Scriptures are actually liturgical documents. It is in great part the praying Church that teaches us in the New Testament.[1] The ministry of sacraments was not without the ministry of the word. Ability to witness and to teach was the prime qualification for authority in the community (Acts 1:21–22; 6:4).[2] The success of the community was expressed in terms of effective teaching (6:7).

The teaching office in the early Church was not relegated to a "department"; the community itself was magisterial. The good news was lived in a spirit of proclamation so that the life of the Christians provided an instruction on the nature of the Christian way. The community, seen as a concrete and living norm of Christian existence, came to be called "the Way" (Acts 9:2). Thus, the Way was persecuted (22:4) and evil was spoken of the Way (19:9).[3] So closely identified was the living body of Christians with the Christian message that Ignatius of Antioch could refer to the Church itself as "the agape."[4]

The early magisterium, therefore, was liturgical, ecclesial, vital. It enjoyed, initially, an admirable dynamism and simplicity. Simple credal formulae and symbols were a favored technique.[5] Simplicity, however, was short-lived. The message was poured into the ears, cultures, philosophies, and languages of Parthians, Medes, and Elamites. Divisions and factions grew up in the Way. Apostles and elders soon found it necessary to meet in council to settle questions rising not so much from the kerygma as from the clash of Jewish and Hellenic cultures (Acts 15). The credal formulae grew longer and more complex.[6] Biblical language was not found suited to meet the philosophical critics of Christianity and the Church agonized in conscience at the necessity of restating Christian teaching in new words and new symbols.[7]

Councils and synods have always been a favored technique for tapping ecclesial wisdom and for revealing the Church's current state of doctrinal consciousness. Particular weight was also attached to the traditions of the communities in the great cities which had been the starting points of Christianization. Irenaeus, for example, stressed the sureness of the traditions of communities which boasted a directly apostolic foundation.[8] At times, the most important magisterial figures on the scene were individual bishops who through their eloquence and extraordinary abilities obtained a voice and influence not suggested by their sees.

One such was Caesarius of Arles. The bishop of Rome urged Caesarius to care for "the affairs of religion, both in Gaul and in Spain."[9] Caesarius showed something more than alacrity, dispatching emissaries throughout Gaul, Spain, and into Italy itself.[10] His leadership was felt in thirteen church councils held between 506 and 541.[11] Chrysostom, Epiphanius, and most especially Augustine had an influence on Church teaching that was nothing less than massive.

In the period from the sixth to the eleventh centuries, the monasteries attained magisterial prominence. The penitential books wrought by the monks were widely used to guide confessors. They were a most important means in those centuries for the teaching of morality in the Church. This type of magisterial operation was not highly centralized; communications and sociological conditions did not permit it to be. Some advantage accrued to this as when, for example, the Irish, cut off from the penitential practices of Rome and the continent, developed the more benign systems of private penance that eventually prevailed.[12] Centralization became a notable phenomenon in the modern Church with teaching and administrative burdens shifting more to the Roman See. This situation has scarcely been altered by an application of the principles of collegiality and subsidiarity, announced but not realized in Vatican II.

At any rate, no study of the magisterium can ignore the variety of form that has characterized the magisterium in history. It is not enough to look to conciliar or Roman decrees to know what the Church has taught.

Our specific concern here is with the Church teaching morality. The nature of morality is such as to present special problems and to justify a distinct consideration of the Church's authentic teaching competence in this area.[13] It is instructive to see how the hierarchical magisterium has functioned in special moral questions in the past to see how the magisterium can effectively function in the modern. After seeing the magisterium in action, in our concluding section I will explore the theological implications of the historical data.

The Church on War and Peace

History shows no one Christian position on war and peace.[14] On this most crucial moral issue Christians have shown neither consistency nor unity. New Testament teaching did not answer the problem of war. War was a reality from which Jesus felt free to draw parables (Lk 14:31–33). He marveled at the centurion's faith without questioning his military profession (Mt 8:10). In spite of the absence of ethical casuistry, the New Testament was not irrelevant to war. Its appreciation of the dignity of persons and the need for societal justice points to the genuine source of peace; in addressing our sinfulness it calls for surgery on the radical causes of war. The sermon on the mount gives the maximal goals of justice and peace, to be fully realized on "the new earth where justice dwells;" but to be worked toward now in creative tension. The Christian scriptures yield a vision of harmony and love but do not tell us how this vision can be realized in the perplexing situations of a sinful world. This scriptural revelation asks questions of the moralist; it does not provide the answers in the "deposit of faith."

Not surprisingly, early Christian reaction to war was mixed: some would serve in the army but most would not. So many would not serve that the philosopher Celsus had the impression that all Christians were pacifists.[15] Origen, responding to Celsus, supports this impression by saying that Christians do not fight under the emperor even if he should require it.[16] There is ample evidence, however, that many Christians, especially in the frontier provinces, served in the army without scruple.[17] (See Chapter Four for a fuller treatment of this history.)

Pre-Constantinian Christian literature was not so ambivalent as practice. When Irenaeus wrote that Christians do not know how to fight and when struck offer the other cheek, he was speaking the language of Justin, Athenagoras, Tertullian, Cyprian, Origen, Minucius, and Arnobius.[18] The pacifism of these men was rather untested, however, because they spoke of peace when the *Pax Romana* had banished all major wars. What is clear is that the Christians had brought from their encounter with Christ an unprecedented sensitivity to the horror of bloodshed and they enunciated its basic incompatability with the gospel ideal. Even when they were later forced to bend their principles to the needs of new situations, they usually insisted that the ministers of the sacraments abstain from war to maintain some minimal witness to the peacefulness of Christ.

A perceptible change took place with the coming of Constantine. When Jesus was credited with the military success, Christians leapt from persecution to preferment. After this, their voices did not sound the same.[19] In East and West the new regime was hailed in eschatological terms.[20] The sword had become a friend and Christians began to glory not in infirmity but in power. The sensitivity to military service so completely disappeared that by the time of Theodosius II only Christians were permitted to serve in the army.[21] The earlier Christian tension had disappeared. A new situation had yielded a new morality.

If the Scriptures did not have an ethics of war, pagan antiquity did, and Christians did not hesitate to borrow from it. Augustine, whose magisterial contribution in this matter has been endorsed by centuries of acceptance in the Church, fashioned a theology of war. With the barbarians pressing in Europe and Africa, Augustine the moralist concluded that love dictates not only rules but also painful exceptions. In a world where God is not yet all in all he could see that even gospel morality is susceptible to human compromise. And so the just war theory was baptized, without being fully evaluated.[22]

Saddened by the need for violence in view of the gospel ideal, Augustine, who would not allow a private citizen to kill even in self defense, tended to blend the Old Testament idea of the God-inspired war with the idea that the power of the state comes from God. Thus the soldier preserved his innocence by the right order of obedience.[23] Surrender of personal responsibility to government and the holy war are foreshadowed here. This note would have a congenial ring in subsequent centuries of Christian history.

Aside from the military threat, the barbarians were a cultural and moral threat to the civilization they began to overrun. Knit into their culture was a creed of violence that was bereft of nuance or nicety. This creed would compete with the Christian creed and show that there are competing leavens in the batch of society and that the Christian leaven does not always raise the dough.

As this cultural invasion progressed, some Church efforts were made to resist. With the frenzy of violence mounting, the penitentials continued up until the eleventh century to prescribe penance for soldiers who had killed in battle, however just the cause.[24] The participation of the clergy in war was never really sanctioned. The Truce of God was a colossal, if belated, attempt to educate men to peace. But, as Stanley Windass remarks, "The disease was too radical to respond to such first aid."[25]

In effect, the Church chose to divert the violence which it could not subdue. This was the story of the Crusades. The sword was given a prime role in establishing the kingdom of God. The Crusades aimed at reuniting Christendom and establishing Jerusalem as the center of Christian holiness. With this rationale battle against the infidel came to achieve a salvific importance. Fulfilling the expressed hopes of Pope St. Gregory VII, Blessed Urban II launched the crusading movement at the Council of Clermont, *toto plaudente orbe catholico*.[26] A plenary indulgence graced all who died in these wars that the Church began in the name of Jesus.[27] Pope, bishops, and monks scurried around the continent preaching the crusade.[28] A cargo of noses and thumbs sliced from the Saracens was sent back as gory witness of crusading zeal.[29]

The consecration of violence was further formalized by the founding of the Knights Templar, who vowed to fight in poverty, chastity, and obedience.[30] Swords were blessed with liturgy. And not only infidels were struck with them. Indulgenced warriors struck at the Cathari in southern France. When the papal legate was asked how to distinguish between the Cathari and the Catholics, his reply shocked no one: "Kill them all; God will know which are his."[31] The important *Decretum* of Gratian said that to die in combat against the infidel is to merit heaven.[32] In a violent age, the Church was violent in word and in deed. A new situation had yielded a new morality.

Prophetic figures and sects within and without the Church arose to reassert the claims of the gospel of peace. With their plea made plausible by the collapse of Christendom and the rise of national power, reform was slowly brought about. But the road from Clermont to Vatican II was tortuous and many feel that an insensitivity to war and a sacralization of national policy linger on in the Christian conscience, an unhappy legacy of the crusading period.

I rehearse this material on war in this discussion of teaching authority to show that claims of infallible teaching in morals, given this history, are incredible. How can there be a claim to infallible supernatural teaching power in morals in a church which has staggered from one position to another over twenty centuries on so vital an issue as war and peace?

The Church and Sexual Ethics

The New Testament does not provide a full ethics of sex, although it says much that is relevant to sexual ethics. Its view of marriage as an example of the love of God for humankind and its concept of agapic love challenge the insight and discernment of the ethicist.[33] The idea of personhood which emerges from its pages has endless ethical implications.[34] But the problem of applying the profound personalism of the gospels to the intricacies and subleties of sexual questions in a complex and evolving world remains to bother the Christian conscience.

In facing this problem, Christians did not hesitate to turn to the existent and popular moral philosophy of the non-Christian world, Stoicism. The Stoics had an ethics of sex. The Stoic anthropology exalted nature, reason, and decorum. It downgraded the emotions—*perturbationes*, Cicero called them[35]—and dependence on others. The emotion-laden phenomenon of sexuality thus needed a justifying rationale. The decision of the Stoic sages was this: "The sexual organs are given us not for pleasure, but for the maintenance of the species."[36] Nothing but the decent and reasonable need to procreate could justify sex. There was no link between love and sex. (This rigorous view of sex seemed all the more agreeable to early Christians in the face of the libertine gnostic reaction within the Church.[37])

Stoic rigor was not only generally accepted in the Church but was even intensified. Chrysostom could cite the Greek ideal of continence: "to fight desire and not be subservient to it . . . but our ideal is not to experience desire at all."[38]

However grim a view of sex this was, it had the undeniable advantage of ethical simplicity. The procreation rubric made it easy to ban non-marital sex of all forms and contraceptive sex in marriage. Small wonder that by the time the mighty Augustine appeared on the scene he could accept the Stoic rule as traditional teaching.[39] The rule also provided a perfect retreat for Augustine from the morbid Manichean resistance to procreation. On matters of sex and marriage, however, Augustine the Christian was never fully freed of Mani. "In intercourse," he said, the human person "becomes all flesh" (Sermons 62.2, PL 38:887). This he said in commenting on the biblical notion of man and wife as "one flesh." Nothing was more devastating to the masculine mind than "female blandishments and that contact of bodies without which a wife may not be had" (Soliloquies 1.10, PL 32:878). Only procreation could justify marriage, sex, or even women. "I do not see what other help woman would be to man if the purpose of generating was eliminated" (On Genesis According to the Letter, 9.7, CSEL 28:275).

Concupiscence and sexual pleasure are suspect in Augustine's eyes. In the unredeemed, in fact, concupiscence is equivalent to sin. After baptism, "the concupiscence of the flesh" remains, "but it is not imputed as sin" (Marriage and Concupiscence 1.25.28, CSEL 42:240). Original sin is transmitted by the exercise of concupiscence and, were it not for Adam's fall, there would be no "concupiscence of the flesh" involved in generation (ibid. 1.18.21, CSEL 42:233).[40]

This is the Augustine who wrote the influential The Good of Marriage (1, CSEL 41:187). Not surprisingly, proles come first in his formula for the goodness of marriage. This formula, proles, fides, sacramentum (ibid. 29.32, CSEL 41:227), was to echo through the centuries and would, as late as 1930, provide a structural scheme for Pius XI in his Casti Connubii.[41]

Caesarius of Arles did much to maintain Augustine's historical resonance in the area of sexual ethics. With him, also, only the intention to procreate could justify marital intercourse. Following the Stoic bent for agricultural analogies, he compared intercourse to the sowing of a field and added his prestigious voice to those condemning intercourse during pregnancy; he even seemed to condemn frequent intercourse as un-Christian.[42]

Caesarius was no outrider on this question of intercourse during pregnancy. John T. Noonan finds no Christian theologian before the year 1500 giving complete approval to this practice. Up until that time it was an integral part of the teaching of the ordinary magisterium of the Church.[43]

Pope St. Gregory the Great brought into the Christian scene an austerity that made Augustine look benign. In his *Pastoral Rule* he had admonished couples not only that pleasure is not a fit purpose for intercourse, but also that if any pleasure is "mixed" with the act of intercourse the married have "transgressed the law of marriage." They have "befouled" their intercourse by their "pleasures" (3.27, PL 77:102). The *Pastoral Rule* was an important magisterial document, as was also Gregory's letter to St. Augustine, archibishop of Canterbury. Augustine wondered whether he could teach "the rude English people" that they could receive communion after marital copulation. Gregory's answer was negative. It was as impossible to have intercourse without sin as it was to fall into a fire and not burn. Only a miracle could save you in either case (*Epistles* 11.64, PL 77:1196–1197).

This extraordinary doctrine proved magisterially viable. In the twelfth century. Huguccio, Gratian's chief commentator, taught that coitus "can never be without sin" (*Summa* 2.32.2.1). Innocent III, an expert theologian in his own right, thought of this opinion as beyond question.[44]

The somber thoughts of Jerome, Augustine, Caesarius, and Gregory were given prominent play in the penitentials and in the instruction of the people. Preachers like Bernardine of Siena proclaimed this news with eloquence. To have intercourse "too frequently or with inordinate affection" was wrong (*Seraphic Sermons* 19:3). "Of 1000 marriages," St. Bernardine declared, "I believe 999 are the devil's."[45]

We have already mentioned the unanimous disapproval of intercourse during pregnancy.[46] Other striking opinions took root and were propagated. The Augustinian doctrine about the need for procreative purpose to free intercourse from sin grew in Christendom until we find it the established opinion with few dissents by the twelfth century. The classical canonists and theologians of the thirteenth century reaffirmed it, and it became common teaching through the fourteenth and fifteenth centuries.[47] Theologians who followed St. Thomas (*On the Sentences* 4.31, "Exposition of the text"; II^a II^{ae}, q.154, a.11) taught that intercourse that deviated from the position of woman beneath the man was a mortal sin. It was commonly taught for centuries that intercourse during the time of menstruation was sinful. Indeed, some important figures held that it was mortally sinful.[48] All these opinions have since been abandoned.

Gradually, new insights begin to appear in the Church. The Council of Trent, in 1563, was the first ecumenical council to stress the role of love in marriage.[49] Modern popes, keeping step with theological developments, stress this theme.[50] Vatican II shows some of the more recent progress and reveals the depth of change in the Church's outlook on marital sexuality. It reflected and crowned a recent theological development by acknowledging the coital expression of conjugal love as a substantial value independent of procreation.[51] Until Vatican II it was customary to refer to procreation and education of children as the primary end of marriage (cf. Code of Canon Law, c. 1013, §2 and the encyclical *Casti Connubii*). Due to advances in the appreciation of the other "ends" of marriage, this concession of primacy to one end was deliberately discontinued.[52] The implications of this and other advances in the understanding of marriage and sexuality are slowly finding clarification and expression in the Church. Again, the record is anything but supportive for any who would claim that the Church basks in supernatural powers of moral insight, free from the stumbles, errors, and pitfalls that plague all other mortals.

The Question of Usury

We are indebted to John T. Noonan for his careful studies of the Church's condemnation of usury.[53] Taking 1450 as a year when the Church's strong stand against usury was in fullest vigor, Noonan explains what was meant by usury.

On a loan to a poor man, or a rich man, to help the starving or to finance a mercantile enterprise, nothing could be sought or even hoped for. The risk inherent in lending was not a ground for taking interest; . . . Interest could never be lawfully sought as profit. To hope for interest, to seek profit, was to commit the sin of mental usury. Usury, mental or actual, was a mortal sin against justice.[54]

The unanimous stand against usury was grounded in the unanimous interpretation of five scripture texts (Ex 22:25; Lev 25:35–37; Ps 15:5; Ez 18:5–9; Lk 6:33–35). The three men who were most influential in shaping morality in the western Church—Ambrose, Jerome, and Augustine—gave strong witness against usury. In the East, Clement of Alexandria, Basil, and Gregory of Nyssa could find no room for interest-taking. Increase on a loan, as Gregory saw it, was a "wicked union, which nature does not know"; such fertility is proper only to sexually differentiated animals (*Homily 2 on Ecclesiastes*, PG 44:674). Three ecumenical councils lent their authority to this teaching, Lateran II, Lateran III, and Vienne.[55] Four popes had especially clear statements to make on the subject: Alexander III, Urban III, Eugene III, and Gregory IX.[56]

As far as can be determined, theologians and teachers all concurred in his teaching. Discontent arose, finally, from those who had experience in finance, the bankers of Siena and Florence. The first theologian to challenge the long accepted interpretation of Luke 6:35 was Dominic Soto in the sixteenth century.[57] In the same century John Medina defended risk as a ground for charging interest. One hundred years later a Roman congregation accepted this position; and, of course, by the time of the great modern social encyclicals all scruple about taking legitimate interest had disappeared from the teaching of the magisterium.[58] Again, we witness here no infallible and error-free passage through history.

The Moral Question of Self-Incrimination

Since the early 1700s English law has guarded the accused from compulsory self-incrimination. The notion was incorporated into the United States' Federal Constitution by the Fifth Amendment in 1791. Moralists unanimously hold today that this right to silence flows from the fundamental dignity of the human person.[59] Yet it was not until 1917 with the promulgation of the Code of Canon Law that the Church guaranteed this right to the accused in ecclesiastical trials.

Going back into Church history we see not only that the accused was denied the right to silence but also that even torture was used to induce self-incrimination. Pope Nicholas I in 866 had condemned legal torture as immoral.[60] His intervention, breaking free as it did from the contemporary outlook, had a prophetic quality, but it did not take root in the magisterium of the Church. Patrick Granfield notes that medieval justice, "both civil and ecclesiastical," considered torture an indispensable part of court procedure:

The ordeal, with its hot iron, molten lead, and boiling water, became commonplace. From the eighth to the thirteenth century it was accepted by many local ecclesiastical courts with the approval of their bishops, who felt that it was a reliable way to discover the judicium Dei.[61]

Pope Innocent IV contradicts the opinion of Nicholas I, teaching in his *Ad extirpanda* that heretics should be forced "without loss of limb or danger of death" to admit their errors and denounce their accomplices. The pope imposed the same obligation on thieves and robbers.[62] The Catechism of the Council of Trent (Catechism of Pius V) denies the accused the right of silence. The Jubilee Decrees of 1749, 1775, and 1824 reaffirm this teaching.[63] As late as 1910 the Roman Rota issued norms which again did not exempt the accused in criminal trials from confessing his own guilt.[64] Canon 1743, §1 of the old code changed this teaching. The change, Father Granfield notes, was "abrupt." "In all the pre-Code documents there is either an explicitly or implicitly presumed affirmation of the necessity of self-incrimination.[65] Again, it is not infallibility but movement from darkness to light, from error to correction, often at a slower pace than the rest of society that characterizes Church history.

Religious Liberty and the Rights of Conscience

Progress in the moral teaching of the Church concerning religious freedom is easily illustrated. Pius IX in his *Quanta Cura* condemns:

that erroneous opinion which is especially injurious to the Catholic Church and the salvation of souls, called by our predecessor Gregory XVI *deliramentum* [insane raving], namely that freedom of conscience and of worship is the proper right of each person, and that this should be proclaimed and asserted in every rightly constituted society (Denz. 1690; cf. 1613).

The striking change is seen in the words of Vatican II:

The Synod further declares that the right to religious freedom has its foundation in the very dignity of the human person. . . . This right of the human person to religious freedom is to be recognized in the constitutional law whereby society is governed. Thus it is to become a civil right.[66]

The Syllabus of Pius IX provides many opportunities to study the change in moral judgment that has marked the teaching of the pilgrim Church (Denz. 1700–1780).[67] Much that Pius IX taught in his Syllabus of Errors was rejected at the Second Vatican Council.

The Theology of the Magisterium

The theology of the magisterium has been until recently one of the most important and most neglected areas of Catholic theology. Customarily the magisterium is spoken of as either *ordinary* or *extraordinary*. The extraordinary magisterium comprises the *ex cathedra* statements of the pope and the solemn statements of bishops convoked in council in union with the pope to define the faith. The ordinary magisterium refers to the normal daily teaching of the bishops throughout the world.

As regards infallibility, the ordinary magisterium was considered infallible when there was "unanimity of the episcopal magisterium."[68] The concept of an infallible ordinary magisterium presents some critical problems. First of all, the determination of what constitutes unanimity is not always an obvious matter, especially in specific questions of morality. Secondly, unanimity or consensus can be of various kinds. There can be reflective or non-reflective consensus. Unanimity on some moral matters might represent a legacy received uncritically from another age. This is a non-reflective consensus, and it represents not an accumulation of serious human acts of moral evaluation but rather the absence of such. Such a consensus has serious limitations.

At any rate the infelicitous discussion of infallibility comes to center more on the extraordinary magisterium. This is the case, or example, in the *Pastor Aeternus* of Vatican I, which undoubtedly provides the boldest expression of the consciousness of the Church concerning its magisterial role. This constitution centered, with unfortunate exclusiveness, on the infallibility of the pope. Since, however, the council emphasized that the pope had the same infallibility that Christ willed his Church to have, its statement does afford us much insight into the understanding of infallibility in general that existed in the Church of Vatican I.

The Council declared it a divinely revealed dogma:

> that the Roman Pontiff, when he speaks *ex cathedra*, that is, when in discharge of the office of pastor and doctor of all Christians, by virtue of his supreme apostolic authority, he defines a doctrine regarding faith or morals to be held by the universal Church, by the divine assistance promised to him in blessed Peter, is possessed of that infallibility with which the divine Redeemer willed that his Church should be endowed for defining doctrine regarding faith or morals; and that therefore such definitions of the Roman pontiff are irreformable of themselves, and not from the consent of the Church.

> But if anyone—which may God avert—presume to contradict this our definition; let him be anathema.[69]

This definition was the result of prolonged and intense conciliar discussion and debate. Its meaning is precise and finely nuanced, but a study of the text alone would not reveal that. The context must be carefully considered if we are to capture the meaning of this important

definition. This is needed all the more today inasmuch as the Constitution on the Church in Vatican II repeats the words of Vatican I, without, of course, assuming the theologian's task of analyzing their
original import.

Competent theological inquiry has never neglected the task of research into the *acta* of Church councils in order to discover the true
significance of conciliar texts. Thanks to new understanding of the evolution of doctrine and of the historical and cultural conditioning of
human thought and language, modern theologians are becoming more
aware of the need for contextual analysis of past magisterial pronouncements. Recent advances in the interpretation of Scripture have
also been instructive in this regard. Vatican II gives this advice to the
biblical exegete:

The interpreter must investigate what meaning the sacred writer intended to
express and actually expressed in particular circumstances as he used contemporary literary forms in accordance with the situation of his own time and
culture. For the correct understanding of what the sacred author wanted to
assert, due attention must be paid to the customary and characteristic styles
of perceiving, speaking, and narrating which prevailed at the time of the sacred
writer. . . .[70]

Since magisterial Church pronouncements are no more immune to
the influence of context and culture than are the Scriptures, the task
of the theologian is obvious. S/he must face the problems of language,
the influence of epistemological and theological presuppositions, the
presence of limiting polemical perspectives, and the reality of dogmatic
development. And when past magisterial pronouncements on morality
are involved, the theologian must consider the statements in the light
of the development of moral insight and the circumstances and conditions that affected the statements. To do anything less is to strip the
original statement of its reality.

Debate at Vatican I was acrimonious. One bishop found the lament
of Isaiah applicable: "*Videntes clamabunt foris, et angeli pacis amare fle-
bunt.*"[71] Relative peace might have obtained if the original plan of the
council had been followed. It had been proposed to develop a vast
schema on the Church of Christ. Chapters one to ten would treat of
the Church in general; eleven and twelve would treat of the primacy
of the pope. Through internal and external pressures, the decision was
made to drop all the chapters except those on the pope.[72]

Many of the bishops felt that a separate discussion of the infallibility
of the pope without treatment of the role of the bishops was ill con-

sidered. Bishop Moriarity of Kerry, for example, testified that in the Irish Church neither the ordinary preaching nor the catechisms stressed the infallibility of the pope, but that the subject of infallibility was always said to be the Church. In practice this meant the bishops in agreement with the pope.[73] The proposed definition seemed to be giving a power to the pope which was too "personal, separate, and absolute." These words were spoken in concern by so many that Bishop d'Avanzo remarked that the council could become known in history as "the council of three words."[74] To quell these anxieties, the Deputation of the Faith, the committee which had drafted the document, gave close attention to the clarification of these terms as well as to the notion and object of infallibility in the Church.

Speaking for the Deputation, d'Avanzo stressed that the anti-Gallican expression of the definition *ex sese non autem ex consensu ecclesiae* did not purport to separate the pope from the Church. He pointed out first that it was the same holy Spirit who was operative in pope, bishops, and faithful.[75] Secondly, the pope teaching infallibly did not do so in virtue of a new revelation but rather, with the help of the Holy Spirit, his role was to discover the truth already contained in the fonts of revelation.[76] Thirdly, it was obvious that the pope did not work privately with the holy Spirit, but rather that he must seek out the truth in the living witness of the Church.[77]

A more complete elucidation is found in the monumental speech of Bishop Gasser, the outstanding theologian and spokesman of the Deputation. He centered his discourse on the "three words." The infallibility of the pope was "personal" only in the sense that the pope was a public person and head of the Church.[78] This is better explained when he discusses the second word, "separate." He begins by saying that the word "distinct" would be more precise. The pope is part of the Church, and indeed when he speaks infallibly he speaks as one who represents the universal Church. The essential concurrence and cooperation of the Church is not excluded by the definition.[79] Since the pope has no new revelation on which to base his statement, he is bound to seek out the truth in the Church by various means. This is an obvious duty which binds him in conscience.[80]

Is the definition, then, really maintaining a union between the pope and the consenting Church? Yes. Anything other than such a union is unthinkable.[81] What kind of consent does the definition exclude? It excludes consent of the extreme Gallican style (cf. Denz. 1322–1326). It will not make it a "de iure conditio" (Mansi 52:1208). To insist on such a thing would create insoluble problems, such as determining how many bishops had to be consulted, and so forth.[82] When the truth is obvious it would be foolish to bind the pope to an extensive investigation. It is in this limited sense that the consent of the Church is not required.[83]

Concerning the question of infallibility. Gassar said: (1) Absolute infallibility is ascribed only to God. The infallibility of the Church is limited; (2) the limited infallibility of the Church, whether exercised by the pope or in some other fashion, extends to the same ambit of truths; (3) it certainly extends to the revealed truths contained in the deposit of faith; (4) the infallibility extends to those truths which, though not revealed, are necessary for the defense and explanation of the deposit. Whether the infallibility extended to these matters in such a way as to constitute them dogmatic truths (the denial of which would be heresy) was an unsolved theological question and the Deputation decided unanimously to leave the question open.[84] Doctrines noted as theologically certain (or with lesser notes) are not within the range of *de fide* infallible statements.[85]

Thus did Vatican Council I explain itself. Its explanations merit attention from modern theologians. More space than is available here would be required to discuss the total context of Vatican I and the deficiencies under which the council labored. The Church's present understanding of the doctrines discussed at Vatican I has grown and widened. As Vatican II says, "there is a growth in the understanding of the realities and the words which have been handed down."[86] Important areas touched by Vatican I have known vast development: the interpretation of Scripture, the relationship of Scripture and tradition, the concept of "Church" including the acknowledgment of genuine ecclesial reality in the Protestant Churches, the increased respect for the *sensus fidelium* and the magisterial role of the laity.[87] We cannot concede the genuine ecclesiality of the Protestant Christian Churches and then deny them magisterial significance. The doctrinal positions of all Christian bodies must now be viewed with a new seriousness.

Let us, however, at this point focus on certain elements of the teaching of Vatican I that are vital to our understanding of the moral magisterium. It is an important fact that Vatican I did not give special attention to the distinct problems involved in teaching morality. This was to be expected. The nineteenth century might indeed represent the nadir of Catholic moral theology. As Noonan remarks: "In the entire nineteenth century it is difficult to name a single person who displayed genius in its study and exposition."[88] Repetitious manuals that taught morality like a code had trained the council bishops and theo-

logians. The in-depth expositions of Aquinas or Liguori were not seminary fare.[89] Until the *Aeterni Patris* of Leo XIII in 1879, a heavily
Cartesian spirit pervaded Catholic thought. The Cartesian stress on
clarity as the mark of truth did not dispose its students to grasp the
ambiguities and complexities that are met in applying moral principles
to the infinitely diverse circumstances of life.

Given the inevitable dependence of a council on the philosophical
tools and principles available to it, it is perhaps not useless to speculate
momentarily on how a strong Thomistic revival before Vatican I would
have influenced the outcome of that council. The council bishops
would have been well served by St. Thomas' reminder of the *quasi
infinitae diversitates* that characterize the material of ethics (S. Th. II^a II^ae,
q. 49, a. 3). Thomas' realism about the nature of ethics is an extraordinary insight which has never had sufficient impact on Catholic moral
theology.

Following Aristotle, Thomas saw that moral principles were not the
principles of speculative reason, which admit of universal application.
The principle of non-contradiction, for example, properly understood,
will admit of no exception. Moral principles, on the contrary, proceed
from practical reason. They are indeed valid principles embodying eternal values, but since they are concerned with the contingencies of human behavior, the more one descends into the particularities of life the
more one is likely to find exceptions. Pressing the point, Thomas explains that the most general moral principles (do good; avoid evil; love
God and neighbor) admit of no exception.

However, when one must decide by what he calls "secondary principles" how, in the concrete, one does good and loves effectively—and
this is the heart of ethics—it is discovered that these principles are
applicable most of the time (*in pluribus*); in particular cases (*in aliquo
particulari et in paucioribus*) they may not apply (I^a II^ae, q. 94, a. 4, a. 5).
Thus, he says that it is a good principle to return things to their owner;
but, enter the ethically significant circumstance of the owner's manifest
intention to do serious harm with the object held, and the principle
can be seen as nonapplicable. A more important value takes precedence
(cf. *ibid.*, a. 5). This is true for all of ethics. Monogamy is clearly a value
which may be expressed as a moral principle; yet St. Thomas notes
that particular circumstances may in fact permit a plurality of wives
(*Supp.*, 65, 2).

Clearly Thomas does not support the attempt to do ethics by the
deductive use of principles conceived as static derivatives of an im-
mutable nature. "The nature of persons is mutable" (II^a II^ae, q. 57, a.

2, ad 1). Unlike the divine nature, our nature is variable (*Supp.*, 41, 1, ad 3, 65, 2, ad 1; *De Malo*, 2, 4, ad 13). Almost anticipating the modern realization of the difficulty of teaching morality transculturally, Thomas wrote that law is not everywhere the same "because of mutability of human nature and the diverse conditions of people and of things, according to the diversity of places and of times" (*De Malo*, 2, 4, ad 13).

This Thomistic view obviously does not lead one to expect pronouncements on morality that would be infallibly true for every time and place without exception. Neither do recent biblical studies encourage such expectations. The Bible itself attempts no such thing. We no longer look to the "deposit of faith" for specific answers to modern ethical questions. The temptation to feel that a system of ethics relevant to all times is contained in revelation, to feel that the answers are there to be wrenched out by exegetical wizardry—such a temptation has happily been conquered. For example, no longer does anyone look in Scripture for explicit answers to questions of interest-taking.

Jesus neither affirmed nor denied the right to private property.[90] We have seen that revelation did not answer the multiple questions of sexual ethics, the moral right to silence, or religious liberty. We need hardly mention business ethics and international law. Even when Jesus was apparently quite specific on the divorce issue, he did not close the case.

Father Schillebeeckx writes:

It is important to bear in mind that, although Christ declared that marriage was indissoluble, he did not tell us where the element that constituted marriage was situated—what in fact made a marriage a marriage, what made it the reality which he called absolutely indissoluble. This is a problem of anthropology. . . .[91]

The so-called "Pauline Privilege" (canons 1120–1124, 1126), which permits a person to contract a second valid marriage for reasons of faith while the first partner still lives, is not found in St. Paul. Schnackenburg points out that the permission is based on 1 Corinthians 7:15 ff. However, "Paul is dealing with the question whether separation is permissible in such a case; he does not speak of remarriage."[92] In other words, the Church went beyond Scripture here and decided that the ideal of indissolubility did not apply in this case. In this instance divorce with remarriage was seen as a value even though without scriptural warranty.

Clearly then, the "deposit of faith," whatever riches it contains for morality, does not do the moralists' work. Yet Vatican I defined that infallibility in faith and morals extends to guarding and exposing the deposit of faith (Denz. 1836). Obviously the infallibility does not extend to answers that are not there. Gasser, however, explained that it extends in some theologically undetermined fashion to those matters that, though not revealed, are necessary to guard, explain, and define the deposit of faith (Mansi 52:1226).

It would be no simple matter to show that the various moral questions we have mentioned above are necessary for guarding, explaining, and defining the deposit of the faith. Indeed Cardinal Berardi, immediately after distribution of the final schema for the infallibility definition, pointed out the vagueness of the definition with regard to practical moral matters. He said that the wording even implied that the infallibility did not extend to decisions about the morality of actions "viewed in their concrete reality."[93] His difficulty was not relieved the next day by the final exposition of Gasser.

Whatever problems the definition presents in this regard, one thing is clear: the council intended to say that in some way the teaching authority of the Church does extend to the area of morals. The practice of the hierarchical magisterium at the time and the general tone of the council leave no doubt that this was being taught. What the council did not do was explain how this teaching competence is best realized and best explained. This problem still remains and now commands our attention.

Traditionally the Church has claimed authority to teach "faith and morals." What is meant by "morals" in this expression is not clear, but the dominant opinion of late has been that it refers to the general and specific questions of natural moral law. Recent papal teaching has asserted this unambiguously.

Pius XII said:

The power of the Church is not bound by the limits of "matters strictly religious," as they say, but the whole matter of the natural law, its foundation, its interpretation, its application, so far as their moral aspect extends, are within the Church's power.[94]

Pope John, speaking of the moral principles of the social order, said:

For it must not be forgotten that the Church has the right and the duty to intervene authoritatively with her children in the temporal sphere when there is a question of judging the application of those principles to concrete cases.[95]

Recent discussions, however, comes to center more and more upon whether to term this competency "infallible." Gregory Baum writes:

I realize that not a few authors in recent years have claimed that the Church, in interpreting the natural law, is indeed infallible. This is wrong. . . . The Church speaks with great authority in the area of human values but when she is not dealing with the ethics revealed in the Gospel, she is not exercising an infallible teaching office.[96]

John J. Reed, S.J., quite as apodictically, asserts the infallible competence of the Church in this area. Since the Church is entrusted with the whole of revelation, it seems obvious to Father Reed that it may teach the natural law infallibly. In some way the natural law is contained in revelation. Since this allegation is bristling with difficulties, Father Reed explains: "Evidently, as with matters of dogmatic truth, a particular demand of natural law may be contained only obscurely, implicitly, or virtually in the deposit of revelation."[97] Richard A. McCormick, S.J., applauds the position of Father Reed and notes that the disagreement between Baum and Reed "is representative of a growing body of opinion on both sides of the question."[98]

I think that the term "infallible" does not in fact aptly describe the nature or function of the moral magisterium, and that we should discontinue using the term in describing the moral magisterium. My reasons are the following:

(1) It is commonplace in discussions of infallibly defined doctrine to refer to the norm of canon 1323, §3, which said that nothing is to be taken as a definition unless it is seen to be such beyond all reasonable doubt: *nisi id manifest constiterit.* Certainly since Vatican I, and even before that council, it is difficult to find an example of a pronouncement in the area of natural moral law that meets this requirement. The lack of examples in the writings of the defenders of the infallible moral magisterium is thus not surprising.[99]

The Church's non-use of the prerogative of infallibility is theologically instructive. This seems to mean that in practice the Church has recognized that it has a firm grasp of the moral vision of the Gospel and that it can and should make rich and meaningful judgments on specific modern problems: but the Church seems to realize further, though the theologians have been slow to acknowledge it, that it does not enjoy an infallibly guaranteed competence to apply the moral vision of the Gospel to complex natural law questions such as are presented by medical ethics, genetics, business ethics, international law, social reconstruction, and war and peace. To allege that the Church can teach the natural law infallibly suggests the weird spectacle of a Church that has the power to settle these questions in a definitive fashion and does

not do so. It is also a position that must suffer considerable embarrassment from the data of history.

The infallibilist position has other problems. It claims that the natural law is contained implicitly or virtually in the deposit of revelation.
This is not a little baffling. All ethical theory grants that concrete and
changing circumstances enter essentially into the constitution of the
"moral object." Hence there is an essential presentiality in the natural
law which precludes its being pre-given, even in an implicit and virtual
way, in any "deposit."[100] Knowledge of the empirical data is essential
to moral judgment; no moral judgment may be made without such
knowledge.

Moral principles and examples may be pre-given; they may have
been acquired from past experience or revelation. They enter into moral
judgment but they are not the only requisite for ethics, which is not
simply a deductive science. For particular demands of the natural law
to be contained in revelation it would be necessary to say that a foreknowledge of the ethical implications of the particularities and circumstances of subsequent centuries is somehow contained in that
revelation. I do not know how such a contention could be supported.
It is certainly not supported or established by an uncritical repetition
of past magisterial formulations. It is furthermore not at all supported
by the Church's abstinence in the use of this infallibility. (We will consider below Baum's suggestion that the Church is infallible in teaching
the ethics of the Gospel.)

(2) As noted above with regard to the Thomistic notion of ethics,
moral principles are, by reason of ethical implications of circumstances,
not universally applicable. The completely general principles such as
"Do good and avoid evil" can be called absolute and universal precisely
because of their lack of circumstantial content. When, however, you
begin to apply specific principles to particular contexts, they admit of
exceptions. They evince a certain essential plasticity.

This does not mean that there are no stable values in the moral
realm. The sacredness of personal life must always be respected, for
example. However, in certain cases a person may kill. The ethical task
is to determine what instances of killing are, because of special circumstances, compatible with a respect for life. A knowledge of the circumstances and the ethical implications thereof is essential to this ethical
task. To say in advance that no circumstance whatever could ever justify a particular action implies a foreknowledge of the ethical import
of all possible circumstances. The epistemological problem here should

be obvious. In actions involving other human beings, history should have taught us that the unpredictables and imponderables should not be adjudicated in advance.

Indeed, it can be stated that as the complexity of life increases, "exceptional" cases become more frequent. As Karl Rahner says: "What used to be an extreme borderline case in a moral situation which hardly ever occurred, has now become almost the 'normal' case."[101] Compare the ethical problems of a general store in the country a century ago with the ethical problems of a corporation like General Motors today to see what complexification does to ethics. Infallible guidance is not anticipated in such a situation. What is needed and to be anticipated in this situation is a meaningful and effective dialogue of experts in particular fields with moralists and other representatives of the moral magisterium of the Church. We shall return to this.

(3) The very nature of truth should make us cautious in speaking of infallibility. Reality always exceeds our conceptualization and knowledge of it. As Piet Fransen writes, the magisterial ministry "is a *diaconia* of the Holy Spirit and also of divine truth. This truth possesses the Church but we do not possess it."[102] Morality involves the mysterious truth of personal contact and relationship of God and us. The mystery of morality is radically ineffable. No matter how wise we become in explaining this mystery, we remain unprofitable servants and we still know, in Paul's words, only "in part." "The truth lives in us as something open, a disposition for more truth, for correction and completion."[103] In a sense, human knowledge is never free of error inasmuch as it is never complete. This is not to say that it is invalid; it embodies the real, but for *homo viator* it is never complete or entirely error-free.

This notion was quite alien to the men of Vatican I, who sought to grasp truth *nullo admixto errore* (Denz. 1786). The term "infallibility" seems to imply a completion that our groping knowledge of reality does not allow. It conforms better to Cartesian assumptions than to modern views of truth.

(4) There is a conflict in the concept of an infallible statement made through the medium of fallible language. A form of words can symbolize "an indefinite number of diverse propositions."[104] The intrinsic ambiguity of language is such that many propositions can "fit the same verbal phraseology."[105] Communication, which is the goal of language, can be blocked by "a lack of shared presuppositions or shared universe of discourse."[106] Meaning has a tendency to slip out from under verbal formulae; through usage, new meanings succeed in attaching them-

selves to old expressions. It can happen that a verbal change is essential to recapture and conserve the original meaning. Change, in this case, is conservative.

This appreciation of the character of language is not entirely new. St. Thomas, for example, taught that the act of the believer did not terminate at the proposition but at the reality (II[a] II[ae], q. 1, a. 2, ad 2). But it is modern linguistic analysis that has presented this insight with force.

(5) Even the brief look at the history of our moral teaching with which we began this chapter should prompt us to describe our teaching competence in more modest terms. Either we must admit a drastic relativism which would allege that all of that teaching was right in its day or we must admit the presence of error in the history of the pilgrim Church. To stress this point: The *Decretum* of Gratian which taught that it was "meritorious" to kill the infidel, the teaching of Gregory XVI and Pius IX that it was "madness" to allege religious freedom as a human right and a necessity in society, and the proclamation of Vatican II that such freedom is a right and necessity in society—such teachings are not consistent or mutually reconcilable.

Even full recognition of the historical context that spawned these statements does not establish doctrinal continuity. The change on interest-taking cannot honestly be explained by alleging simply that the nature of money has changed. Interest-taking could have served some economic purposes in the fifteenth century at the height of the Church's condemnation. Certainly the nature of sexuality has not changed so much as to permit our justification of the opinions once taught by the universal ordinary magisterium. Similarly for the right to silence, and the others.

This, of course, is not to deny that notable good often resulted from positions taken. So, for example, the ravages of a usurious economy that have wracked other civilizations were largely averted. The attitude toward contraception did much to underline the sacredness of life and the life-giving processes. Analysis of the historical context often makes it quite understandable why a particular position was taken.

Still, to assert that in all of this there is not change but simply development is to play semantic games. There has been development from blindness to sight, from incompleteness and error to fuller perception of the truth. Our reaction should be not to cover over the change, but to thank God with humility that we have allowed God to lead us into the light. We can resist God. That is the tragic mystery of sin. Our history proclaims our resistance. Let us react with penance, not rationalization.

Some react to the discovery of past error by insisting that the doctrine in question was not infallibly taught. When the doctrine has come to be seen as largely wrong, its non-infallibility is hardly debatable. Behind this protest, however, there seems to be a docetist tendency to deny the incarnationalism of the Christian experience. It seems to deny the essential characteristics of human thought and language. Implicit in it is the failure to see us as we are, a pilgrim people who move slowly and not always directly toward the beckoning God of truth.

(6) The *acta* of Vatican I show that some of the bishops were not at all happy with the word "infallible."[107] Furthermore, the use of the word "infallible" in conciliar discussion shows marked ambiguity. Gasser explained that infallibility—which had become by this point synonymous with the teaching authority of the Church—extended also, in some way, to positions noted as rash, scandalous, or dangerous.[108] Such plasticity is not suggested by the word "infallible." It is difficult to describe a doctrine as infallibly rash or infallibly dangerous and scandalous. Clearly Gasser intended to assert teaching competence concerning matters related to the data of revelation. Describing this as yet theologically unrefined competence as "infallibility" was not felicitous. We are not, of course, bound to this expression.

(7) We have already noted some of the difficulties encountered by the defenders of the infallible moral magisterium. We touched upon the position of Father Reed, who maintains that the natural law is contained implicitly and obscurely in the "deposit." Of interest here are the remarks of Richard A. McCormick as he comments with regrettable brevity on the position of Gregory Baum. He says: "The Church's prerogative to propose infallibly the gospel morality would be no more than nugatory without the power to teach the natural law infallibly."[109] This statement cannot be swallowed whole. (Indeed, as we shall suggest, the infallibility proposed by Baum is "nugatory.") But to proceed from that indictment to "the power to teach the natural law infallibly" is a huge and unwarranted step. McCormick argues from the ambiguous position that the natural law is integral to the Gospel. Hence the Church can teach it infallibly. (McCormick is close to Reed here, whose article he finds "thoroughly competent and well-documented" and a "very helpful essay."[110])

Saying that the natural law is integral to the Gospel could mean that principles concerning human dignity, the sacredness of life, the idea of morality as an operation of love, and the like, are integral to both natural law and the Gospel. From this it does not at all follow that the Church has the power to proceed infallibly through the multiple judgments and informational process required to apply these natural and gospel values to special natural law problems. The Christian experience is certainly an enrichment of the natural law. The magisterium, if it is faithful to this experience, has much to offer those who struggle for the realization of human values. Its contribution, however, need not be infallible to be of value.

McCormick further elaborates his argument by saying that natural law is essential to the protection and proposal of Christian morality. He concludes again that particular demands of the natural law are capable of definition. Given the many meaningful and important ways that the Church can treat natural law questions, and given the way that it does in fact treat them, this seems to be a case of *qui nimis probat nihil probat* (whoever proves too much proves nothing).

McCormick's concluding statement is more helpful.

Would not, therefore, the ability to teach infallibly the dignity of man (certainly a revealed truth) without being able to exclude infallibly forms of conduct incompatible with this dignity be the ability infallibly to propose a cliché?[111]

There seems to be a legitimate concern here to avoid an irrelevant proclamation of the gospel ethos without applying it to modern life. One can readily agree that the Church must enter into the specific questions of the day in a quite specific fashion. The Church must recognize in so doing, however, that the position it in good faith assumes may, as has happened often in the past, later have to be changed because of subsequent data and insights. Infallibility is not the only escape from platitudinous clichés.

A final word on McCormick's statement about excluding forms of conduct that are incompatible with a proposed ideal: the claim that this can be done is more modest and nuanced than "teaching the natural law infallibly." The essential problem, however, remains. The Church might declare with much certitude (infallibly, if you will) that murder (unjust killing) is incompatible with human dignity. This statement is self-evident if not tautological. It is a general statement which allows for certitude precisely because of the lack of circumstantial content. To be certain about this does not mean that you can be equally certain (or at all certain) that a particular instance of killing is murder. The certitude of the general principle does not pass over into the discussion of cases as the morality of certain abortions or pills that prevent im-

plantation. Here moral intuition, empirical data, philosophical prob-
ings, and various forms of expertise are relevant, and the certainty of
unapplied principles does not obtain.

Gregory Baum's view of the magisterium has the merit of an historical consciousness. He observes:

We must face the fact that the development in the understanding and presen-
tation of the Gospel has not always been positive in the Church and may not
always be positive. It would not be difficult to establish the fact that certain
themes of divine revelation have not always been announced and taught by
the ecclesiastical magisterium with the same clarity.[112]

He still feels bound to assert some area of infallibility, and he for-
mulates the idea that the Church is infallible only in regard to the ethics
revealed in the Gospel. Such an infallible power would be, as Richard
McCormick observed, nugatory since most of the current ethical questions are not answered in the Gospel. Much of the ethics of the Gospel
is applied to the situation existing at that time and must be reapplied
today to be of value. If Baum meant to say that the Church can be
hoped to have a basic sureness about the Gospel's moral ideas he might
well have stated it without resorting to infallibility, and balanced it off
with his realistic perception of how the sinful Church can at times
obscure the gospel light.

(8) In the polemics of the past century the word "infallible" has
acquired connotations that are offensive and confusing to many. "The
manner and order in which Catholic belief is expressed should in no
way become an obstacle to dialogue with our brethren." Catholic doctrine should be presented "in ways and in terminology which our separated brethren too can really understand."[113] Words, like persons,
have a history and a set of relationships from which one may not prescind. There is probably no word which more readily suggests to non-
Catholic Christians the objectionable aspects of Catholic pre-conciliar
mind-set than this word "infallible." The word should be dropped from
the Catholic lexicon.

The Authentic, Non-Infallible Magisterium

Since the question of infallibility has tended to loom over Catholic
moral theology, casting an inhibiting shadow, it was necessary to deal
with it at some length. Of more practical importance, however, is the
"authentic" and admittedly fallible magisterium. In the Constitution on
the Church, Vatican II speaks of this magisterium and the response
due it:

In matters of faith and morals, the bishops speak in the name of Christ and the faithful are to accept their teaching and adhere to it with a religious assent [obsequio] of soul. This religious submission [obsequium] of will and mind must be shown in a special way to the authentic teaching authority of the Roman Pontiff, even when he is not speaking *ex cathedra*.[114]

Pope John XXIII wrote:

It is clear, however, that when the hierarchy has issued a precept or decision on a point at issue, Catholics are bound to obey their directives. The reason is that the Church has the right and obligation, not merely to guard the purity of ethical and religious principles, but also to intervene authoritatively when there is question of judging the application of these principles to concrete cases.[115]

We will impose upon John Reed again for an example of the way in which many theologians explained the effect of the authentic, non-infallible magisterium. From such teaching, he says, "two consequences follow, one external and absolute, the other internal and conditional. In the external order there results the obligation not to contradict the doctrine in public speech or writing." Theologians may enter into a "speculative discussion" of the doctrine taught, "supposing a discreet selection of audience and method of discourse." Still, even in such discreet discussions the matter in question "is not to be approached as something on which either side is of equal standing or could be equally followed."

So much for the external order.

In the internal order there results per se the obligation of intellectual assent to and acceptance of the teaching. But since, in the supposition, the teaching is not infallible and there remains the possibility of the opposite, there must remain also the absolute possibility that someone, exceptionally qualified in some aspect of the question upon which the conclusion depends, may have grave reason to think that the proposition is not certainly true. In this event the individual, while bound by the teaching in the external order, would not be obliged to yield internal assent.[116]

Before commenting on this particular approach to the papal and episcopal magisterium it seems necessary to introduce more recent philosophical and theological perspectives without which the discussion is doomed to become a narrow exercise in legalistic quibbling.

The Office of Teaching in the Church

Catholics have always believed in ecclesiastical offices, and linked these offices to a teaching role. It is partially in terms of teaching that theology explains the nature of the offices of deacon, priest, bishop, and pope. Catholic theology has emphasized those scriptural texts that seemed to promise the grace and blessings of God upon the preaching and teaching officers of the Church (Mt. 16:18; 28:19; Jn 21:15 ff; 1 Tim 4:14; 5:22; Tim 1:6; 2 Pt, *passim*.). In Short, there has been no lack of stress upon the powers and prerogatives of the teaching officers.

As often happens in any science, certain aspects of a truth might be overly stressed due to cultural and polemical factors, with the result that other elements are neglected and an imbalance ensues. Regarding the ecclesiastical office, theological science should be especially wary. There is a deep-rooted tendency observable in human religious history to magnify the role of religious authority figures and to view their teachings as oracular. A rather clear example of this is found in the history of the Church. The proclamations of councils in the early Church came to be viewed as inspired by the Holy Spirit. It became a widely held view that the first four councils were inspired and on a par with the four gospels. Pope Gregory the Great was merely continuing an established tradition when he asserted: *Sicut sancti evangelii quattuor libros, sic quattuor concilia suscipere et venerari me fateor* (I profess that I accept and venerate the four councils just as I do the four books of the holy gospel).[117] This tradition continued through the middle ages and was carried on by various synods and popes as well as by canonists and theologians. Only after Trent did all traces of the tradition die out in Catholic theology.

To preserve us from a false estimation of the authority of the teaching office in the Church the office must be seen not only in terms of a *gift* of the Spirit but also in terms of a *task* imposed by the Spirit. We must continue to stress the supportive presence of God in the teaching Church: "And know that I am with you always; yes, to the end of time" (Mt 28:20). At the same time, we must acknowledge that the divine assistance is not foisted upon us without our cooperation and a disposition of openness on our part. It is given, in Trent's phrasing, *secundum propriam cuiusque dispositionem et cooperationem* (in accordance with the disposition and cooperation of the recipient) (Denz. 799). Neither history nor theology will permit us to say that constant fidelity to the Spirit is guaranteed by the promise of the ultimate victory of Christ. We believe that the gates of hell will not prevail against God's work and we are supported by the vision of God becoming all in all. Until this is achieved, however, we must never forget the crippling and darkening reality of sin. We must never forget that the Church which is holy by the presence of God's Spirit is sinful by our presence. Perhaps the early Church was more aware of its frailty. Augustine wrote:

Wherever in my books I have described the Church as being without spot or wrinkle, it is not to be understood that she is so already, but that she is preparing herself to be so when she too will appear in glory. For in the present time, because of much ignorance and weakness in her members, she must confess afresh each day, "Forgive us our trespasses."[118]

St. Thomas wrote in a similar vein:

That the Church may be glorious, without spot or wrinkle, is the final goal to which we are being led through the passion of Christ. It will be so only in our eternal home, not on our journey there during which, if we said we had no sin we should be deceiving ourselves, as we are told in the first Epistle of St. John.[119]

The ability of the Church to be unfaithful to God and to impede God's saving and teaching work is a truth that we must confess. The Spirit of the Lord is with us, ready to lead us to all truth, but we can refuse to be led. "The Church is a sinful Church: that is a truth of faith, not just a fact of her primitive experience. And it is a shattering truth."[120] If we forget this truth of faith in our discussion of the magisterium, as though the magisterium were removed from the possibility of sin, we imply that God's help is given without human cooperation. This would be magic. The teaching office is not just a gift; it is a task at which we can falter.

This consciousness of sin should not cause us to overreact and lose all love for and trust in the Church as a work of God. It should prompt us rather to a realistic sense of penance and to an examination of ourselves and of the Church and of the magisterium. We should confidently expect to find in the Church the fruits of the Spirit, but we must be ready also to find the spot and the wrinkle. To remove the spots and smooth the wrinkles that we find in ourselves, in the Church, or in magisterial pronouncements is a service to the God who works with us.

The Notion of Teacher

Discussions of the Church teaching tend to ignore how equivocal, mutable, and culturally conditioned the notion of teacher is. Even theologians writing to emphasize the magisterial role of the laity, and trying to temper a purely hierarchical conception of the magisterium, seem unduly concerned with finding examples of active lay participation in doctrinal developments in Scripture and in the history of the councils.

Admittedly, such testimony is useful. However, recognizing with the second Vatican Council that "the human race has passed from a rather static concept of reality to a more dynamic, evolutionary one,"[121] we should be less likely to expect that teaching should occur in the same fashion in every time and culture, that it should be achieved now as it was in New Testament times or in the middle ages.

In this respect the teaching offices in the Church must be seen in an evolutionary perspective. The way they should function in the modern world will be as different as the modern world is different from the past. "The living conditions of modern people have been so profoundly changed in their social and cultural dimensions, that we can speak of a new age in human history." Thus Vatican II.[122] A new mode of teaching in this new age should be expected. It might differ from the past forms as profoundly as a forty-year-old man differs from the infant he once was—*without loss of identity.*

In a paternalistic culture where there was general illiteracy, little insight into God's presence in non-Catholic and non-Christian experiences, and a view of truth as something static and given, paternalistic magisterial figures were understandable. They could take over the task of reflection, formulation, and preservation of the faith; their teaching was truly analogous to the work of a shepherd feeding his sheep.

The laity today are not aptly compared to sheep, and the Church in dialogue should not present itself in the guise of the all-knowing schoolmaster. In moral matters in the past, Church leaders could be expected to act like a parent dealing with immature children who need extensive help in making particular decisions. Today, however, Vatican II emphasizes that not even children are to be treated the same.

This holy Synod likewise affirms that children and young people have a right to be encouraged to weigh moral values with an upright conscience, and to embrace them by personal choice, and to know and love God more adequately. Hence it earnestly entreats all who exercise government over peoples or preside over the work of education to see that youth is never deprived of this sacred right.[123]

The right to weigh values and make personal decisions in moral matters is, in the council's words, "a sacred right." Those who would deprive people of this right on grounds that they would abuse it or are too immature to exercise it responsibly certainly bear the burden of proof. What the council says of children is obviously more true of adults. We can expect the maturing hierarchical Church to give fewer detailed rules of conduct to the maturing laity and to teach rather by giving broad outlines. Growing up is a painful process and people can be expected to resist the burdens of responsible freedom and the agonies of decision-making. Bishops and popes will share the experience of good parents who hate to see the children grow up. These problems are to be expected and faced.

Vatican II's reminder is a good one here: "Let the laity not imagine that pastors are always such experts, that to every problem which arises, however complicated, they can readily give a concrete solution, or even that such is their mission."[124] Moreover, what their pastors on the scene cannot do should not be expected from the bishop or the pope. The nature of ethics in a world of mounting complexification makes this quite impossible.

It seems today that the notion of teacher does not imply the imposition of information and decisions on largely passive recipients. Rather, the effective teacher in this age should be a stimulator of thought. S/he should seek to dissipate the immature desire for unreal certitudes. S/he should seek always to enlarge a debate and not to close it.

Let it not be thought that we are suggesting here that the hierarchical magisterium make an instant conversion to a kind of non-directive counseling technique. Whatever the ideal and whatever the progress thus far, many people will continue to function at an immature level and will continue to look for specific directions. We have not sufficiently encouraged the laity to be mature and cannot call for immediate maturity. But as we attend to these needs which our pastoral practice has helped to create, let us see the situation for what it is.

Ethics and the Expansion of the Sciences

Regarding the various sciencs, there is an expansion not only of data and expertise but also of our appreciation of the ethical significance of the sciences. Acknowledgement of this is frequent in the documents of Vatican II. We are directed to the many new colleagues of theology: psychology, sociology, the social sciences, the science of communications, and biology.[125]

A further quite relevant observation is the following:

Today it is more difficult than ever for a synthesis to be formed of the various branches of knowledge and the arts. For while the mass and the diversity of cultural factors are increasing, there is a decline in the individual person's ability to grasp and unify these elements. Thus the ideal of "the universal person" is disappearing more and more.[126]

So too is the ideal of "the universal magisterium" disappearing.

Magisterial pronouncements will perhaps have an even greater value in such an age, as our social consciousness grows and our need to tap communal wisdom is more felt. The magisterium must try to provide this wisdom by being as sensitive as possible to the movements of the ubiquitous Spirit. Still, both moralist and moral magisterium will have a very new look.

In a simpler age the moralist could attempt to acquire enough technical expertise to make judgments about the moral problems of the scientist. Technological growth and "the information explosion" make this impossible. In facing the moral questions posed, for example, by the science of genetics, two possibilities are conceivable: the moralist must become a geneticist or the geneticist must be made morally alert by a continuing dialogue with the ethical experts. The second is obviously preferable. The geneticist must not prescind from the moral dimensions of his/her science (and indeed s/he does not, even if s/he pretends to). The moral questions cannot be answered by the scientist alone; but they cannot be answered without the scientist.

The Ecumenical Approach to Moral Truth

This point about ecumenism can be made briefly. The Church has entered into dialogue with other Christians, with non-Christians, and with non-believers. This means that we have something to learn from them. None of the faithful, lay or clergy, can ignore the witness of these people in the pursuit of moral truth—although emotionally, it would seem, we are more ready to say this than to do it. The hierarchy may not merely proclaim their teaching prerogatives if they are not engaged in *real* dialogue with the laity, theologians, and all others who are also anointed with the spirit of truth and prophecy.

With these considerations in mind it is hoped that we will attain to some useful refinements by turning to the statements of Reed and McCormick concerning the authentic magisterium. John Reed asserts that, given a prounouncement of the authentic magisterium, there is an "obligation not to contradict the doctrine in public speech and writing."[127] This statement, for some years, was a truism among Catholic moralists and canonists. It is hardly defensible today. Reed, we saw, says that theologians may enter into speculative discussion about magisterial statements "supposing a discreet selection of audience." Presumably, if discussion is called for, theologians around the world can hardly communicate by word of mouth. They must write, and by now it would be obvious that there is no written word on theological subjects that might not be proclaimed from the housetops. Vital theological discussions can no longer be kept "under wraps." Pastoral difficulties result from this and must be met, but this new fact of life must be accepted.

More important is the internal intellectual assent which Reed states is *per se* due magisterial statements (p. 59). Enlarging on this Reed says that "it will not easily or commonly happen that the ordinary faithful, the ordinary priest, or even the ordinary theologian will be in a position to depart from the sort of authentic teaching at issue here" (p. 60). Those who go against a particular moral teaching would appear to be imprudently exposing themselves to the danger of violating the moral law" (p. 57). The reason: "For the assistance of the Holy Spirit is always present to the vicar of Christ and the other bishops, and in their purposeful pronouncements they will have used more than ordinary human means as well" (p. 57). (Since the Holy Spirit is also present to the laity and theologians and non-Catholics, this reason is limp. It also ignores the times when hierarchical teachings were amended at the initiative of the faithful.)

Reed does, however, make an important admission. There is an "absolute possibility" that someone "exceptionally qualified" could disagree with the teaching in question and even act according to "his" own opinion as long as "he" does not shake "the external order" (p. 59). This, of course, is "a rather extraordinary thing" (p. 60).

This admission, I repeat, is important. It is, I think, quite gratuitous to assert that it is "a rather extraordinary thing" to find persons sufficiently qualified to dissent with a particular teaching. In the present question of contraception, for example, given the wide publicity afforded important studies on the subject and the deep convictions of the persons and groups with whom we are in dialogue, it seems to me that the number of those "exceptionally qualified" to dissent could be quite large. Clearly it is a matter of judgment. Reed mentions the possibility that the Church could in a particular case wish to impose a norm of conduct by using its "jurisdictional authority." If we apply this possibility to the contraception question, then the debate is no longer about natural law but is a case of positive law; positive law, of course, is open to the soothing influence of *epikeia*.

Several points made by Richard McCormick deserve attention. He writes: "Certain truths about man's nature penetrate his consciousness gradually by historical processes and for the same reason are maintained only with difficulty."[128] He points out that it is not always easy to demonstrate the reasonableness of certain moral evaluations. Because of this, an authoritative magisterium makes sense.

It is certainly true that it is not always easy to give a fully satisfactory explanation of certain moral convictions which emerge gradually in human consciousness. The magisterium can exercise an important preservative influence here. It can preserve these nascent appreciations from an iconoclastic rationalism. We would only add to this that the developing understanding in history of a truth can also be arrested at a particular point by an inflexible magisterium which is not open to the implications of an expanding historical consciousness. The magisterium can easily fall prey to a bad spirit of conservatism. This too should be admitted and guarded against.

McCormick continues:

Is it not, up to a point, precisely because arguments are not clear, or at least not universally persuasive, that a magisterium makes sense in this area? At what point does our healthy impatience to understand muffle the voice most like to speed the process? (p. 613)

Three comments suggest themselves here. First, precisely because the arguments are not clear it makes sense for the magisterium to be flexible and open to the possibility that when the arguments are clarified another position may be indicated.

Secondly, precisely because the arguments are not clear, that magisterium, however forcefully it presses its position, may not impose a certain obligation that only clarity makes possible. *In dubiis libertas* contains an insight that may not be invalidated by any juridical power.

Finally, one should view history closely before saying that the magisterium is "the voice most likely to speed the process." At times, it has been such a voice, but at other times it has failed.

To conclude this section on the authentic, non-infallible magisterium: how should we react to this kind of papal and episcopal teaching? Pius XII in *Humani generis* said that "if the supreme pontiffs in their official documents purposely pass judgment on a matter debated until then, it is obvious to all that the matter, according to the mind and will of the same pontiffs, cannot be considered any longer a question open for discussion among theologians" (*quaestionem liberae inter theologos disceptationis iam haberi non posse*).[129] Vatican II, as we have seen, said that the ordinary magisterium of popes and bishops should be met with a *religiosum obsequium* (in *Documents of Vatican II*, "obsequium" is translated "assent" and "submission," perhaps not too felicitously). To determine the authority of papal statements which are not *ex cathedra* the council offers some criteria: they are to be adhered to in accordance with the "manifest mind and will" of the pope (same paragraph). "His mind and will in the matter may abe known chiefly either from the character of the documents, from his frequent repetition of the same doctrine, or from his manner of speaking" (The Constitution on the Church, #25, p. 48).

Concerning the celebrated statement of Pius XII in *Humani generis*, Ford and Kelly are ready to concede that "even a non-infallible pronouncement can close a controversy among theologians." They add something of a reservation:

We feel sure, however, that the pope himself would agree that this decisive character of the pronouncement must be evident. That is in accord with canon 1323, §3, which states that nothing is to be understood as dogmatically declared or defined unless this is clearly manifested. The canon refers to infallible teachings; yet the same norm seems to apply with at least equal force to the binding character of non-infallible teaching, especially when there is question of pronouncements that would close a controversy.[130]

We need not belabor the problems of such a position. *An admittedly fallible statement could close off discussion of the question among theologians with the possibility of error thus going unchecked.* The reservation expressed by Ford and Kelly indicates that they were not unaware of this difficulty. They do not, however, exclude the possibility of closing a controversy with fallible teaching.

John Reed prefers to translate the final words of the statement from *Humani generis* in this way: "cannot be any longer considered a matter of open debate."[131] He feels that Pius meant that the debate could go on but that both sides of the question cannot "be held and followed with equal freedom."[132] The precise cause of this limitation of freedom is not made manifest. It seems to me that whatever the presumptive value of a particular fallible papal teaching and however respectfully one receives it and studies it, it is difficult to see why the discussion should thereby have been rendered less free. At any rate, I do not think that many theologians would deny that the theology of the magisterium has advanced considerably since *Humani generis*, and that the magisteriological controversy was obviously not closed by that encyclical.

The statement of Vatican II concerning the criteria for judging the binding power of the authentic papal magisterium is not satisfying. It seems to say that the teaching is as binding as the pope wills it to be. This would be voluntarism. It also would lead theologians into fantastic probes to discover the mind and intent of the pontiff on certain questions. Some theologians, for example, trying to discover the mind of

Pius XII on psychiatry after he had warned against certain attitudes and techniques, felt the need to do more than analyze his text. They also sought out "a subsequent 'inspired' comment in the pages of *L'Osservatore Romano* [which] made it very clear that he had not intended to condemn psychiatry in general or psychoanalysis in particular."[133] They also thought it relevant to report that "his *cordial* reception of the psychiatrists and psychoanalysts and the friendly words with which he closed his address showed a spirit far removed from hostility to this modern branch of science."[134]

Let us think of the statements of Pius IX on religious freedom. His manner of speaking, his frequent repetitions, and the solemn character of the language he used indicated the utmost seriousness of intention. I would not be inclined to say that those who respectfully disagreed with Pius' stand, preferring something more akin to the subsequent teachings of Vatican II on religious liberty, would have deserved any reproach.

The language of the code of canon law on the related question of the episcopal magisterium seems better: "While the bishops, whether teaching individually or gathered in particular councils, are not endowed with infallibility, yet with regard to the faithful entrusted to their care they are truly teachers and masters (*veri doctores seu magistri*)" (canon 1326). The pope and the bishops are truly teachers. Their teachings should receive deep respect. Their statements represent serious interventions by officers of the Church. Hopefully, these teachings are representative of ecclesial wisdom and thus merit religious reverence, but it is religious also to recognize that they are not infallible; they might at times come from a period when vitally relevant data, since come to light, were lacking. These teachings, after all—and we must say this to avoid a kind of magisteriolatry—are not the word of God. Indeed they must stand under the judgment of the word of God. It is not an act of disloyalty but rather a duty of the theologian to test these statements to see if they can withstand the cutting power of the two-edged sword.

To develop a new kind of magisterial approach to a new kind of world is a massive task. A thousand questions beginning with "how" await research and reply. Here I presume only to persent certain terms which might more accurately describe the essential characteristics of the Church's moral magisterium. Two terms seem particularly apt: prophetic (closely allied to creative) and dialogical.

Prophetic: The magisterium is called to prophecy. The prophet is distinguished not so much for insight into the future as for insight into the present. The prophet is called to pierce the blinding clouds which inevitably envelop human consciousness. Inherent in our history is a tendency to develop a myopic and insensitive code morality which evades the agonies of the moral call to authentic personhood. This insensitive ethos tends to grip society and defy penetration. The prophet must see and penetrate.

The Church in history has had great moments of powerful prophecy. In the early centuries it became a powerful social force, championing the dignity of persons, the rights of conscience, and the power of unselfish love. It was its religious and moral intensity that made it so important on the imperial scene that Decius himself had to admit that he was more concerned over the election of a bishop in Rome than over the revolt of a political rival.[135] It was not Constantine who gave the Church status. Historians tell us that: "Sooner or later some emperor after Constantine would have had to seek an understanding with the victorious Church."[136] The Church's work in education and the care of the sick and the poor gave many effective, prophetic lessons in compassion and love of truth to the medieval world. The social encyclicals in modern times that braved charges of left wing radicalism to call for social reconstruction were genuinely prophetic. Recent papal calls for peace merit the same encomium.

On the other hand, prophecy melted in the warmth of Constantinian favor. In the medieval age of violence the Church imbibed the barbarian spirit of violence. It did not pierce the enveloping cloud. Christian consciousness was seduced by the rigors of Roman law and Stoicism for centuries. It followed when it should have led. The treatment of "heretics" and unbelievers was harsh and often ruthless. The use of torture and the ordeal provide us no happy memories. The lessons taught by these practices were not prophetic or Christian. The evils of anti-Semitism, colonialization, slavery, righ wing totalitarianism and racism were not met with distinguished prophecy.

The bane of prophecy, often enough, is a stifling traditionalism which confuses tenure with authenticity, forgetting that error too can become traditional. Traditions must be respected; they must also be critically examined to see if they enshrine insensitivity and blindness.

The true prophet is creative. The Church teaching must not detach itself from the human scene, and act as though it were called to pronounce *licets* and *non licets* from a distance. Its role is creative more than judgmental. It must not simply worry over the dangers of progress, but participate in that progress so as to minimize the dangers.

A timid and negative magisterium is the irrelevant voice of uncreative fear.

Ethics can be radically divided into an ethics of survival and an ethics of creativity. A cringing, self-centered ethics of survival can never befit the Christian. And yet the way of creativity is difficult.

Sometimes the creative word will be called utopian because its hour has not yet come. Pope John's encyclical on peace was thus described by Paul Tillich at the *Pacem in Terris* convocation at the United Nations. Yet the prophetic word must be spoken and inserted into the stream of human thought so that it might slowly achieve dynamic influence.

Creativity breaks through the status quo. An institution which has allowed itself to center on survival will thus be tempted to crush the creative spirit. The long list of creative theologians who have been condemned shows that this danger is not illusory in the Church. The harassment of theologians whose work was later to find conciliar blessing in Vatican II gives a poignant lesson in this regard.[137]

Dialogical: Truth is not reached in soltitude but in the process of communitarian existence. If the Church would bear witness on the human scene, it must recognize itself as a participant in these processes. It must not enter conversation trying to say the last word; rather it must say meaningful words drawn from its vast memory and rich Christian experience. The magisterium must be honest and not pretend to data it does not have. Obviously the moral magisterium must not feel bound, by a kind of institutional pride, to past magisterial documents that through lack of insight and information taught something that can now be seen as inaccurate and unacceptable. Respect for the wisdom of the past does not impose the perpetuation of past deficiencies.

An example of a dialogical magisterium can be found in the statement on the Vietnamese war issued by the American bishops in November, 1966. Indeed, it could serve as a classical paradigm for the Church teaching on many moral questions:

We realize that citizens of all faiths and of differing political loyalties honestly differ among themselves over the moral issues involved in this tragic conflict. While we do not claim to be able to resolve these issues authoritatively, in the light of the facts as they are known to us, it is reasonable to argue . . .

The bishops then went on to acknowledge that Catholics were free to be conscientious objectors to the position that their bishops had presented. The bishops did not content themselves with reiterating the gospel message of love and peace. They made an effort to see how this applied to the present war situation. But they allowed that Catholics with other viewpoints and insights could responsibly reach another position.

There is no reason why this approach could not be taken in other areas. The doctrine of conscientious objection involves a respect for the individual conscience and for the complexity of ethical decision making. These factors obtain in questions other than war. Persons of all faiths and differing loyalties differ among themselves and with us on issues such as contraception, abortion, divorce, civil disobedience, political philosophy, business ethics, etc. With the same honesty that our bishops showed in this instance, all spokespersons for the teaching Church should admit that we do not have a comprehensive knowledge of all the factors needed for a solution to these questions.

In these matters it could be said with the bishops: "While we do not claim to be able to resolve these issue authoritatively, in the light of the facts as they are known to us, it is reasonable to argue . . ." Then, acknowledging with consistency that individual Catholics might disagree, the possibility of respectful conscientious objection to the announced position should be admitted. Any other practice pretends to an omniscience regarding all relevant essential circumstances and places an obstacle before the guidance of the Spirit whose grace is the New Law.

Furthermore, should a dialogical statement such as that of the American bishops have to be amended in the light of new information, the change would not be a clumsy retreat from a position too apodictically assumed. It would represent, rather, a new phase in the enriching dialogue. It will occasion no loss of prestige among honest people. Other Christians and non-Christians will be inspired by our openness to their views and will thus be inclined to share more deeply in our experience of truth.

We are not suggesting that the Church succumb to the weakness of consensus politics and become an insipid and bland voice. Dialogue cannot always be reserved or agreeable; neither can it be reduced to a gentle, inoffensive bleating geared to the creation of a false unanimity and fellowship. Its prophetic character would thereby be lost. However, it must acknowledge a *de facto* pluralism in many moral matters, especially those which have been profoundly affected by changing conditions and new knowledge. It is naive and self-deceiving to seek one "official" Catholic position on all questions. (It would, for example, be naive and self-deceiving to allege that Catholics are one in theory and

practice on the question of contraception.) However, in such less ambiguous questions as racial integration, and even in ambiguous questions, people in the Church should speak out with sufficient force and
specificity to be influential in national and international discussions.

Agencies should be erected also to make it possible for strong minority opinions in the Church to enter the public forum effectively as
"Catholic." (The bishops' statement on Vietnam in November, 1966,
did not represent the views of large segments of the Catholic population, who are thus left to protest "unofficially" without the important
sociological influence of institutional prestige.)

A dialogical magisterium does not forget the integral magisterial role
of the laity. The laity, Pius XII said, "are the Church" (*AAS* 38: 141).
Vatican II taught: "The body of the faithful as a whole, anointed as
they are by the holy One, cannot err in matters of belief."[138] Neither
the magisterium nor the Church is simply hierarchical. If the laity,
therefore, feel that the Church is not being effective or true to its mission they are not free simply to criticize the hierarchy. We usually get
the leadership we want and then ease our consciences by criticizing it.
The laity, quite as much as the hierarchy, too often work under the
illusory impression that initiative and creativity always come from
"above." The impression is a kind of infantilism and has been repeatedly discredited in history.

Finally, the magisterium must be served by a vigorous theological
community. Theologians, bishops, and laity must concur in the service
of the word. In fact, since there are and should be various agencies of
witness and influence in the Church, it would be better to speak of
the *Magisteria* of the Church. We would then consider not just the papal
and episcopal magisteria but the equally authentic magisterium of the
laity and the magisterium of the theologians. Each of these has a role
of creative service to the truth; none can be considered as having a
quasi-juridical power to stifle or invalidate the other. Each magisterium
must be seen as open to the corrective influence of the other magisteria.
Freedom and mutual respect must characterize this service. The theologian must respect the bishops' concern for the integrity of the kerygma; bishops should presume a similar concern on the part of
theologians. Episcopal ordination does not convey theological expertise. Neither does election to the papacy.

Theologians whose teachings or prudence is questioned should
have the advantage of judgment by their peers. Those not active in the
theological community might easily miss the implications of current
debate and judge people unjustly. Error is inevitable in the develop-

ment of any science. The only way to stop it is to stop all thought. It should be noted too that bishops who create a repressive atmosphere for theologians are thereby inviting non-experts and the popular press to address themselves to the neglected subjects. Theologians, on the other hand, must respect the pastoral needs and concerns of the bishops. Mutual respect for the distinct but complementary authorities of bishop, theologian, and layman must be the goal.

Will a moral magisterium that does not call itself infallible command respect? Yes. Will an authentic magisterium that is conscious of its limitations as well as of its strength be able to exert a positive influence? Yes. In the first place, it will spare many Catholics the anguish of unexpected change that wracks so many of our people today. Unaware that the Church can in many ways change—and has changed often in the past—many Catholics today are shaken in their faith. Future Catholics, schooled in the reality of being a pilgrim people, will greet progress with joy and not with panic. Formal magisterial pronouncements which give faithful voice to Christian consciousness will be received with respect. In matters moral, such pronouncements will be treasured as an expression of the wisdom of the Christian people. Such teaching will be seen as an invaluable aid but not as a substitute for conscience, since no agency can substitute for the unique role of conscience.

Secondly, non-Catholics will react to our honesty as they did to the honesty of Vatican II. Prophets of doom feared the self-revelation that was inevitable in the council; they have not yet changed their triumphalist stance. No persons of good will will think less of us if they hear in our voices the echo of him who was meek and humble of heart. A Church that is distinguished by a fervid religious life and an unmistakable concern for the good of humankind will be a powerful force for good. Its involvement, its love, and its absence of pretense will give it superb credentials in the modern world.

Catholic moral teaching will be more realistic and pertinent. The collegial character of the magisterium will free it from the impossibilities attached to overcentralization and the attempt to impose moral absolutes universally and transculturally without sufficient regard to varying contexts. The magisterium will not be thought of as merely papal or merely episcopal. Rather, the service of the hierarchy will be to vitalize and encourage the primary witness of the Church, the liturgy and lives of the people of God. This is the magisterium, the Church that will serve the world without pretension.[139]

Part 7

OF MORALS AND METHOD

Arguments are like waves. Assumptions are like tides. A study of ethical
method is primarily a study of assumptions. In Part Seven, I look first to the
possibility of a Moral Creed to which all Christians could say "Amen!" Are
there assumptions that should underly all debate among Christians? I argue
that there are, in Chapter Sixteen. In Chapter Seventeen, I offer a portrait of
a working ethicist to illustrate what method in ethics is all about. Chapter
Eighteen looks at the massive assumptions of the popular behaviorist psychology of B. F. Skinner. Chapter Nineteen recognizes that ethics is not a
matter of simple calculation. All our faculties, sensitivities, and feelings are
needed for good moral choices. Ethics, especially philosophical ethics in the
Anglo-American school, often works at the dry-bones level of a disembodied
rationality. The tedious results bear little fruit in moral wisdom. The critical
fault in such ethics I have called "the intellectualistic fallacy." The fallacy is
in failing to see the linkage of moral wisdom to the affective, mystical, and
even contemplative dimensions of human moral experience. Chapter Nineteen looks at the neglected but essential role of the affections and "heart" in
ethical discernment.

CHAPTER 16

A Moral Creed for All Christians

A failure of nerve can lead to a failure of insight. In the face of a noble challenge, if we dare not see, we will not see. And then, in self-defense, we will lose sight of our failure of nerve and failure of vision, and an entombing comfort will seal us off from any cleansing experience of guilt. Contemporary Christian decadence illustrates that.

If talk of decadence seems unduly harsh, let us turn to the observable fact that Christians are not conspicuously committed in their behavior to the quintessential values of their moral creed. Decadence is one term that fairly describes that condition. Decadence is descriptive too of what W. D. Davies indicts in his study *The Sermon on the Mount:*

. . . with a few notable exceptions, interpreters of the New Testament have been largely absorbed in kerygmatic or strictly theological questions. The moral teaching of Jesus, although acknowledged, has been sharply distinguished from the kerygma of the Church and often treated as a Cinderella. Scholars have sometimes been even self-consciously anxious to relegate his teaching to a markedly subordinate place in the exposition of the faith of the New Testament.[1]

For anyone aware of the centrality of Jesus' moral message and demands in the experience of the New Testament, Davies' judgment should be unbelievable. For most early Christians, the moral demands of the Gospel were at the heart of the exciting and foundational revelation that the reign of God was upon them. Morality could not be shunted aside by dogmatic or theological considerations, for such considerations would be form without substance if severed from the penetrating demands communicated by Jesus.

As if Cinderella experience were not enough. Gospel morality has suffered in other ways at the hands of scholars. (These errors, of course, are not limited to the scholars. Scholars are ever prone to give expression to the more formless errors of the masses. For Christian scholars, this means that they are more often the *vox populi* than the *vox Dei*.)

Scholars have raised the question of whether there ever is such a thing as a distinctively Christian ethic. The fact that this question would be asked is significant; the answers to it are even more so. Catholic University theologian, Charles E. Curran answers that a Christian may know moral truth in a thematically and explicitly Christian way. "But what the Christian knows with an explicit Christian dimension is and can be known by all others."[2] Elsewhere he writes: "Obviously a personal acknowledgment of Jesus as Lord affects at least the consciousness of the individual and his thematic reflection on his consciousness, but the Christian and the explicitly non-Christian can and do arrive at the same ethical conclusions and can and do share the same general ethical attitudes, dispositions and goals."[3]

More commonly, the answer given to this question is that Christians and non-Christians have the same material content ethically speaking (they perceive the same concrete obligations), but that Christians have distinctive attitudes, dispositions, intentions, and goals. These, however, will not yield something distinct from the human. As Richard McCormick says explaining this view: "This is what nearly everyone (e.g., Fuchs, Aubert, Macquarrie, Rahner) is saying these days. The light of the gospel does not bring something distinct from the human, but helps us to discover what is authentically human."[4]

These positions have much in them that is laudable but also much that potentially dulls the impact of the "good news." What these authors are up to cannot be understood apart from three factors: (1) the florid and belated ecumenical spirit of our time; (2) the collapse of dualistic and supernaturalistic explanations of salvation; and (3) the demise of fundamentalism and naive biblicism.

First, to ecumenism. In this day, it would seem at least unfriendly to present Christian morality as a superior moral *gnosis* which contains a wisdom unavailable to the non-Christian. This represents a worthy concern. As H. Richard Niebuhr said, Christianity is "one of the distinctive ways of human existence." He goes on: "Whether it is better or worse than other styles is a question neither Christians nor others are in a position to answer, since men lack standards by which to judge their standards."[5]

However, the issue for Christians (and for anyone who seeks awareness within a specific tradition) is not whether we are better than others in our moral perceptions, but what it is that our perceptions are. The challenge is to appropriate and share what is viable and best within our experience, not to initiate an impossible competition with other experiences. In the dialogue that follows sharing, ideas will be modified or will yield to or blend with more humanizing possibilities that appear in other traditions.

Ecumenism should not press us into blurring our differences. Ecumenism is after all our natural state; it is rooted in our ontology. As St. Paul said with masterful epistemological insight, "I know in part" (1 Cor. 13:12). In real ecumenism we serve the truth by becoming more conscious of our "part" while opening ourselves to other parts. This imports as much interest in differences as in common ground. To minimize those differences evacuates the ecumenical process.

To say that there is something special and distinctive about Christian morality is not a show of *hubris*. It is, rather, an expression of awareness rising out of a tradition that has its own story to tell and is as ready to tell it as it is to listen and learn from other traditions where revelation is also anticipated. God was ecumenical before Christians were, and so we can look for God's presence and word in other religious traditions.

Second, as to dualistic and supernaturalistic explanations of revelation. To explain how God touches us in the creative relationship that we call grace or salvation is a gigantic challenge that has staggered theology. One way of understanding God's initiative has been to dichotomize drastically the natural and the supernatural, the native endowment and the superadded gift. The error was well motivated. The desire was to show the gratuitous and gifted quality of God's creative will. We could not *deserve* to be or to be sustained. To symbolize the initiative of the divine giving and our impotence to merit it, theologians repaired to the categories of nature and supernature. In this unrealistic distinction, nature suffered by comparison. There followed more emphasis on the *divinization* of human persons than their *humanization* in the encounter of God with us.

In the atmosphere of this theology Christian morality was radically severed from the natural and the human. It could not, as it were, "come naturally." To emphasize the "gift" idea regarding Christian morality it was presented as somehow superadded to our merely human nature.

This theology has been largely abandoned. Joining in the rush from it, are those who write on the distinctively Christian ethic. They evince a welcome recognition that if Christianity does not beckon to a fuller more authentic humanness, it is irrelevant. If it does not make us to be *us* in a truer way, it is intrusive. Grace enhances the human, it does not substitute for it.

This does not mean, however, that there can be no distinctively Christian moral experience or that Christian moral existence cannot be a distinguished species of the genus human. Neither can Christianity be segregated somehow and stored away in uninfluential attitudes and intentionalities which never bear fruit in distinctive practical conclusions and attitudes. Moral experience is too deep in mystery, too broad in experiential scope, too infinitely variable to be identical in any two individuals or in any two groups.

Just look at what morality involves. It has its beginnings in a foundational, prediscursive (intuitive) faith experience of the value of persons and of the possibilities and meaning of existence; it involves sensitivity to our multifaceted, value-laden context with all the empirical complexity, and the symbols, stories, and paradoxes thereof. Moral consciousness unfolds in imagination; in humor; in suffering; in unique personal encounters; in study and in syllogism; in affectivity; and in peak, mystical experiences. Moral consciousness takes shape in a specific field of action and reaction to unique and unrepeatable challenges and in a web of collective and interpersonal relationships never found before or afterwards. It is sheer abstraction to think that any two moral experiences or *ethic-s* could be identical, materially or otherwise.

The debate that has gone on in this regard in Christian ethics could profit greatly by being plugged into the research done on human mores in the social science of anthropology. That it has not done so sufficiently is but another example of the enervating isolation of all the academic disciplines from one another. The debate among Christian theologians has been narrowed by the particular conversations in which they have found themselves, with Marxists, humanists, and other Christian groups. However significant, these have not been broad dialogues.

Anthropologists have long ago dissipated all notions of moral sameness throughout the human race. Moral diversity is enormous. Some, of course, have stressed the common moral grounds of all peoples. Franz Boas, for example, wrote that: "There is no evolution of moral ideas. All the vices that we know, lying, theft, murder, rape, are discountenanced in the life of a closed society."[6]

Ralph Linton also is interested in noting the almost universal moral standards. As he observes: "The values on which there is most complete agreement are those which have to do with the satisfaction of the primary needs of individuals."[7]

However, Abraham and May Edel point out that "contravention of our attitudes—to adultery, or truth-telling or killing or toward virtually any rule we accept—are extremely common among the peoples of different cultures of the world."[8] More importantly, other authors point out that there are differences even within apparent commonalities. Clyde Kluckhohn, for example, sees the need to analyze psychological, biosocial, and historical factors and finds "somewhat distinct answers to essentially the same questions."[9] Look-alike answers may be quite different upon further analysis. Morris Ginsberg points to differences in the very conception of the human person. The conception of human personhood, of course, is foundational for ethics. Deriving from it are the notions of obligation, ethical motivation, and indeed, the actual meaning of the root category *moral*. Differences at this level cannot be hermetically sealed off from very practical implications at the level of the "material content" of ethics.

Ginsberg also stresses the contrast between an abstract notion of virtue or vice which stretches almost to universality and a more specific and concrete concept which takes special shape from the particular circumstances and relationships of a group.[10]

Thus, it seems to me to be a kind of epistemological docetism to say that different moral experiences arising out of different cultures, histories, and challenges are "materially" the same in content though they may vary in ideals, goals, and intentionalities. They may and probably will reach conclusions which are on the surface similar regarding killing, truth-telling, and other basic values. However, if we look beyond all of this, if we peel away the skin of their superficial similarity, and analyse their conceptions of personhood, or their view of the nature of the undergirding principle of existence (God); or if we see what they care about and why, who their significant persons are, why they oppose murder and stealing etc., and how they define them; if we see where their emphasis falls in the dialectical tensions between fatalism and creative, hopeful activism, between the Apollonian and the Dionysian, the cynical and the sanguine, the universalist and the exclusivist; and if we enucleate the dominant value-themes of their ethical ambience, the differences in their moralities are likely to be enormous and critical.

One can look in Christianity and in other human traditions for distinctive moral riches and still agree with anthropologist Ralph Linton when he writes: "The peoples of the world must find common areas of understanding or die."[11] Common areas of understanding regarding moral values, however, do not require the impossible—i.e., the homogenization of distinctive ethical realizations. Moral evolution proceeds through the blending and cross-fertilization of diverse traditions, not through the negation of fruitful diversity.

Third, as to the demise of naive biblicism and fundamentalism. The downplaying of the distinctively Christian ethic relates also and finally to the demise of fundamentalism. Critical studies of scripture have established for many, as W. D. Davies says, "that the Gospel tradition preserves only the whisper of the voice of Jesus."[12]

Some form critics attribute not only the preservation of the Christian biblical tradition, but even the very creation of most of it to the Church. For many, the rug has been pulled out from under the Christian revelation. They look at the scripture scholars and lament: "They have taken my Lord away and I don't know where they have put him" (John 20:13).

Following upon this has been a reappraisal of just how "God was in Christ Jesus." It is remarkable that a scholarly article in the prestigious Jesuit journal, *Theological Studies,* by Seely Beggiani of The Catholic University of America could raise new and radical questions about the divinity of Jesus and create no widespread stir.[13] Beggiani raised the question in his lead article as to whether Jesus was exclusively the "divine son." The article hypothesized that every person has a potential for a union with the Logos such as that found in Jesus. In Beggiani's words, all persons have innately "the possibility of hypostatic union." He continues: "Having said this, we do not claim that in historical fact anyone other than Christ has fulfilled the potential of hypostatic union, but the possibility is there."[14]

These thoughts would have brought the author to the stake in an earlier day. Today's context entertains them. Obviously, if the distinctiveness of Jesus can be questioned, the distinctiveness of the Christian ethic is not enhanced.

Nevertheless, the passing of naïveté in our understanding of the foundational literature of Christianity and the appearance of variant Christologies do not mark the end, but hopefully a new beginning of Christian experience. In this phase new boundaries between heresy and orthodoxy will emerge. In the new Christianity those who believe that Jesus is God will co-exist with those who do believe that "God was in Christ Jesus" but do not find it meaningful to say that Jesus was and is God. Hopefully the new Christianity will be slow to banish those who, while not thinking of Jesus as divine, believe that Jesus was the significant symbol of God in our historical experience. It is to be hoped that the Chalcedonians will break bread with those who simply but significantly believe that Jesus was the form and exemplar of our encounter with God and that in him we see something of the shape and hope of humanity in the Kingdom of God.

The new scriptural scholarship is not a doomsday machine. In the scriptures we have as much as we ever had, the literary expression of the religious consciousness of the early Christian Church. Even though we know the evangelists were not stenographers of Jesus providing us with a transcript of his remarks, we do have their extraordinary accounts of that religious and moral revolution in which Jesus was central. There is no bankruptcy.

Presuppositions of a Christian Moral Credo

Before suggesting the lines of a Christian moral credo, we should look at the special problems and pitfalls that greet the Christian credalist. First of all, if one thinks of a moral credo as a moral code, Jesus will be of disconcertingly little help. Even when Jesus seemed quite case-oriented and code-minded as on the issue of divorce, his teaching comes up wanting. For permanent marriage he certainly was, but as the Dominican scholar E. Schillebeeckx writes: "although Christ declared that marriage was indissoluble, he did not tell us where the element that constituted marriage was situated. . . ."[15] Thus we are thrown back on our own resources in deciding whether a particular union which is *legally* marital is *actually* marital and thus a potential manifestation of indissoluble love. Jesus is clear on the ideal but no help in deciding whether, with a particular couple, incompatibility or immaturity or sinfulness makes divorce more morally commendable than unpromising and probably destructive efforts at marital union. The early Church does not portray Jesus as a codifier. Sean Freyne writes: "There is no rigid adherence to the letter of what the master said, for the early Christian teachers, least of all Paul, cannot be regarded as Christian scribes who interpreted the words of Jesus in a casuistic manner. Rather his sayings could be interpreted, adapted and applied to new situations."[16] Whatever the moral credo will be then, it will not be a tidy list of do's and don't's. The spirit of Christ was upon the early Christians but a specific code of Christ was not.

The instinct for neatness and order is also frustrated by another fact of Christian moral experience. There is room within Christian ethics for a degree of pluralism. In truth we are still parties to the early Church's debate over the one and the many gospels. There was a strong desire in apostolic times for one single gospel that would put the story of Christ in order. The multiple gospels were severely criticized. Celsus reflected this criticism when he said that the Christians had treated the Gospel "like drunkards" by "recoining it three and four and many times."[17]

This one-Gospel movement, however, came to be seen as heretical. As Oscar Cullmann writes: "It is no mere accident that the men who were responsible for the various attempts to replace the four Gospels by a single Gospel upheld a conception of Christian teaching differing from the New Testament, and were therefore heretics."[18] Orthodoxy held that "it was impossible for this revelation, which claims to be more than mere biography, to be reproduced by one person in all its fullness. . . ."[19]

It was also impossible that the various renderings of the significance of Jesus would not contradict one another and clash in important ways. Paul's "I know in part" was as true of himself as it was of all other scriptural and subsequent Christian writers and interpreters. Disagreement, it seems, is not incompatible with the Kingdom.

These lessons are applicable to those who would address the necessary task of reconstructing the Christian moral credo. Efforts to establish a one-rubric approach which would harmonize all the disparate elements of the Christian moral heritage are in vain. Some try to unify the biblical elements under a single umbrella such as liberation maturity, covenant, responsibility, prophecy, new being in Christ, etc. The danger here is noted by Catholic University theologian Charles E. Curran: "Especially in the light of the fads which have existed in theology in the past few years there remains the constant danger of taking one aspect of the biblical message and making it so central and exclusive that the full biblical message is not properly understood."[20]

Eclecticism is also a word that imposes itself on the Christian moral credalist. When we realize that Christian experiences is not all contained in the Bible and that revelation is an ongoing and enriching part of human life, the area to be surveyed is vast. We should be prepared for the fact that there will be much within that area that we might best repudiate rather than appropriate. Walter Rauschenbusch may have been unfair to Paul when he said that Paul was a radical in theology but a social conservative, but the spirit of Rauschenbusch is correct: in shaping our Christian understanding, we may have to prefer James to Paul on certain issues.

And when we look for elements of Christian moral heritage beyond the foundational biblical literature in the historical unfolding of Christian living, more eclecticism yet will be in order. Revelation may be serene and unific in its gracious source, but since it is poured into the bumbling and sinful receptacles of humankind, we may not approach it unless the one hand is as ready to filter as the other is to receive. This, of course, presents the problem of finding the criteria whereby we reject or receive. We must turn to that issue momentarily. For now, it is well to see that when we enter the storehouse of Christian experience, we encounter sin as well as inspiration. We are faced with contradictions which make selection unavoidable. On top of this, historical Christian traditions vary. Roman Catholics and Quakers, Episcopalians and Baptists do not have the same story to tell. Four Gospels came to be seen as enough for the early Church. There is more pluralism than that today. Much of that pluralism is the product of obstinacy and sin. But much is also the natural product of the inevitable ramification that marks the unfolding of life whether physical or spiritual. At any rate, even under the sign of Christ, there will be more drummers than we can or would want to follow. Therefore, sorting and picking are part of the process of appropriation which issues into a moral credo.

A final caution is in order. Becoming steeped in Christian wisdom does not include a dispensation from homework. In setting up a moral credo, we are setting out as best we can the essential lineaments and specifying themes of Christian living. This, however, does not set us up for instant ethics. Morality consists (as does ethics, which exists to bring discernment to moral experience) in a dialogue between one's ideals, principles, and all of those things that shape our world view on the one hand; and the empirical order, which is bursting with moral meaning, on the other. The moral credo adds to the first side, but does not relieve us from wrestling with the empirical order in which moral values take on flesh. A particular moral experience such as is found in Christianity may also influence our empirical search by prolonging hope, stimulating imagination, prodding our creative powers, and explicitly valuing life, work, beauty, etc. Still, one's credo does not do one's empirical hunting, gathering, and analyzing. Not by credo alone is concrete policy wrought. Examples may illustrate this:

At the calculated risk of giving aid and comfort to bigots, let us say that one might find segregation a clear-cut violation of the inherent dignity of persons as experienced in the Christian ethos. To conclude from this, however, that busing is the only Christian response in a particular city at a particular time may be invalid. Indeed, it may represent a well-intentioned failure of imagination, and imagination ranks high in the credo of those who believe themselves made in the image of the Creator God. Of course, the failure to do anything in the face of segregation would unambiguously represent apostasy from Christianness. But searching empirical work may uncover several options other than busing that may merit Christian blessing. Shunting students from one inferior school to another may not represent the highest soaring of the human spirit and may indeed show a reluctance to do what is needed by way of radical assessment of social priorities and budgetary allocations. Where one's heart is there will his budget be. In the concrete, busing may represent the refusal of a society to correct the structural injustices which bring daily assaults on the dignity and rights of minorities. Instead, "the powers that be" prefer to shuttle lower economic level whites and blacks from school to school while suburban whites watch from afar. It would be dangerous to bring Christian morality in as the prop for such mischief.

At the same time, it may be that resistance to a specific plan such as busing may be unchristian, given the carefully studied empirical realities. Christianity does not dwell in inaccessible and inapplicable light. Thus, *Christianly perceived values are at times at issue in specific policy decisions.* And in such cases they are present in such a way *that failure to respond merits the title of sin and apostasy.* To deny *a priori* the possibility of this is to minimize the relevance of Christianity to the world of concrete decision where values ultimately come to roost.

What has been said here regarding busing as an example could be said also for other matters. To leap from the Christian moral credo to a certain form of socialism or a certain form of capitalism as the only orthodoxy, is unsound. Also, new sexual life styles may or may not be depersonalizing and desocializing and thus wrong, but the point will not be made simply by by-passing the gritty work of analysis to flaunt one's credal stance as an adequate base for judgment.

In general, it can be said, that the more specific the policy directive or moral stance, the more dangerous it is to overleap the empirical analysis. And the more overleaping we do, the more discredit is brought to our beliefs and the less are they useful for serving the process of humanization.

Shaping a Credo

Sheer eclecticism is chaos. There must be some base upon which we stand to do our choosing; otherwise we would be rudderless, judging without criteria. We must look for a theological base with which the various specifying themes of Christian moral existence link and interrelate. Ideally, this base would appear as foundational and central in the Christian story. Such a critical base is available, I submit, in the notion of the Kingdom of God. Alan Richardson writes: " 'The Kingdom of God' is the central theme of the teaching of Jesus, and it involves his whole understanding of his own person and work."[21] The reign of God is central both as subject and as motive in the preaching of Jesus. In Schnackenburg's words: "Generally speaking, the principle subject of Jesus' preaching, the reign of God and its advent, also provides the most powerful of motives."[22]

Though the language of the kingdom is most characteristic of the synoptics (it is found only twice in John and ten times in the Pauline literature), the thought within this language is a pervasive theological presence in the early Christian experience. In this theological sense we can understand why T. W. Manson could cite as "fact" "that the ethic of the Bible, from beginning to end, is the ethic of the Kingdom of God."[23]

The pregnant notion of the reign of God put Jesus into basic conflict with Judaism, for Jesus used it in setting himself up as a rival authority to the Law.[24] Indeed, it set Jesus in confrontation with the world beyond Israel. As Richardson observes, Jesus used it to make it clear "that he was concerned with nothing less than the renewal of the world on the lines of God's original purpose."[25]

Several things about this rich notion must be seen at the outset. It has important meaning in two tenses. In the present it says that God is perceived as active in history and in the moral vision of Jesus. However, God is not yet all in all. It has not yet appeared what we will be. The idea of the reign of God makes us Christians kin of Herbert Marcuse when he says with meaningful enigma: "That which is cannot be true."[26] The presently given is not enough, not definitive. The now is heavy with the not yet. God has begun, but in so doing God summons us to radical openness to the future. The reign of God is a call to adventure, not a stabilization of the *status quo*. As such it is profoundly relativizing. Present structures, perceptions, and pieties may not lock us in and stifle us, for the reign of God is movement which brooks no atrophy.

The application of this idea is revolutionary. We are immersed personally and socially in false absolutes and this doctrine accosts them all. Philosopher Eric Voegelin writes: "The Christians were persecuted for a good reason; there was a revolutionary substance in Christianity that made it incompatible with paganism. . . . What made Christianity so dangerous was its uncompromising, radical de-divinization of the world."[27] The Kingdom of God was no harmless flight of idyllic rhetoric in the early Christian vocabulary. "Thy Kingdom come" is an unsettling aspiration.

The Kingdom, of course was not formless, and this is why it grounds the shaping of a moral credo. There were certain qualities and themes that would mark its unfolding. First of all there is hope.

The God whose Kingdom this is, is a "God of hope" whose creative spirit "will remove all bounds to hope" (Rom. 15:13). The end for the Christian is not death, but resurrection—a decidedly hopeful posture. Hope defines three things about which everyone must decide: the stance before *tragedy, the suicidal option,* and *fate.*

Tragedy is so real that it is by no means obvious that hope is sustainable. At this writing, thousands of mangled bodies are being collected after a Guatemala earthquake. Orphaned and bleeding children, looking out from the rubble that was their home, face television cameras with stunned faces and broken hearts. Tragedy is the denial of hope, and they exemplify it. In the sight of such, can we babble on about our "God of hope"?

Christians acting Christianly do *not* do certain things in the face of tragedy: they do not pretend to understand how God could let it be; neither do they retreat to the mechanism of denial or to the obnoxious insipidities of "a blessing in disguise." What they do first of all is to respond to the victims of the tragedy, and, not letting themselves "drift away from the hope promised by the Good News" (Col. 1:23), they fix their pained vision on the preciousness that coexists with tragedy and seems ultimately more real. Christian hope is no bland optimism. It is even compatible with turbulent streams of despair. It survives amid chaos and bears the wounds that are the insignia of that chaos. It is ultimately more impressed with good than with evil, with what is and can be rather than with what is not. It is convinced that, whatever chaos is, it is not the name of God.

Hope has an activist quality in the Christian ethos. It is the vigorous alternative to the suicidal option. In the words of the Christian existentialist philosopher Gabriel Marcel, hope "underpins action or it runs before it . . . it is the most active saints who carry hope to its highest degree." Thinking of hope as an inactive state of the soul comes, says Marcel, "from a stoical representation of the will as a stiffening of the soul, whereas it is on the contrary relaxation and creation."[28] Hoping Christianly is not standing on the sidelines pining for the best. It is rather a drive toward action that comes with believing one's self to be, in the striking phrase of Thomas Aquinas, "a participator in divine providence."[29] In this sense hope is the antithesis of the suicidal option. I do not refer here to the physical termination of life,[30] but to the gradual, psychical withdrawal from life by someone who is more impressed by life's negativities than by its possibilities. The marks of the suicidal option are the marks of death: detachment, coldness, insensitivity. Overwhelmed by the anomalies, the suicidal option says no. Hope, struggling in the darkness of faith, says yes.

Hope is also thus the alternative to fatalism, for which there is no room in the Christian credo. H. Richard Niebuhr writes:

[Jesus] sees as others do that the sun shines on criminals, delinquents, hypocrites, honest men, good Samaritans, and VIP's without discrimination, that rains come down in equal proportions on the fields of the diligent and of the lazy. These phenomena have been for unbelief, from the beginning of time, signs of the operation of a universal order that is without justice, unconcerned with right and wrong conduct among men. But Jesus interprets the common phenomena in another way: here are the signs of cosmic generosity. The response to the weather so interpreted leads then also to a response to criminals and outcasts, who have not been cast out by the infinite Lord.[31]

Notice the practical conclusions (material content) that flow from Jesus' hopeful interpretation of reality. In the heart of all human experience is a contest between hope and fatalism, between confidence in life and cynicism. Christianity comes down mightily on the side of hope, believing as it does that unconcern is not the last word of reality, but rather, that "deep down things" there is love, supreme artistry, and gracious creativity. This good news points toward and should yield practical fruits in creative response, in lived concern, and in increasing harmonization of all that is, animate and inanimate, within the Kingdom.

Love

Love is a many-caricatured word. Every moral tradition must speak to its meaning, since being moral means loving well. Christianity has spoken to it, and in a revolutionary way. Christianity gave human life a value that it did not have in a world where it was dwarfed by the *polis* and the *cosmos*. In Christianity, human life, including individual human life, was so valuable, so worthy of love, that even in death it would not perish. Hannah Arendt writes: "the Christian 'glad tidings' of the immortality of individual human life had reversed the ancient relationship between man and world and promoted the most mortal thing, human life, to the position of immortality, which up to then the cosmos had held . . . only with the rise of Christianity, did life on earth also become the highest good of man . . . [the modern age] never even thought of challenging this fundamental reversal which Christianity had brought into the dying ancient world."[32]

That the value of human life verged on the absolute was stressed in other ways. Loving as Jesus loved was paradigmatic. Laying down one's life for friends not only made sense; it was the apex of love. God is love and would hold us as a mother or father does an infant. In God's eyes the very hairs of our heads are numbered and we are called by name, not lost in the mass. In Christian loving all divisive and superficial distinctions melt, such as those between Jew and Gentile, freedman and slave. "National interest" pales in this universalist élan, as does every other form of private or collective egoism.

And Christian love, like Christian hope, is activist. Lived love, not piety, holds the primacy in this view. Significantly, apart from the great commandment where loving God and loving people are indissolubly conjoined. Jesus nowhere spoke explicitly about loving God.[33] It is too easy to liturgize or pietize loving feelings, to exhaust their fire in gestures or while offering gifts at the altar. Liturgy has its place, to re-enforce the habit of contemplation, to remember, and to celebrate, but without lived love, it is not worship. The test of love is action.

Prophecy

In Jewish and Christian thought, the prophet stands out as the *social conscience* of the people.[34] Jesus was perceived as a prophet and Christian morality is essentially prophetic. A prophet is one who stands at the piercing point of evolving social conscience. The prophets animating genius is *sensitivity* and *compassion*, especially for the *anawim*, the benighted poor, the powerless, the exploited base of society. Prophecy excoriates those "who trample on the needy and try to suppress the poor people of the country" (Amos 8:4). The prophet discovers the Uriahs and the Bathshebas of the world and accosts the Davids who would use and abuse them.

The prophets were *political* beings, who perhaps could distinguish but could not separate the terms *moral* and *political*. In politics is the life blood of the *anawim*, and so prophetic religion is political by definition.

The prophets were *eccentric* if not bizarre by the standards of the contemporary society. They were at odds with the current respectability and were, for their own purposes, troublemakers. "He is inflaming the people . . . from Galilee, where he started, down to here" (Luke 23:5). If they were at times outrageous in word and action (Isaiah "walked about naked and barefoot" for three years) it was, perhaps because they sensed that only outrage speaks to outrage, only outrageous symbol speaks to outrageous insensitivity.

And they had *courage*, that rare virtue that is so discountenanced in decadent times, but which represents the flowering of Christian moral existence. The prophets knew that you had to hate your life to find it. Isaiah was sawed in half; Jeremiah was stoned to death; Jesus was crucified. History is splattered with prophets' blood.

The prophets were *traditionalists* too. In Israel, they did not call for the abandonment of origins but for renewal in continuity with the best moments of the past. They called Israel back to her promising origins when God spoke to her heart and she listened.

Prophecy is a rich tradition which takes unique form in the Jewish and Christian religions. It is clearly a mark of the Kingdom and must be an informing presence in any Christian moral creed. (See Chapter Two, "The Primacy of Justice in Moral Theology," for a development of the biblical prophetic spirit of justice.)

Joy

Joy is also a property of the kingdom, proleptically present now and pointing to greater fulfillment. Joy is not superficial effervescence. It springs, rather, from the perceived possibilities of the reign of God. As such it is a child of hope. It is also a sister to prophecy, for it is not egoistic joy, but rather essentially social. It cannot be full while sisters and brothers are in misery.

In the Christian vision, joy is normal and normative. The normalcy of joy is a minority report filed by Christians and little children. For most of the rest, pessimism and gloom seem more normal and accurately reflective of the really real. Gloomy fatalism is rampant even where not thematically professed. The normalcy of misery is the gospel of "the world."

Misery in the Christian view is not normal; it is not the product of inexorable *karma* or all-powerful unfeeling fate; it is, rather, to be attacked.

In summary, joy in the Christian ethos has a vibrant social conscience. It is rooted in hope and prophecy and confidence in the reign of God. Only with this in mind could we make sense of Schnacken-burg's comment which would otherwise seem superficially lyrical: "What Jesus in fact wanted was not to revive penitential practices wher-ever he went, but to spread joy."[35]

Creativity

Made in the image of the Creator-God, we are by destiny creative. We may of course fail that destiny, but the Christian views himself (herself) as a co-creator, co-provider, and trusted steward within the kingdom. Christian genius and work must not be seduced into an adul-terous union with the *status quo*. Christians are committed to escaping the stranglehold of the currently given, whether in their mind, insti-tutions, or in any aspect of life. The glory of personhood is in per-ceiving not just what is, but what can be. A person who is fully alive is committed to the discovery of the more that is implicit in the less. Lived Christianity is a creative nuisance for all who have yielded to the competing gospel of low expectations.

Peace

In much of modern thinking as in classical Greek, peace denotes the absence of conflict. It is negative in its primary meaning. Peace as a development of the Hebrew *shalom* is a positive and comprehensive notion. It signifies "the untrammelled free growth of the soul (i.e. per-son) . . . harmonious community; the soul can only expand in con-junction with other souls . . . every form of happiness and free expansion, but the kernel of it is the community with others, the foun-dation of life."[36]

Peace then implies the experience of a community knit together with self-giving, agapaic love. Fed by the vision of the Hebraic proph-ets, the word peace was bursting with meaning for the early Christians. It was a summation word of their moral beliefs, appearing prominently in their liturgies, as well as in greetings and in epitaph. To die "in peace" implied a fulfillment of Christian living.

Reconciliation

Peace is closely tied to the idea of reconciling and to the experience of God as one whose distinctive act is reconciliation. To recognize this God is to be targeted as ambassadors of reconciliation; and directed against all hostile divisions, whether they be among or between persons, or between persons and the parent earth.

This list of the specifying themes of Christian existence is offered as suggestive, not exhaustive. The themes of the credo as presented are biblically rooted but not biblically confined, since revelation is not a prisoner of the Bible and theology is not the art of repetition. These themes are here presented as developed both by biblical exegesis and, one hopes, by creative theological reflection upon the ongoing revelation. Theological attention should be focused now upon the specifying themes of the Christian moral experience. Christian theologians should at least recognize with James Gustafson, "that if one experiences the reality of God, particularly in the context of Christian history and life, there are or ought to be consequences for the sort of person one becomes morally. . . . In the conviction that certain experiences of the Holy, certain beliefs about God, are valid, persons and communities see (understand, interpret) the significance of historical events, of man's relationship to nature, of themselves, to be different from what other persons do."[37] Recognizing that, the prime theological task becomes one of specifying what is "different." In theological ethics this means attempting, as I have done, to plot out the shape of a Christian moral credo.

The question for Christian ethics is not whether there is a distinctively Christian ethic, but what it is. Also, this discussion should not be further impaled on the epistemologically untenable position that there may be distinctively Christian attitudes, dispositions, intentions, and goals without resonating distinctiveness at the level of "material content." Taken as a totality, the themes of the Christian moral experience are distinctive. Whatever common ground may be found, no other tradition has the identical system of symbols, heroes, motives, hopes, and inclinations. In no other system does an identical personology (or an identical conception of the *humanum*) emerge, and person is the key term from which all ethics derives.

Christians and others will come to many similar conclusions and do many similar things, but the fruits of each will not be growing from the same soil nor will the goodness of each fruit be based on sameness. Christians living Christianly will have their own way of caring and daring, persisting and hoping, enduring and rejoicing. This may not make them better, but it will make them different at the level of practical moral judgment as well as at the practical behavioral level. A great creed married to conscience is not without distinctive issue.[38]

CHAPTER 17

Service on the Common: A Portrait of the Ethicist

Ethics is a critique of conscience. Like conscience, it is a zone of episte-mological complexity, breadth, and mystery. The joy and the pain of ethics is that everyone is at it. Ethics is the common where all of life meets. We are "the valuing animal," as Schopenhauer put it, and while we live, we breathe and evaluate with equal inevitability. The problem is that it is the way of the lay to operate with no examined method, but with tacitly controlling methodic assumptions. The ethicist is the method-ist, the professional who is to show others what they are doing and how they might do it more sensitively and freely. Our prime yield is method. Our prime temptation is issue-hopping.

Issue-hopping is evasive action for ethicists since our elucidations of how we moral mortals know is our first service. Our conclusions flow from our method and are integrally intelligible only in the light of it. The issue-fixated ethicist is like an oceanographer who studies only waves while ignoring the tides and currents that carry the undular surface. We should not have to guess at the methodic assumptions of well-published ethicists or to comb their writings to know what implicit method operates there.

In my *The Moral Choice* (1978) and in the central chapters of *A New American Justice* (1979) is the heart of my recent service to method. I start with the assumption that moral truth has a special sublimity. To know that water boils and freezes and that metal expands when heated is a solid experience of truth and can be proved in kitchen or laboratory. But to know that promises must be honored, even when the promisee is dead, or that persons are worth suffering for and even dying for, or that the white male monopoly must be dismantled, or that political and economic power must serve the internationalization of community or be resisted—the *knowing* involved in all of that is not a *quantum* but a *quale* leap, a leap in kind, beyond scientific knowing. Reductionism here is unforgiveable.

The foundational experience of moral knowing, I argue, is an affective-mystical, faith process of knowing (1978, Chapter Three, "The Meaning of Morals").* The experience of the value of persons and their environment, which is the ground of moral knowledge, is all of that. This does not condemn us to "moral sense" or emotivist simplisms. The foundational moral experience which is born at the precordial levels where affection and cognition cannot be neatly severed rises to expression and is served in its effability by logic and reasoning, by principles and metaphysics. But the effable and the ineffable of it is served, too, by creative imagination, by experiencing life in and through communities, by the sense of the tragic and the comic, by feeling, by the arts, and by the trusting discovery of reliable authorities. The shape of all of this an ethical method must try to sketch. In doing this, it must avoid any one-rubric approach which would put all stress on consequences or on reason or on feeling or on intuition or on sectarian experiences. The quest of ethics reaches into mystery; an holistic and humble approach is the methodic ideal.

The Intellectualistic Fallacy

Speaking of method has already led to the affections that cradle moral knowing. The ethicist must know that ethics rises from caring and caring is cognitive. Missing this leads to what I have called "the intellectualistic fallacy" (1982b). A denuded rationalism pervades much of philosophical and theological ethics. By ignoring the affective animating mold of moral knowledge, ethics is shrunken and sight is lost of the relationship of moral awareness to mysticism, contemplation, faith, and religious experience. Such fleshless rationalism also leads to the adoption of false paradigms for moral knowing drawn from science, mathematics, or linguistics.

To allow for the affective dimension of moral knowing, to speak with the Thomistic school of the "affective knowledge" of the good and the sacred, takes much of the tidiness out of ethics. For ethicists bent on tidiness, this is clearly a shame. But if life is sloppy and ethics neat, the two will only happenstantially meet.

---

*References are listed at the end of this chapter.

A lot of cognitional action is missed by the intellectualistic fallacy. The epistemology of ethics is also an epistemology of affect. Great moral truths are felt before they can be brought to articulation. Emotive, affective uneasiness is often the penumbra of major criticism. Myth, ideology, cognitive moods, and conscience-numbing biases operate for good or for ill in the powerful netherlands of affect. The affective orientation called character must also be appreciated as an active hermeneutical agency. Worst of all, the intellectualistic fallacy misses the centrality of creative imagination in ethics. The divine task of creative imagination, "the supreme faculty of moral persons," is to "find the possibilities of order in 'the formless void' and begin the rout of chaos" (1978, 189). But the creative *eureka* is an *affective* explosion of intelligence. "Creativity is imaginative insight born of the emotions of love and desire" (1978, 198).

Where Knowing is Also Believing

My next book is tentatively entitled *A Moral Creed for All Christians (and Other Practitioners of Humanity)*. (For those familiar with my wheel model of method, this will be the tire on the rim.)

St. Paul saw only half the truth when he said that the just person lives by faith. So too the unjust. Faith is not antithetical to knowledge; it is what we know believingly. Faith is an affective-cognitive role beyond the simplicities that are available to sight and proof. Human life (and ethics) is founded on faith-knowledge. Whether we speak of the Revolution of the Proletariat; of Liberty, Fraternity, and Equality; or of Life, Liberty, and the Pursuit of Happiness; the epistemological happening is in the realm of faith. We can prove none of these things, but we can know them passionately through faith.

Faith is ubiquitous in the human nousphere. Anyone who knows that persons are worth justice, or that "the rule of law" is better than "the rule of man," is a believer. To aver with Socrates that it is better to suffer injustice than to perpetrate it is a faith stance. Even the most abstracted analytical ethicists—with their coded messages and all—are head high in faith. What you believe about persons and their environment is controlling in even the most reduced modes of ethics.

And so my next book. Although many of my writings are explicitly credal and steeped in Judeo-Christian-Catholic traditions, *The Moral Choice* was offered as "philosophy," as I reached to all interested in moral truth. Yet *The Moral Choice*, as ethics, was implicitly faith-full. By definition. Needed now, a further and formal explicitation of the faith that is in me. I will seek to do two things in this aborning book: explain the theology that is in philosophy (and elsewhere) and chart out the core moral beliefs of Judeo-Christianity. (See Chapter Sixteen above.)

Theology is a bruised term and needs redefinition. It is used derogatorily in much political science and sociological writing—as a kind of intransigent, impervious, and fact-shy ideologism, the opposite of clear and hard-nosed realism. By philosophers, "theology" is generally ignored—seen as more devotional than bright, even though the major developments in ethical method of late have come under "theological" rather than under "philosophical" auspices.

My effort is to show that philosophy and theology are unnaturally divided. Their divorce was made in hell. My definition of theology, I know, will raise the protectionist hackles of those who ply philosophy in today's terms. Nevertheless, descriptively and insistently, I see theology as this: a quest to know whether things ultimately make sense. It is a probe into the truth which always escapes even our best answers. It is concerned with the ultimate and questionable reliability of reality and the plausibility of sustainable hope. It pokes curiously into the mystery that envelops all of our debates. Theology insists that awe is central to any authentic wisdom. Sometimes it uses God-talk; sometimes not. Theology is not the ward of the churches or synagogues, which are often enough its tomb. Sometimes it is called practical wisdom; sometimes philosophy. Often it goes forth in deceptive drag and operates in social sciences, constitutional law, and economics. Theology is both practical and theoretical: practical inasmuch as the choosing animal makes choices that build or unbuild our planetary *polis* and that enhance or sabotage the sharing patterns that are the conditions of human life. It is theoretical because it probes consistencies, apparently revelatory events or "peak experiences" of meaning-making, and past moral and religious articulations in their inevitable partiality and incompleteness.

But, then, all of this could be worthily pursued by any holistic and sensitive "philosophy". That is the point. Philosophy and theology are as one. The current division, I submit, is an historical accident. Both are works of logic, reasoning, and metaphysics, but also of faith in and affective appreciation of the human mystery. Both stand humbly before that mystery and make of it what they can. Specializations there must be—given the breadth of the quest and the creativity of the participants—but the enterprise is one.

I recognize with appropriate hopelessness that such ideas threaten havoc to the sacred structures of disciplines and departments and could not, without breach of reverence, be entertained. Instead, philosophy and theology shall go forward like separate nation-states, with their borders guarded, ignoring their natural commonality and shared vocation. The honest searcher for truth, however, need not be imprisoned by in-structured falsity.

Meanwhile, theology has the advantage. We can explore and test the faith that *we* admit is in us, purging out the old leaven while growing, in true traditionalism, with what is best in our historical credal resources. The creed I am working on is Judeo-Christian, taking full account of the fact that Jesus was more Jewish than Christian—as the latter term is often used. The creed seeks out the essential specifying themes of a Judeo-Christian moral vision. (For my explicit development of the Judeo-Christian dimension of a specifically Christian ethics, see 1974, 1976, 1980, 1983a). The reign of God, a rich category that births a worldview, is the first article of the creed. Justice is the hallmark of the reign; it is incipient love and the only form thus far that love takes in the political and economic order. Other themes such as prophecy, hope, love, the normative normalcy of joy, creativity, peace, reconciliation, and others will flesh out the moral creed. The creed seeks out the good news that we can share with "every creature" (Mk. 16:15) and then listen to their gospels to find what God has wrought elsewhere while we Christians were otherwise engaged.

The Priority of Issues

The whole world is the ethicist's oyster, and so priorities are a must. Let me dare to suggest where our energies are most needed.

(1) *Racism.* Black persons are the perennial orphans of American conscience. Even the Reagan-engineered ending of the second short civil rights movement in our history moves us white ethicists only slightly. On justice issues I contend that we suffer from an *al di là* complex, a preferential absorption in issues that are *al di là*, way out there. We prefer Chad to Watts, Afghanistan to Brooklyn, Santiago to Milwaukee's inner core. There is some apparent sense to this. After all, nuclear war and international revolution seem more important than rat bites and joblessness. But might I preachily suggest that the white Christian ethics establishment should know that prophecy begins at home and then moves on to the massively important issues that exist *al di là*. The test of the prophetic spirit is in the prophet's response to the *anawim* at the doorstep. In the United States, the quintessential *anawim* are black, and yet they remain invisible in much of our eco-

nomic, political, and ethical analysis. Their *qualitatively* distinct plight is not acknowledged.[1]

(2) *Feminism.* Sexism is original sin, the perversion of the male-female dyad that constitutes the human molecule. Its fallout touches *all* our institutions and products (1982a).

Feminism is of particular urgency in Catholicism where exclusivist masculinism reigns from the altars to the heavens. I have urged Catholic ethicists and prelates to candid service on the institutionally dangerous issue of reproductive ethics (1983b). Abortion, particularly, has become the orthodoxy stakeout in today's Catholicism. Truth and justice cry for candor and courage here. There is no one normative Catholic position for all abortion decisions. The anguished minority of women who face abortion decisions have a right to know that. Justice too is owed to the Mansours, and Drinans, and to the Sisters of Mercy who have wounded in various ways on the reproductive issue. Tenured Catholic scholars who find this issue too hot to handle, or just uninteresting, are not on my "most admired" list.

(3) *Peace. Shalom* is the only permissible single-issue fixation. Militarism is the alternate faith option to Shalom; it is faith in arms. The militaristic faith option sucks out some forty million dollars per hour twenty-four hours a day from the American bloodstream. It is militarism which is a major cause of hunger, a symptom of malignant tribal-nationalism, a perversion of political power, and a distraction of creative intelligence. The ethical agenda is urgent and enormous.

In Fine

Let me conclude by singing lauds to our profession. Theological ethics has moved from micro- to macro-ethics. We are now less like those German chaplains who accompanied the *Wehrmacht* in the invasion of the Netherlands warning the soldiers against the Dutch prostitutes while overlooking the Second World War and the Holocaust. We are less inclinded to ignore the institution of slavery while quibling about the number of slaves that can be humanely carried on a slave ship. We are looking more to our roots in the rich Judeo-Christian traditions. That is progress. And yet, for all of that, we must admit to "unprofitable servant" status. Our ministry on the common of life remains too meager by far.

References

1974 "Dreams and Facts in Church and State". *The Saint Luke's Journal of Theology* 18/1, 21–37.

1976 "Credal Conscience: A Question of Moral Orthodoxy". *Anglican Theological Review,* Supplementary Series 6, 37–54.

1978 *The Moral Choice.* Garden City: Doubleday, 1978; Minneapolis: Winston Press, 1979.

1979 *A New American Justice: Ending the White Male Monopolies.* Garden City: Doubleday, 1980; Minneapolis: Winston Press, 1981.

1980 "Ministry and Morals". *Ministries* 1/4, 11–13.

1982a Chapter Nine, "Feminization of God and Ethics."

1982b Chapter Twenty, "The Knowing Heart and the Intellectualistic Fallacy."

1983a Chapter Two, "The Primacy of Justice in Moral Theology". *Horizons* 10/1, 72–85.

1983b "Abortion: A Question of Catholic Honesty". *The Christian Century* 100/26, 803–07.

CHAPTER 18

Pigeon Ethics: The Moral Philosophy of B. F. Skinner

The story is told that Jonathan Swift once sat in a village square watching a fishmonger as she prattled and chatted through an afternoon of business. When his bemused and reveried watch was over, he passed by and mystified her by saying: "Would that I could be as sure of one thing as you are of everything." After reading *Beyond Freedom and Dignity*, I would address a similar comment to Burrhus Frederic Skinner. The world of Skinner is a simple one. Unfortunately, the world in which we dwell is not.

Subtle and sensitive minds have long pondered the human mystery and have wondered over the meaning of phenomena such as culture, creativity, heroism, sacrificial love, transcendence, freedom, personal dignity, religion, patriotism, and guilt. Skinner would see all these ponderings as the myopic gropings of prescientific persons, for Skinner has the answers to these and to most other questions tidily wrapped and scientifically boxed.

No one can be unimpressed by the ingenious work that Skinner the scientist has done. But this is not a book of experimental science. This is a book of philosophy and of ethics, a book which theorizes about what we are and what we ought to be.

Skinner is here philosophizing on and applying to the human scene what he has learned in his laboratory. He is not, however, really alert to the fact there is a qualitative leap involved when you move from the behavior of pigeons to the behavior of people. He does, indeed, allow that "pigeons aren't people," but the unwritten premise of his book is the *people are pigeons*. From this premise flow the remarkable simplicities that lead Skinner beyond freedom and dignity and even beyond common sense.

All of which raises the very fair question: why has Skinner been able to cause such a stir and to summon response from so many fine and learned minds? Partly this is due to the fact that there is a perverse and rare delight involved in encountering someone who is, on so many basic human issues, so outrageously and unabashedly wrong. But there is more to the Skinner event than that. It might indeed be that there is a small amount of Skinner in the moral and educational philosophy of the best of us that makes us all uneasy when the real Skinner stands up in full view. The questions, then, are two: what is Skinner saying and why are we reacting to it? Both questions can be answered by looking at both Skinnerian wisdom and Skinnerian nonsense.

Skinnerian Wisdom

First of all, and happily for all of us, no one is all wrong. Skinner is no exception to this. Much of what he says makes good sense. For example: when he says "complete individualism or complete freedom" is wrong, he is right. Any value absolutized becomes demonic, including freedom. Human freedom is not absolute or complete; it is limited by the right and needs of others. Bigots defends racism in the name of freedom. American business speaks of "free trade" to defend the exploitation of economically weaker nations. People speak of "free love" to dignify exploitative sexual encounters. Freedom covers a multitude of sins in our culture and Skinner does well to highlight the natural limits of freedom.

Skinner is right again when he urges that rewards work better than punishment and that "when treated aversively people tend to act aggressively." This is true. Harshness and violence tend to be counterproductive. That gospel should be welcomed, by whomever it is preached.

Again, if we prescind from the totality of control that Skinner gives the environment, we can accept new emphases on the fact that environment does exert major controlling influence. A truly human environment will promote behavioral patterns that are more human. Here is a lesson that many institutions (prisons and schools, for example) are slow to learn.

Finally, Skinner does well to point out how much "aversive" and unjust control people put up with too willingly. "Many people have submitted to the most obvious religious, governmental, and economic

controls for centuries, striking for freedom only sporadically, if at all."
It is a work of prophecy to call attention to the fact that obedience to
oppressive political, religious, and other authorities is objectionable. It
is another manifestation of the cowardly tendency of all of us to sacrifice both freedoms and justice to security.

Skinnerian Nonsense

Unfortunately, these good suggestions in Skinner are not developed
and are presented in the shadow of his master image of person as
pigeon.

The moral philosophy of B. F. Skinner can be captured under four
rubrics: all power to the environment, "psychology without a psyche,"
ethics without morality, and life without mystery.

All power to the environment! In simple terms, what Skinner is telling
us is that people are Charley McCarthys and the environment is Edgar
Bergen. Prescientific children used to personify Charley and attribute
his words and movements to what they thought to be his *self*. Scientific
person knows that Edgar was doing it all the time and that Charley's
activities were the product of a "controlling environment." And so
Skinner says that the prescientific view was that "a person's behavior
is at least to some extent his own achievement." Not so. As science
advances, we move to the conclusion that "the achievements for which
a person himself is to be given credit seem to approach zero. . . ." As
far as human behavior and achievements are concerned, "A scientific
analysis shifts both the responsibility and the achievement to the environment." To the environment also goes all blame or credit: "A scientific analysis shifts the credit as well as the blame to the environment.
. . ."

*"Psychology without a psyche."** For Skinner, all behavior is reduced
to interaction with the external environment. There is no internal environment, no inner self, no mind, no personality. In a word "we do
not need to try to discover what personalities, states of mind, feelings,
traits of characters, plans, purposes, intentions, or the other prerequisites of autonomous man 'really are' in order to get on with a scientific analysis of behavior."

Once upon a time, says Skinner, simple people used to explain
physical events by attributing human qualities of will and emotion to

---

*The term is used by Peter Caws, a philosopher who teachers at Hunter College, in a
piercing review of *Beyond Freedom and Dignity* in *The New Republic*, October 16, 1971, pp.
32–34.

things. For example, ancient physics taught that a falling body accelerated because it grew more jubilant as it found itself nearer home. Thrown objects were said to acquire "impetuosity." Good, scientific physics stopped attributing human qualities to inanimate objects. Likewise psychology will advance if we stop attributing "human behavior to intentions, purposes, aims, and goals." As philosopher, Peter Caws, summarizes Skinner's psychology, scientific progress will follow in psychology "if we could stop attributing human characteristics to human beings." So there it is: it was good physics to depersonalize inanimate things (we can only agree); it is good psychology to depersonalize persons (we can only gasp).

Ethics without morality. Ethics is a large problem for Skinner. He does ask the classical ethical questions: "Can we define the good life?" "What, in a word, is the meaning of life, for the individual or the species?" He does not answer these questions. Instead, he assumes that people would naturally agree on what the good life is and then he goes on with his call for an environment that will produce this good life.

His treatment of particular moral values is not so much true ethics as it is true mechanics. In fact he calls it "a technology of behavior." It is also a kind of unrefined Ayn Rand program of selfishness. The reason you should not lie or steal is that it will cause you trouble. You will suffer disapproval and punishment. The result is a superficial, self-centered, pragmatic explanation of moral obligation. "If you tend to avoid punishment, avoid stealing." "If you are reinforced by the approval of your fellow man, you will be reinforced when you tell the truth." If you do not behave monstrously with your fellows, it is not because of "a sense of responsibility or obligation", neither is it because of "loyalty or respect for others." It is simply "because they have arranged effective social contingencies." Furthermore, "we should not attribute behaving for the good of others to a love of others." All such behavior "depends upon the control exerted by the social environment."

All complex explanations about civil religion, the experience of the sacred, and transcending self-sacrifice are swept away with staggering simplicity. "A person does not support his government because he is loyal but because the government has arranged special contingencies." "A person does not support a religion because he is devout; he supports it because of the contingencies arranged by the religious agency." (One wonders where Skinner found either governments or religious agencies organized enough to organize all those contingencies.) A man "behaves bravely when environmental circumstance induce him to do so." What then, we may query, makes a hero? A hero is someone who is addicted to and controlled by the reinforcements of praise and adulation. Thus reinforced, the Hero "takes on more and more dangerous assignments, until he is killed." (It seems that a greater "ego trip" than this no one has—to lay down life for one's friends.)

The behavior of the hero is not unlike the phototropic behavior of the moth whose proclivity for light "proves lethal when it leads into flame." So much for the hero as a phototropic moth. So much too for an "ethics" without freedom, virtue or evil, without love, respect, or generosity, where all credit and all blame belong to the environment.

Life without mystery. Hamlet refers to a humanity "sicklied o'er with the pale cast of thought." Skinner offers a humanity "sicklied o'er with the pale cast" of technology. There is no mystery of love in Skinner. Indeed there is no love; there is only response to environment. Skinner does no justice to the strange capacity that people have so to value one another that they can transcend the narrow structures of egoism in the marvelous phenomenon of benevolence. We can discover in the world of persons values so great that, when they are at issue, we will die to all "reinforcements," including life, to defend them.

There is also the mystery of beauty and the ecstasy that beauty provokes in the beholder. Skinner's soulless technology has no light to shed here. Human dignity is also emasculated in Skinner's terrible reductionism. It becomes the grasping of environed people for credit to which, controlled as we are, we ultimately have no right. Admiration becomes a pale thing, the product of ignorance. It seems that "the behavior we admire is the behavior we cannot yet explain." Whole philosophical systems which grappled with the human mystery such as "idealism, dialectical materialism, or Calvinism" are simply "the effect of environmental conditions which it would not be hard to trace, but the conditions must have existed and should not be ignored." (Is this a science if it conceives a theory and then says that the supporting data now hard to trace must have existed?!)

There is another mystery to which Skinner's theories blind him . . . the mystery of evil. Ever since Freud revealed the nature of neurotic guilt, there has been a tendency to forget that there is such a thing as real, un-neurotic guilt. The nether but real side of our capacity for greatness is our capacity for evil. This, too, is part of the human mystery. Dietrich Bonhoeffer wrote: "One is distressed by the failure of reasonable people to perceive either the depths of evil or the depths of the holy." These and other depths remain unplumbed in the unreal and mystery-free simplicity of Skinnerism.

The Skinner in our closets. It would be well for educators to acknowledge that they are in the business of control. Education, whether done in family or in school, is in fact, one of the most powerful forms of control in society. Even in the current educational climate, where it is more and more recognized that students are persons and not products and where the image of teacher as martinet is passing, the controlling influence of a teacher is enormous. We control by what we tell and by what we do not tell. We open some doors and leave others closed and unmentioned. We communicate attitudes, values, and myths. In a word, we exert major control not only on *what* a student knows, but, more importantly, on *how* he or she knows. It is the *how* that usually endures and controls when much of the *what* has slipped through memory's fragile grasp.

Sometimes the controlling power of education is acknowledged, though described in terms less offensive than *control*. This is so in religious education where certain values are overtly professed and the instruction geared to promote some patterns of behavior and exclude others. In so-called secular or public education, however, the control is not acknowledged and is therefore probably more powerful since it operates in the guise of unalloyed and unbiased objectivity. A popular illusion exists that public education can be "objective" in the sense of value-free and that this is something of an Americn democratic ideal. It is, of course, neither an ideal nor a fact. Human consciousness is not value-free and neither are human schools. In a true sense, all schools are parochial in that they represent a particular and inevitably limited view of reality and of values. This view is communicated and exercises a considerable control over the perceptions and behavior of students. (Middle Americans, for obvious example, are learning more than the three R's in the public and private schools of this land. They are learning the values and creeds that are woven into the American culture and the American civil religion.)

At any rate, although the controlling influence of education has limits and can be transcended, it should be recognized as real and, to some degree, inevitable. If our educational institutions are not to be Skinnerian boxes in which our pigeons do figure eights without any critical intelligence operating, then moral evaluation must be an active part of every curriculum. Ethics should not be an isolated elective which ponders the thought of dead men but an alert discipline that analyzes the value judgments that roam controllingly in the humanities and social sciences. The alternative to that is provincialism and control.

CHAPTER 19

The Knowing Heart and the Intellectualistic Fallacy

There are three areas which are most revealing of a systematic ethicist's methodological hand. Even if the ethicist does not offer us an explicit unpacking of his/her method and presuppositions—which at some point the ethicist should—the treatment of *guilt*, *moral principles*, and *practical reason* will tell much of the tale. Each of these issues is at the crossways of so many methodological considerations, that there is no hiding if these issues are addressed at any significant depth.

My subject is practical moral reasoning, and, as my opening comment suggests, my treatment will be broad, since it is my foundational asumption that you cannot touch so critical a category without unveiling your underlying epistemological assumptions. My initial focus will be on Thomas Aquinas and his idea of *ratio practica*. In the Thomistic line, *ratio practica* is reason at work in the service of ethics. The concept of practical reason, however, is suggestive and complex. Mainly and clearly in Thomas, practical reason, while not beyond the gravitational pull of speculative necessities, must do its work amid the only somewhat predictable contingencies of the moral order. Beyond that, however, practical reason has ties to the volitional and the affective that are too rarely noted. The question to which I am pointing here is that of the affective component of moral consciousness and moral judgment. Thomas moves in and out of this aspect of moral knowledge but he never offers us a systematic development of it. Also Thomas did not separate theological ethics from his overall systematic theology. His moral theory is broadly diffused throughout his work. He has no separate and coordinated treatment of the methodology and epistemology of ethics.

Let me then be clear at the outset about the claims and disclaimers of this paper. First I shall discuss the role of practical reason in Thomas as Thomas uses this term to cope with the natural contextualism of the ethical enterprise. Next I shall move to the affective component of moral knowledge in Thomas. I will explore those elements of this that are present though not systematically developed or coordinated in his work. I shall look at one of Thomas' principal commentators, John of St. Thomas, a seventeenth century writer, who avowed that he strayed not at all from Thomas in developing a concept of "affective knowledge" of the good and the sacred. Then I shall move off from these Thomistic roots to offer my own position on the implications of the affective aspect of moral knowledge, building upon what I have done in my book *The Moral Choice*. Practical moral reasoning is an important category because it implies the question of the nature of moral knowledge. It points us to the foundations. Practical moral reasoning invites us to consider the question of what I will call the *intellectualistic fallacy*.

This fallacy, which finds broad and frequent expression in a narrowly and nudely rationalistic, analytical, and intellectualistic approach to ethics, ignores the animating affective mold of moral cognition. It represents an epistemology of ethics that is at once reductionistic, simplistic, and jejune. Such an approach leaves untouched the mystical and contemplative dimensions of moral consciousness. It offers little grounds for speaking of the linkage between religious and moral experience or of the natural rapport between faith and moral judgment.

I will argue for the affective base of moral awareness and knowledge and submit that this in no way imperils the work of reasoned debate and rational moral discourse. The practical import of this is not slight. It is not for nothing that the rationalist is upset by the inclusion of affectivity in the concept of moral knowledge. Affectivity imports mystery and depth. We can feel more than we can see or say. Tidy schemes and ethical blueprints are threatened by the "intrusion" of the mystical and affective aspects of moral awareness. The temptation to intellectualistic reductionism is understandable. Still I submit that a recognition of the affective-intellectual nature of moral knowledge is essential not only for an understanding of ethics itself, but for the unveiling of hidden ethical postures in the social sciences and elsewhere. Knowing how we know is the beginning of wisdom. Epistemological reductionism does not do justice to our minds nor to the God in whose image those minds were fashioned.

It must be noted forthwith, given the attention that practical reason in Kant has had, that *ratio practica* in Thomas and practical reason in

Kant are not the same, even though in both thinkers practical reason is the opposite of speculative or pure reason. Thomas may even at times sound close to Kant as when he speaks of practical reason's first duty being *imperare*, to command.[1] One might also see Kantian glimmerings in Thomas' contention that "reason is the rule and measure of human acts" and the "first principle of human acts," but the similarity would be largely superimposed.[2] As I have said, practical moral reasoning is a revealing category, epistemologically speaking, and the epistemology of Thomas is simply not that of Kant—partly because of the affective component in moral knowledge that Thomas' thought allows for. Revisionist studies may suggest that more parallelism exists between Kant and Thomas than orthodoxy has heretofore allowed. I am sympathetic with such an effort, since both Kant and Aquinas have been pigeonholed too neatly by their commentators. That said, however, I suggest that the distinctiveness of the elements that follow in Thomas are notable.

Judgment Amid Contingencies

Practical reason, for Thomas, does not enjoy the ultimate simplicity of speculative reason. Speculative reason is concerned with the necessities, with those matters that could not be other than they are, whether or not everyone knows this. Thus it is true for all that a triangle has three angels which together equal two right angels. Practical reason does not enjoy such universality or necessity. Practical reason can achieve valid generalizations, such as *act according to reason*. However, as soon as you try to specify the dictates of reason in a particular situation, the generalization limps. Thus, says Thomas, it is a specification of the need to be reasonable to say that "things held in trust should be returned upon request." That is a fine generalization which normally encapsulates proper moral counsel. But, and here is the rub, not always. The more specific principles of practical reason experience *defectus*, deficiency. The more you take them into the contingencies and vagaries of life, the more likely is it that the counsel of those principles will be inadmissible and inapplicable. Thus if you held a sword for someone and he was going to misuse it in a gross way, you should not return it, even though he asks for it and it is held in trust. To do so would be "harmful and consequently unreasonable."[3] Thomas' very notable conclusion is this: "In speculative things, truth is the same for all persons. . . . In matters of behavior, however, truth of practical moral rightness is not the same for all with regards to that which is particular but only with regard to that which is in common . . ."[4] Thus did Thomas' use of practical reason lead him to acknowledge the meaningfulness of that which is unique and special and ungeneralizable as well as that which is generalizable. If all moral meaning were generalizable, then the truth would be the same for all persons and Thomas' dramatic statement would not be necessary.

Note, too, that Thomas did not leave this discussion of exceptions to moral principles without some quite specific examples. He allowed that in certain circumstances, one might take the property of other persons, have sexual relations with someone other than one's wife, and even directly kill one's self or other innocent persons. Thomas wanted to justify the deeds of certain biblical figure and saints of the Church. Samson had committed suicide by pulling the building down on himself; Abraham consented to directly kill his son, Isaac; Hosea seemed to have been implicated in sexual sin. Thomas took the sting out of these exceptions by stipulating the necessity of a "divine mandate" to know that these exceptions were good. However, he did not lapse into a crude nominalism. As an ethical realist, Thomas held that nothing could be commanded unless it was good. God too is bound by the order of justice and "beyond this order God can do nothing."[5]

Practical moral reasoning in Thomas is tied to some recognition of the circumstantiality of morality. In a critical question of the *Summa*, Thomas is most explicit about this. *That is good which is according to reason.* However, reason has its work cut out for us because only in God is goodness substantial and constitutional. With us, goodness or badness depends on the circumstances. With us, goodness is not *per se*, but *"secundum diversa."*[6] "Human actions are good or bad according to their circumstances."[7] That is good which is in accordance with reason but reasonableness is circumstantially discovered.[8] This does not mean that Thomas is consistently "contextual" in our sense. It also does not mean that Thomas denies the existence of constancies or principles in moral life or that he is never an absolutist on particular moral issues. It does reveal in Thomas, however, critical awareness that practical moral reasoning must take it judgments according to the diversities and circumstances of life, whatever *constancies* it may happily find there.

Affectivity in Moral Knowledge

It would be mistake to think that Thomas and the Thomistic school limited the specialness of *ratio practica* to decision-making amid contingencies. Speculative reason, by its nature, merely apprehends; practical reason not only apprehends—it also causes things to happen. Practical reason not only knows; it directs events.[9] As such, then, practical reason is not just a function of intellection, but also, in some way, of volition and affection. It does not just know; it "commands," "petitions," "begs," and "orders" things toward some perceived good.[10] It is essentially *ad bonum*. It pursues the good as good, and not just the true as good. Reason is the rule and measure of moral actions and the primary principle of moral actions because it is the essence of practical reason to order behavior toward the good.[11] This link to good is integral to practical reason. Because of this link Thomas can say that law is binding only if it is reasonable and geared to the good.[12] For this reason it is quite accurate to say that, for Thomas, *the truly reasonable is the truly good*. A strict rationalist might say that too, but the difference with Thomas is that the affections are implicated in the work of practical reason, in the determination of reasonableness. Practical reason working well imports an attitude of will and not just an attitude of intellect.

I am not saying here that Thomas explicitly posed the question of "affective knowledge" in the way that one of his principal commentators, John of St. Thomas, would. In at least one context, Thomas does use the terms "affective" and "practical" as synonymous. In a rather strained effort to explain how angels sin, Thomas uses such expressions as "affective or practical knowledge" and "practical, i.e. affective knowledge," and he speaks of falsity of judgment occuring not speculatively, but "in a practical, i.e. affective way."[13] What he did do is say that the work of reason is to order and direct us toward the good. "*Rationis est ordinare ad finem . . .*"[14] Right reason, perfected by the moral virtues, has a *connatural* orientation toward the good. This link to the good, this rapport of right reason to the good as good, which implies affectional orientation toward the good could not but be illumining. Thomas does not explicitate this, but I suggest that it is an implication of his description of practical reason. This implication is developed in Thomas' treatment of prudence and the moral virtues as perfective of practical moral reasoning. The possibility of a kind of affective knowing is even more obvious in his idea of connaturality through love. It appears further in his treatment of the gifts of the Holy Spirit, especially the gift of wisdom, as supplemental to reason, and in his treatment of delight and of faith. Again, there is not a systematic development here in Thomas, but rather a re-emerging theme. Let me turn first to prudence.

Prudence and Affective Knowledge

Prudence is the virtue which, with the moral virtues, perfects reason so that reason will be a reliable guide toward our moral goals.[15] It should be noted that Thomas does not always use the qualifier "practical" when referring to moral reason. In fact his usage of the term reason is expansive, sometimes meaning openness to reality and at other times practical reason as the opposite of speculative reason.[16] The perfection of reason by prudence and the moral virtues, however, clearly refers to moral reason. How then does prudence perfect reason?

Prudence does this by being conjoined with the moral virtues. "There can be no prudence without moral virtue."[17] The moral virtues, of course, reside in the will, and they serve prudence in these two ways: first, they remove "the impediment of corrupting passions." This may be seen as a somewhat extrinsic role, clearing the way for clear, undistracted judgment. There is more, however. The moral virtues also so attune a person to the morally good that it become "connatural" to judge correctly about the good. A virtuous person judges well about the material of that virtue because it becomes connatural, or second nature to him to do so. He quotes Aristotle to the effect that the kind of person you are determines how you perceive the good.[18] This connaturalizing effect of virtue, which Thomas, as we will see, elsewhere describes as coming about "through love," affects the intentionality and the manner of knowing and perceiving the good. The way of knowing is affectively qualified. Thus when John of St. Thomas claims that his category of "affective knowledge" is grounded in Thomas, he has something of a case. There is, however, more.

Wisdom and Affective Knowledge

In treating the gift of wisdom, Thomas returns to the idea of knowledge by way of connaturality. Correct judgment can come about in two ways, says Thomas—either by a perfect use of reason or in another distinct way, through a connaturality with the subject being judged. Thus, as illustrative of the first way of knowing, someone versed in ethics may judge correctly about matters of chastity. But the chaste person who has the *habitus* of chastity may judge through his connatural attunement with the virtue. Thomas allows the possibility of merely intellectual and rational achievement. True knowledge can be had by that route. However, there is another way. He cites that it was said of a certain Hierotheus who achieved a kind of perfection in divine knowledge *"non solum discens, sed et patiens divina,"* not only leaning, but in some sense undergoing, experiencing, or even suffering the divine realities. This kind of compassion or compatibility or connaturality to the divine comes through love. He concludes that the gift of wisdom that achieves this has its essence in the intellect, but its cause in the will.[19] Thomas adds that the knowledge of the gift of wisdom involves a kind of tasting as opposed to vision.[20]

As I have written elsewhere, Thomas is certainly not clear on the concept of affective knowledge.[21] Also I find his dichotomizing between connatural and discursive, reasoned knowledge overdone and insensitive to the affective component in all moral knowledge. Nevertheless, Thomas is not a purveyor of the intellectualistic fallacy which would imagine moral knowledge as mirror-like representationalism. Thomas is more sensitive to the intrinsic complexity of what we call knowledge and to the interplay of the affective and the rational. His epistemological base is not narrow.

The Gifts of the Holy Spirit and Affective Knowledge

In his general treatment of the gifts of the Holy Spirit, Thomas again introduces the need for some supplement to naked reason to connaturalize us to the good and the holy. Four of these gifts are cognitive—wisdom, understanding, knowledge, and counsel—yet all the gifts are connected in love and none could exist without love.[22] These gifts are described as a special stimulation by the Spirit which render us more promptly and readily obedient to the lead of the Spirit of God.[23] Obedience, however, is not a virtue of the "mind" but of the affections and the will. The gifts, then,—even those which reside in the mind—are essentially linked to love and render us connatural, obedient, and amenable to the movements of the Spirit. The volitional attitude has cognitive impact. There is an affective component in the knowing process. Again, the idea is not developed, but it is present, and the knowledge of good and the holy is not achieved by naked intellection. Knowledge is awareness and that awareness does not come about in a narrowly intellectualistic fashion.

There are other elements in Thomas that are not customarily introduced into treatments of his epistemology. Because they are not seen as integral to his thought, Thomas is often pictured as a narrow intellectualist. Thomas gives special attention to delight as an important phenomenon in human experience. There can be not just sensual delight but also intellectual delight which is experienced in the intellectual appetite, i.e. the will.[24] Does delight have any cognitive import? Obviously it does in an extrinsic way, since we attend more to that which delights us. There is more to it, however. Thomas says that when our activity is connatural to us, it is delightful.[25] This would suggest that what delights the good person is good. Just as Aristotle was willing to say that "truth is that which seems to the good man to be true," so the delights of the good person can be taken as true and properly rooted.[26] The good person who is connaturalized to the good through virtue need not be learned to know. He/she knows by way of connaturality. The reliance would be on the affective orientation. That which is good vibrates and resonates delightfully in the good person. The emotional reaction of delight amounts to an endorsement of that which is perceived. But endorsement procedes from evaluative awareness and implies some kind of knowledge. Endorsement divorced from knowledge is just noise.[27] The cognitive connection is also implied in what Thomas sees as the first effect of delight—a broadening or expansion of the soul. In delighting, we are stretched and enlarged as we strain to contain the new good. It is hard to see how this could be done without a heightening of awareness of the good. If we delight in the value of persons and in those moral values which enhance and protect their preciousness, these values are absorbed into the tonality of our moral consciousness and conscience. *The good delighted in is experienced more expansively and thus is better known.* Obviously, I am building on Thomas here, but I am not contradicting the implications of his thought.[28]

Faith and Affective Knowledge

Faith, for Thomas, also shows the collaboration of affectivity in knowledge. "The knowledge of faith proceeds from the will since only the willing believe . . ."[29] Somewhat mystifyingly, Thomas also says that "faith derives its certitude from the fact that it is outside the realm of knowledge and in the realm of affection."[30] Certitude that derived from the affections, however, would do violence to the mind if it were not traceable to a kind of knowledge—i.e., affective knowledge.

The conclusion is that there are many elements in the epistemology of Thomas Aquinas that lead reason, both practical and speculative, beyond a narrow and nude intellectualism toward a wholistic conception of knowledge that embodies affective appreciation. It is my contention that a narrow viewing of *ratio practica* in Thomas that does not touch down on these other bases of his thought would be reduction-istic. Thomas' philosophy and theology include love not only as a stim-ulator to knowledge but as an illumining factor in knowing. This should not be surprising when we realize with Thomas that "willing and apprehending are diverse faculties, but diverse faculties of the one soul."[31]

John of St. Thomas and Affective Knowledge

Among Thomas' commentators none goes further with these hints in Thomas than John of St. Thomas. The idea of affective knowledge becomes for him the controlling category for an understanding of the gifts of the Holy Spirit. He develops an explicit notion of "affective knowledge." This sounds like a confusion of intellect and will, and John faces up to this objection. He refuses to slip off the hook by saying that affective knowledge is knowledge prodded or stimulated by love. This he would see as love acting as an *efficient cause*. In affective knowl-edge, love acts as an "objective cause," transforming the relationship of the object known to the knower and making for a different kind of knowledge. When the object known is also loved, it is known in a formally distinct way. The affections can *"causally provide greater light"* by rendering the object known more fully experienced. He reaches for images and metaphors other than those customarily used to describe more intellectualized knowledge. Affective knowledge is less like seeing and more like "tasting," "touching," "sensing." That which is loved is "inviscerated" within the knower and experienced as united to the knower with a new and distinct proportion and congeniality. Such knowledge is far from any naked intellection and it is the kind of knowledge involved in knowing the good and the holy.[32] Through love, the person is rendered more subtle and open to the knowledge of things divine and created.[33] Divine truths may be known "experi-mentally and affectively."[34] The good and the holy may be known *"in affectu."* Such truth is knowable and judgeable precisely through this affective experience.[35] This is the kind of knowledge that issues into contemplation.[36] It is in John of St. Thomas that the Thomistic notion of affective knowledge of the good and the holy reaches its most ex-plicit expression.

The Affective Dimension of Moral Knowledge

In my own theory of ethics, I do not employ the term "practical moral reason." I trust, however, that from the aforesaid that it will be clear that I am in debt to the Thomistic tradition of *ratio practica* and to the Thomistic idea of illumination through the connaturalizing love of the good. I begin ethics by posing the question which is regularly bypassed in the rush to issues: what is the foundational moral experience? What is the experience that consitutes us as morally aware, giving meaning to moral language and judgment? Reason in the service of moral truth, whether we call it practical moral reasoning or not, must be understood first in its foundations. Whence comes this kind of truth experience? If I allege that metal when heated expands or water when heated to a certain point boils, I have made verifiable truth statements meriting universal acceptance. But when I say that promises must be kept, what kind of truth statement have I made? How do I know that it is valuable to keep promises and that this value may be *truly* affirmed? Some would say that promise-keeping works better; it is a pragmatic necessity. It enhances the common good and promotes an atmosphere of confident exchange. Certainly it does that, but as W. D. Ross says, "that is not the whole truth."[37] He offers the example of a promise made to a dying man with no witnesses present. Let me elaborate and extend this case. Suppose a dying man asked you to give from your abundant wealth two hundred dollars to a person he cheated some time ago. If you would promise that, he feels he could die in peace. You do so promise. He dies. You could say to yourself: "Well, he got the promise he wanted and died happy. No one heard the promise, so I can just keep my money and forget all about it. The institution of promise-keeping in society will not be affected since no one knows. I am completely off the hook." Or are You? Whence comes that nagging sense of indecency and sleaziness? From custom, or habituation to promise-keeping? Or is it deeper? Does deciding to ignore the promise make you a certain kind of person? Would we want a child of ours to be that kind of person? Clearly we have here a different sort of truth experience. We are far from the impact of heat on metal or water, with the easy and even palpable verifiability such empirical truths allow. It is no great wonder that the emotivists defected at this point into noncognitivism and said there is no truth here, only emotive approbation or disdain. By such a defection, however, intelligence is not served.

Those who would reduce moral truth experience to custom are equally shallow. Since goodness and badness can become customary, relativism does not touch bottom. Equally reductionistic is Ayn Rand's view that the good is that which promotes survival. Survival might be noble or ignoble, and not surviving might be heroically good. The good of surviving is not foundational. Some are edifyingly confident that

God is the foundational base of moral knowledge. However, since we do not see God and since faith in God is inferential from moral and other experience, it is futile to posit God as the *epistemological* grounding of moral consciousness. And then there are the ubiquitous rationalists with their confidence in naked intellectualism, who say that the foundation of moral awareness must be an implicit and universal datum of human rationality. Here the gounds of morals are implicit like the first principles of mathematics or logic. The farmer and the cab driver may never have brought it to conscious expression, but they do implicitly know and operate on the assumption that the part is less than the whole and that a thing may not *be* and *not be* at the same time in the same circumstances. Such truths are universals and imbedded in all human consciousness. The rationalistic purveyors of the intellectualistic fallacy in ethics are sure that something like that is the grounding for all moral consciousness and discourse. *The assumption is that morality becomes intelligible in the same way that mathematics and logic do.* The rationalist who espouses this fallacy is sure that if this assumption is questioned we will plummet into unbridled relativism or a kind of Sartrian antinomianism. If moral awareness is not confined to the universals of speculative reason, then ethical awareness becomes a particular, contingent affair and intercultural conversation becomes impossible. If ethics is not ultimately like mathematics it will perish. This is the import of any rationalistic theory of the foundations of morality. This position is usually assumed and not explicitated.

The debate here is neither donnish nor inconsequential. If ethics is rationalistically conceived in its roots, the gate is opened to simplism and false absolutes. Facile and ungrounded certitudes are likely to abound. The temptation to proceed deductively, as one proceeds from geometric theorem to corollary, will be in evidence. These are the natural hazards of the intellectualistic fallacy which dismisses the cognitive significance of affect in moral knowledge.

My own position is that moral knowledge is born in awe, in affectivity. The foundational moral experience is the experience of the value of persons and their environment. When moral knowledge moves from awe to articulation, it does so within the ambience of this foundational appreciation. As I have written elsewhere: "The foundational moral experience is an affective reaction to value. It is not a metaphysical or a religious experience primordially. It is not a conclusion to a syllogism, though it may be supported by syllogisms and reasoning. The value of persons cannot be taught, subjected to proof, reasoned to, or computerized. It can only be affectively appreciated."[38]

In so saying, I am not lapsing into emotivism which sees ethical judgments as emotional eruptions, not statements that could be true or false. I am saying, first of all, that the foundational moral experience (FME) is cognitive. Of course you do not *know* the value of persons as you *know* the Pythagorean theorem. The knowledge of persons as good, even sacredly good, is infinitely more complex in its etiology than the knowledge of metaphysical and mathematical abstractions. I will trace out some of the differences.

First of all, the FME is *partitionable*. It may be experienced but then barbarically limited to one's own tribe. There may even be partitioning within the partitioning. Females may be less valued than males within the tribe. Those outside the tribe, as anthropologist Ralph Linton describes it, may be regarded "as fair game to be exploited by any possible means, or even as a legitimate source of meat. . . ."[39] By this point the rationalist is already upset. Why am I polluting the theoretical bases of ethics by dragging in anthropological data? Again, the truth is that the FME is not merely theoretical. Neither is it a matter of explicitating implicit principles of the mind. It is a value experience that can manifest itself in observable ways. It can be denied and limited and partitioned as the principle of non-contradiction cannot be without absurdity.

This leads to the second point of difference regarding the universality of the FME. There is the observation of the encyclopedic Arnold Toynbee that "the distinction between good and evil seems to have been drawn by all human beings at all times and places. The drawing of it seems, in fact, to be one of the intrinsic and universal characteristics of our common nature."[40] That, of course, is an empirical estimation. Theoretically, is the experience implicit in all human experience so that we have the grounds for cross-cultural conversation on morality? Yes and no. It is not, again, universally implicit as is the rational principle of non-contradiction. The answer is yes in the sense that this experience is universally available to all persons, and, as I said in *The Moral Choice*, it is not possible to imagine a recognizably human person (free of psychopathy) who would be unaware of the value of at least some persons.[41] *However, the experience is not perceived as necessarily universal.* Universalism has been making slow and tortuous inroads against tribalism in human history. Thus the comparison to abstract rational knowledge is again misplaced. Moral civilization involves the recognition that the FME extends to all persons. Barbarianism, as I use the term, refers to the limiting and particularizing of this experience. However, conversation and moral discourse are possible even with the barbarian who is into the FME in however limited and tribal a way.

Thirdly, *reason* relates to moral knowledge and to abstract metaphysical knowledge in different ways. Some principles are so essentially knit into the power of reason that not to admit them would be irrational. Again, no one can rationally debate the principle of noncontradiction. Anyone who knows what a part is and what a whole is has to admit that the whole is more and the part less. Moral knowledge does not admit of such intuitionism. The experience of the value of persons which waxes deeper and truer from infancy on, attaining mystical and prophetic depths in some souls will not be born of argument. Reason can, however, enhance it and encourage it. Teleological arguments can urge that no other appreciation could successfully ground human affairs. The Teilhardian criteria for truth—coherence and fruitfulness—can be brought to bear on the truth claims of the FME. These services of reason, however, remain extrinsic to the affective appreciation at the core of the FME. Moving off from the FME, reason can discover constancies (principles) about what does or does not befit the value of persons. It can discern reliable authorities and debate the fittingness of accepted judgment on what does or does not befit persons and their environment. Moral debate and argument, the analysis and refinement of morally relevant categories, etc. are all essential to the moral animal. However, the animating mold of this discourse and analysis and reasoning is the affective experience of worth and value without which moral discourse would seem non-sense. Those who would impute a narrow intellectualism to Thomas Aquinas can stress that Thomas does indeed allow for general and thus intellectual knowledge in the strict sense. He does, for example, say that it is true for all persons that one should act reasonably. However, I would insist that, given the affective base of moral knowledge, one might accept that generalization and not know that it is applicable to persons outside the tribe. One must indeed act according to reason with one's own—but with the Iroquois, the *goyim*, or the English? Impairment at the affective roots of moral knowledge could also undermine the universalizability of other principles relating to killing, sexual exchange, and business. The Irish tribalist might concede that two and two are four also for the Englishman, but not that they have the same inviolability regarding promise keeping or violence. If you do not know that caring has cognitive status, your brilliant principleist and rationalistic ethics might subsist in a matrix of sexist, racist, and tribalistic evaluational perspectives.

In the forth place, moral knowledge differs from abstract metaphysical and mathematical knowledge in its unique relationship to faith, mysticism, and religious awareness. Here, I submit, is where the vacuousness of the intellectualistic fallacy becomes most apparent.

Unfortunately, the terms *faith* and *mystical* are in bad odor in our culture. This makes it easier to palm off reductionistic theories of knowledge. Mysticism and faith need reenfranchisement. Jean Paul Sartre once commented on an experience he had while holding an infant in his arms. Suddenly he realized that all that he had ever written or ever done would not tip the scale when weighed against the value of the preciousness he held in his hands. Such an experience is understandable. It seems at times that the sacred value of life is best appreciated in the untainted, uncompetitive, trusting form of childhood. Put next to this the experience of a soldier who refuses to shoot hostages in war time and who suffers execution for his refusal. Could Sartre prove the preciousness of the child? Could the soldier prove that death was preferable to slaughtering the hostages especially since the hostages died anyhow? If, however, you know that Sartre and the soldier were on to something valid and true, you are a believer. Faith is the intellectually normal way of discovering truth that can be neither seen nor proved but which is *known* with sureness. Anyone who knows that persons are worth living for and even dying for is a believer. Paul, the Christian apostle, said that the just live by faith. More precisely and univsersally, the moral animal, i.e. the person, lives by faith. The value of persons and their environment that undergirds all moral consciousness and civilization is believable, but beyond proof. Thomas Aquinas said that faith lends a kind of certitude that is in the genre of affection. Faith is a kind of knowledge that comes from the will and is best described in terms of affectivity. This is the kind of knowing that best describes the FME. Moral truth, foundationally, is faith knowledge. Faith knowledge must be reenfranchised in philosophical as well as in theological ethics.

Mystical too is a word that has suffered unfortunate excommunication. Mystical comes to mean strange, baffling, and unusually mysterious. However, in the Thomistic tradition, the mystical referred to profound affectivity or to what could be called "peak experiences" of the good and the holy. As such it is not abnormal or unusual. Sartre's experience of the value of the child was mystical. At times our love of the human and the terrestrial reaches mystical levels of intensity. Sometimes it is when human life is profaned that we most powerfully experience its value. At any rate, there is nothing abnormal about this. Indeed our tenuous grasp of the sanctity of life must be nourished by some of these mystical moments or it will wane and evanesce. Moral knowledge of its nature is on a continuum that reaches to the mystical. Moral awareness has mystical underpinnings.

I have said too that moral knowledge touches on religious awareness. Moral knowledge is not identical with religious knowledge, even though the good can be experienced as sacred in its preciousness. By religious experience I mean that which relates to God. The knowledge of God is inferential. It is intimated by our primary experiences—including moral experience. The value of persons, the experienced fact that they are even worth dying for, the fact that, as Socrates knew, it is better to suffer injustice than to inflict it, is not only a matter of mystical faith. It is also an intimation of the more that lies beneath the apparent. Teilhard de Chardin felt that "life would be a real factual contradiction, its emergence into consciousness would destroy it, if reflection led us to the conclusion that all our actions were completely contingent."[42] If we come upon values that command our total love, it suggests a deeper reality which validates this unconditioned response. Marjorie Reiley Maguire, in an essay entitled "Ethics and Immortality," argues that altruistic and self-sacrificing behavior is evacuated of meaning if persons have only temporal and temporary value. She sees immortality as the condition of the intelligibility of altruistic love, and from this she postulates the existence of God. She sees faith in immortality as a necessary corollary of moral experience, and faith in God as a corollary of faith in immortality.[43]

At the very least it seems that moral experience is not self-sufficient or complete in its intelligibility unless a deeper Preciousness underlies the preciousness that gives birth to moral awareness. Ethics is quite naturally religious. In my view, to say "religious ethics" is to utter a tautology. How far we are in wholistically understood moral knowledge from the pallid realms of rationalistic thought!

Finally, moral knowledge differs from abstract rational knowledge because moral knowledge is in a special way in process. As such it can recede or it can grow. What is felt and known can be less felt and less known. The experience of war often diminishes what I call the foundational moral experience in persons, leading to an increase in violent crime. Growth in moral knowledge is not just a movement from implicit to explicit. It does not involve just a progression of interconnected insights as in mathematics. Piaget, Loevinger, and Kohlberg have all attempted to trace out the manifestations of progressive moral awareness. Their research underscores the fact that it is no simple thing to know what persons are worth. It involves a long drama in our pluriform consciousness.

Conclusions

Moral reasoning is not just a matter of naked intellection. Neither is it simply comparable to abstract metaphysical thought. We may and must reason and speculate about morality. Ethics is served by metaphysics and speculative reason. But when we ponder moral experience and seek to serve it with our minds, we are affectively implicated. Without that affective base to our moral knowledge, morality would be meaningless. It would be unrealistic and devoid of sense. Does this mean or imply that ethics is ultimately arbitrary and at the mercy of the vagaries of feeling? No. But it does imply with Blaise Pascal that "we know truth, not only by the reason, but also by the heart."[44] It implies also with Henri Bergson that we have a "genius of the will" as well as genius of the intellect.[45] It implies further with John Macquarrie that "all affective and conative experience has its own understanding."[46] It banishes any reductionism in ethics. It makes us wary of those who would shrink ethics to logical, linguistic, or rationalistic analysis. It makes us look to the mystical, the mysterious, the religious, and the contemplative capacities of the human spirit in assessing the full import of the moral.

But does it not after all leave us without the limpid certitudes promised by rationalistic ethics? Not at all. There is room and necessity in ethics for the thundering certitudes of the prophets. The morally good is that which befits persons, and there is much that we can know about that. Negatively considered, there is also much that profanes the human and terrestrial good, and we can know this too with painful certitude. Still, this fuller awareness of what is involved in moral reasoning should make us more modest. The mind of the moralist is not a syllogism unfolding. It is buffeted and conditioned and ever in need of critical and comparative judgment. A wholistic theory of moral knowledge such as that suggested here would make us even more wary of those who offer simple answers to complex moral issues. Infallibility amid ambiguity is anomalous. It would also make us more aware that ethics is not done just by ethicists. Affective ethical biases roam, unto good or ill, amid the sciences and social sciences. A fuller awareness of the nature of moral knowledge, which points to the cognitive affection base of moral awareness, makes us more aware and wary of the disguises that ethical opinionating might take outside formal ethics. If you buy into the intellectualistic fallacy regarding moral values, you will accept the claim of value neutrality too easily. You might miss the fact that the waves of intricate and contrived arguments are carried by hidden affective tides. Obviously, in recognizing the affective side of moral knowledge, one could despair of verification. A criteriology of affect is no simple challenge. Yet to such things our thought must turn. The prime and obvious conclusion is that it is not by ethicists alone that ethics is done. Anthropology, history, social psychology, and the sociology of knowledge will become necessary partners of the ethicist. Universities might turn to the idea of a Center for the Study of Moral Values which would not be a department among others, but a coordinating center for the value inquiry that roams untested and uncoordinated in the many disciplines. Clearly the impact of foundational reappraisals is not slight.[47]

A fuller theory of moral knowledge also makes ethicists natural ecumenists. Like Paul the apostle, we know that we know "in part." We require complementarity and fulfillment. In no area more than in ethics does our fragility appear in such cruel and bright light. Often, with Socrates, the ethicist must know that he/she does not know. But in no area either are we closer to the mysteries that undergird our being.

Notes

CHAPTER 1

1. Aristotle, *Nichomachean Ethics*, 1155a. For a fuller discussion of the foundational moral experience which finds its first articulation in justice, see Daniel C. Maguire, *The Moral Choice* (Garden City: Doubleday, 1978; Minneapolis: Winston Press, 1979), ch. 3. Though *suum cuique*, to each his/her own, is the quintessential statement of what justice imports, the ancient literature offers broader and richer appreciations of the notion. Cicero, who reflects a whole tradition in this matter, says that "justice is a predilection for giving to each his/her own and for protecting generously and equitably the common good of persons." This is my translation of his words: "Quae animi affectio suum cuique tribuens atque hanc, quam dico, societatem coniunctionis humanae munifice et aeque tuens justitia dicitur." *De Officiis*, L. i, Cap. 5, #15. Ambrose extends this tradition. "Justice, which renders to each his/her own, does not lay claim to the goods of another and even neglects its own interests in the interests of an equitable common life." "Justitia, quae suum cuique tribuit, alienum non vindicat, utilitatem propriam negligit, ut communem aequitatem custodiat." *De Officiis Ministrorum*, L. i, Cap. 24, #115. And Ulpian described justice as "a constant and perpetual willingness to give to each his/her own." *Dig*. i, I, 10, pr. Each of these definitions imports the value of every person, the presence of affectivity in the notion of justice, and a concern for the common good. I submit that the theory of justice that I offer in this book and in *The Moral Choice* is an adaptive extension of that tradition. Readers of *The Moral Choice* will notice that I do not follow in a mechanical way the model of method that is the structure of that book. They will also notice, I trust, that no aspect or element of that model of method is unrepresented in this book.
2. See Daniel C. Maguire, *Death By Choice*, 2nd. Edition (Garden City: Doubleday, Image, 1984) for further arguments against the morality of capital punishment.
3. See Giorgio Del Vecchio, *Justice: An Historical and Philosophical Essay* (Edinburgh: University Press, 1952), 53, 68–69, n. 15. See William T. Blackstone, "Reverse Discrimination and Compensatory Justice," *Social Theory and Practice*, 3 (1975): 253–88. Blackstone works off the assumption that there are but two main categories of justice in Aristotle and then exemplifies the weakness of this truncation.
4. An excellent treatment of the tripartite nature of justice is found in Josef Pieper, *Justice* (New York: Pantheon Books, 1955). This has been republished in Josef Pieper, *The Four Cardinal Virtues* (New York: Harcourt, Brace & World, 1965).
5. The confusion on the forms of justice and the befuddling multiplication of these forms resulted from efforts to give justice a new definition in every situation to which it applied—and it applies to the whole of life. To mint a new title for justice in every distinct situation of rendering to each his/her own allows for infinite and unhelpful proliferation. To give a sampling of this melee: I will list some of the kinds of justice mentioned in the literature: vindictive, judicial, familial, antipeponthotic, synallagmatic, commutative, legal, social, distributive, retributive, attributive, recognitive, providential, syndical, corporative, reparatory, penal, and cosmopolitical. The multiplicity bears witness to the breadth of application that justice has as well as to the felt need for meaningful definitions of the term. Justice talk has further been confused by a long tradition of treating justice as universal virtue, the sum of all good-

ness. Plato was a mighty force in this direction. See *The Republic*, I. 6, 331 E; I. 7, 332 D; IV. 10, 433 A. This remained as a tension in Aristotle and also in Thomas Aquinas. Finally, justice was taken as just one virtue among the many, missing the fact that it is the primary and foundational category of communal existence.

6. Thomas Aquinas, *Summa Theologica*, II II q. 51, a.1, ad 3.

7. To the Rev. James Madison, October 28, 1785, quoted in Yehoshua Arieli, *Individualism and Nationalism in American Ideology* (Cambridge, Mass.: Harvard University Press, 1964), 159.

8. Pieper reports this as the opinion of philosophy professor Chung-sho Lo, a onetime member of the Unesco Commission. See Josef Pieper, *Justice*, 116, n. 15.

9. Ronald Dworkin, *Taking Rights Seriously* (Cambridge, Mass.: Harvard University Press, 1977), xi. Dworkin goes on to say that this characterization of rights does not have any "special metaphysical character." Actually, it certainly does have a metaphysical character, showing again how metaphysics is a term on the loose in much philosophical discourse.

10. For this reason, this form of justice has been called "commutative," from the Latin *commutatio*, meaning exchange. This kind of justice regulates the competing claims that occur in exchanges between individuals.

11. Martin Buber, *I and Thou* (2nd ed.; New York: Scribners, 1958), 8.

12. Quoted by Arieli, op. cit., 41.

13. Robert Nozick, *Anarchy, State, and Utopia* (New York: Basic Books, 1974), 169.

14. Aristotle, *Politics*, I. 2. 1253.

15. Jethro K. Lieberman, "The Relativity of Injury," *Philosophy and Public Affairs* (Fall, 1977), 73.

16. Richard H. de Lone, *Small Futures: Children, Inequality, and the Limits of Liberal Reform* (New York: Harcourt Brace Jovanovich, 1979), 179.

17. Koji Taira, "Japan—the New Corporate State?" *The Wilson Quarterly*, 3 (Spring, 1979): 53.

18. A. D. Lindsay, *The Essentials of Democracy* (2nd ed.; Oxford: Claredon Press, 1935), 71.

19. Quoted in Eric Voegelin, *The New Science of Politics* (Chicago: University of Chicago Press, 1952), 56–58.

20. Ibid., 59.

21. I am taking liberties with the term "nation" here, having in mind a distinguishable societal grouping. The grouping may include a number of national entittes which are culturally conjoined. There are various configurations, even hemispheric in breadth, which we might employ as vehicles of interpretation. Certain interpretations of reality are found in nations of the Far East that would not be found in the West. But at any rate we do obey the philosophical injunction "Know thyself!" *through political media* as well as through private and interpersonal forms of sociality. Knowledge is, among other things, political in nature. Since the goal here is an understanding of our ultimate reality and is thus transcendent in its significance, the high stakes are reflected in the language of sacredness. "Everything is full of gods!" as Thales said, and this is certainly so in national self-consciousness. Sacred truths for which people die are at issue. The seriousness is dreadful.

22. Thomas Aquinas, *Commentary on the Nichomachean Ethics of Aristotle*, 8, 9; #1658. *Justitia consistit in communicatione.* I translate *communicatione* with some freedom, but without distortion. The cognate "communication" would be misleading; "sharing" seems best.

CHAPTER 2

1. Stephen Charles Mott, "Egalitarian Aspects of the Biblical Theory of Justice" in *The American Society of Christian Ethics*, 1978: *Selected Papers from the Nineteenth Annual*

Meeting, ed. Max L. Stackhouse (Waterloo, Ontario: Council on the Study of Religion, 1978), 8. Mott has developed this significant essay into a book (available in paperback) which presents a superb and sensitive treatment of biblical justice: *Biblical Ethics and Social Change* (New York: Oxford University Press, 1982).

2. See Mott, "Egalitarian Aspects," 12.
3. What I mean by the prevailing notions of justice in the United States will become clear in the exposition. However, for references to the unsystematized notions of justice that permeate American life and history, see Yehoshua Arieli, *Individualism and Nationalism in American Ideology* (Cambridge, Mass.: Harvard University Press, 1964).
4. Norman H. Snaith, *The Distinctive Ideas of the Old Testament* (London: Epworth Press, 1944 [9th. impression, 1962]), 70. The Aramaic *tsidqah* is equated with "showing mercy to the poor".
5. Ibid., 72.
6. Mott, *Biblical Ethics and Social Change,* 63.
7. See Daniel C. Maguire, *A New American Justice* (Garden City: Doubleday, 1981; Minneapolis: Winston Press, 1982), ch. 2.
8. See ibid., 23, 190. This was the philosophy of John Hay as summarized by his biographer, William Roscoe Thayer, *The Life and Letters of John Hay* (Boston and New York: Houghton Mifflin, 1915).
9. See John Howard Yoder, *The Politics of Jesus* (Grand Rapids, Mich.: Eerdmans, 1972, 34–47.
10. See ibid., 45–46.
11. Thomas Aquinas, *Commentary on the Gospel of Matthew,* 5, 2.
12. The theological principle underlying biblical justice is this: "Human justice is a manifestation of grace not only in the sense that it is provided by a gracious God, but also because it is similar in nature to grace and to grace's expression in love" (Mott, *Biblical Justice and Social Change,* 63).
13. Thomas Aquinas, *Summa Theologica,* II–II, q. 158, a. 4, c.
14. Cited in ibid., a. 8 from John Chrysostom, *Super Mt.* 1. c. nt. 7.
15. Thomas Aquinas, *Summa Theologica,* I–II, q. 47, a. 1.
16. *Ibid.,* II–II, q. 158, a. 8; II–II, q. 157, a. 1 and 3.
17. Chapter Nine, "The Feminization of God and Ethics."
18. See Daniel C. Maguire, *The New Subversives* (New York: Crossroad, 1982), 77–80.
19. The assumption of my exegesis throughout has been that "the good book" is not all good. Much of it is descriptive of the sinful persons and ideas that filled the culture from which the Bible grew.

CHAPTER 4

1. Origen, *Works,* Berlin Corpus, 11: 221–222.
2. See Stanley Windass, *Christianity Versus Violence: A Social and Historic Study of War and Christianity* (London: Sheed and Ward, 1964), 13.
3. Lactantius, *Institutes* IV, XX, 15–17.
4. Lactantius, *Institutes* VI, 20.
5. Minucius Felix, Oct. XXX, 6.
6. Quoted in Origen, *Contra Celsum,* VIII, 68–69.
7. Ibid.
8. Eusebius, *Vita Constantini* 1, 24.
9. Lactantius, *Institutes* VII, 26.
10. Eusebius, *Vita Constantini* 2, 28–29.
11. Ibid., 2, 55.
12. Paneg. 2.

13. Theodoret, *Hist. Eccl.* II, 26.
14. Theodosian Code, xvi, x, 21.
15. Augustine, *De Libero Arbitrio,* Migne, *Patres Latini* 32, 1227–1228.
16. Augustine, *Contra Faustum,* Migne, *Patres Latini,* 42, 449.
17. Augustine, *Epist.* 138, ii, 14.
18. See Roland Bainton, *Christian Attitudes Toward War and Peace: A Historical Survey and Critical Re-evaluation* (New York, Nashville: Abingdon, 1960), 101–111.
19. See *Dictionnaire de Theologie Catholique,* VI, col. 1920.
20. Quoted in Roland Bainton, op. cit., 110.
21. Stanley Windass, *Christianity Versus Violence,* 43.
22. *Calvini opera,* in *Corpus Reformatorum,* VIII, 476; XXIV, 360; XLIV, 346.
23. Roland Bainton, op. cit., 112–13.
24. Ibid., 112.
25. Ibid., 115.
26. Jerry Falwell et al., *The Fundamentalist Phenomenon,* 75.
27. See George Marsden, *Fundamentalism and American Culture,* 52–55, for a description of this.
28. Ibid., 129.
29. Arno C. Gaebelein, quoted ibid., 143.
30. William L. Gaylord, The Soldier God's Minister, "A Discourse Delivered in the Congregational Church, Fitzwilliam, N. H., Sabbath Afternoon, October 5, 1862, on the Occasion of the Departure of a Company of Volunteers for the Seat of War," quoted in James H. Moorhead, *American Apocalypse: Yankee Protestants and the Civil War, 1860–1869* (New Haven and London: Yale University Press, 1978), ix.
31. Ibid., x.
32. Ibid.
33. Tim LaHaye, *The Battle For the Mind,* 218.
34. Ibid. Emphasis added.
35. Jerry Falwell, *Listen, America!* 67 and throughout.
36. Ibid.
37. Ibid., 73.
38. Ibid., 114.
39. Ibid., 84.
40. Ibid., 97.
41. Ibid.
42. Hal Lindsey, *The Late Great Planet Earth,* 155.
43. Ibid., 158.
44. Ibid., 159–160.
45. Ibid., 163.
46. Ibid., 163.
47. Ibid., 164.

CHAPTER 5

1. J. Glenn Gray, *The Warriors: Reflections on Men in Battle* (New York, Evanston, and London: Harper & Row, Harper Torchbook, 1959), 135. Significantly, Gray dedicates his book to "Ursula, my wife, formerly one of 'the enemy'."
2. Henry Kissinger misspoke himself when he wrote: "Power has never been greater; it has also never been less useful" (*The Troubled Partnership* [New York, London, Toronto: McGraw-Hill, 1965], 18). He was falling into the same trap that made Lyndon Johnson complain that he had more power than any person in history, but that he could not use it. The error here confuses power with kill-power. There are other forms of power. Diplomacy is one of them. Kissinger, if he sorted his concepts out, would know that this is power of a still useful sort.

3. Sir Charles Webster and Noel Frankland, *The Strategic Air Offensive Against Germany 1939–45* (London: Her Majesty's Stationery Office, 1962), quoted in Edmund Stillman and William Pfaff, *The Politics of Hysteria* (New York, Evanston, and London: Harper & Row, 1964), 33.
4. Ibid.
5. Robert H. Lowie, *Primitive Society* (New York: Liveright Publishing Corporation, 1947), 399.
6. Ibid.
7. *The Documents of Vatican II*, ed. Walter M. Abbott, S.J. (New York: Herder and Herder, Association Press, 1966), "Pastoral Constitution on the Church in the Modern World, #80, 294. For related condemnations by the popes, cf. Pius XII, Allocution of September 30, 1954, AAS 46 (1954): 589; radio message of December 24, 1954, AAS 47 (1955): 15 ff; John XXIII, encyclical letter "Pacem in Terris," AAS 47 (1963): 286–91.

CHAPTER 6

1. Edward H. Flannery, *The Anguish of the Jews: Twenty-Three Centuries of Anti-Semitism* (New York: Macmillan, 1965), xi.
2. F. Lovsky, *Antisémitisme et Mystere d'Israel* (Paris: Michel, 1955), 113.
3. Raul Hilberg, *The Destruction of the European Jews* (Chicago: Quadrangle Books, 1961), 3–4. Hilberg points out the parallels in Church rulings and Nazi laws and practices on pp. 5–6.
4. A. Roy Eckardt, *Elder and Younger Brothers* (New York: Schocken, 1973), 12.
5. Guilbert of Nogent, quoted in Flannery, op. cit., 90–91.
6. Ibid., 92.

CHAPTER 7

1. Monroe Lerner, "When, Why, and Where People Die," in *The Dying Patient*, ed. O. Brim, H. Freeman, S. Levine, and N. Scotch (New York: Russell Sage Foundation, 1970), 8.
2. Ralph Linton, "The Natural History of the Family," in *The Family: Its Function and Destiny* (New York: Harper, 1959), 52.
3. Morton Hunt, *Sexual Behavior in the 1970's* (Chicago: Playboy Press, 1974), 253.
4. Perry London, "Sexual Behavior," *Encyclopedià of Bioethics*, ed. Warren T. Reich (New York: Free Press, 1978), 4: 1568.
5. Ibid. It would be pleasant and simple if the unitive and procreative powers of sex always coincided happily. They do not.
6. See Marc Bloch, *Feudal Society, The Growth of Ties of Independence* (London: Routledge & Kegan Paul Ltd., 1965), 1: 203, 257–58, 267.
7. Anthony Kosnik et al, *Human Sexuality: New Directions in American Catholic Thought* (New York: Paulist, 1977), 167. This same study has other emphases. See, for example, p. 157. See also my commentary on this book, a book that caused such revealingly anxious reactions in the Catholic world: Daniel C. Maguire, "*Human Sexuality:* The Book and the Epiphenomenon," *Proceedings of the Thirty-Third Annual Convention of The Catholic Theological Society of America*, ed. Luke Salm (New York: Catholic Theological Society of America, 1979), 54–56.
8. I am quoting here intermittently from some of what I wrote in "Human Sexuality: The Book and the Epiphenomenon," 61–63.
9. William Butler Yeats, "The Pity of Love," *The Collected Poems of W. B. Yeats* (New York: Macmillan, 1956), 40.

10. Dorothy Tennov, *Love and Limerence: The Experience of Being in Love* (New York: Stein and Day, 1980).
11. Aristotle, *Nichomachean Ethics*, 1155a.
12. Clearly this listing needs much more fleshing out and defense than the space of one essay allows. The list here is presented as suggestive. I hope anon to develop all of this at book length.
13. For a remarkable and fanciful usage of these symbols, see Sam Keen, "Manifesto For A Dionysian Theology," *Cross Currents* 19 (Winter 1969): 37–54.
14. Ibid., 37.
15. Benedictus Merkelbach, *Summa Theologia Moralis*, Vol. III, Editio Nova, *De Sacramentis* (Brussels: Desclée De Brouwer, 1954), 970.
      Merkelbach does concede in a footnote, p. 970, that this would be a problem only early on in a marriage. He sees men as the more likely culprits in this early excess of enthusiasm.
16. For a fuller discussion of marriage between homosexuals see Chapter Eight, "The Morality of Homosexual Marriage."
17. G. K. Chesterton, *Lunacy and Letters*, edited by Dorothy Collins (New York: Sheed and Ward, 1958), 97.
18. For a study of the positive and neglected role of humor in human experience, see Daniel C. Maguire, *The Moral Choice* (Minneapolis: Winston Press, 1979), 243–69.
19. My colleague from California State University, Fullerton, teaches this in his course on marriage, but he has not yet written on the idea.
20. St. Thomas Aquinas, *Summa Theologiae*, I, II, q. 28, a. 1, ad 2.
21. See note 10.
22. William Butler Yeats, "He Wishes for the Cloths of Heaven," *The Collected Poems of W. B. Yeats* (New York: Macmillan, 1956), 70.

CHAPTER 8

1. On the negative qualities of the macho-masculine, see Chapter Nine, "The Feminization of God and Ethics,"
2. See Walter M. Abbott, general ed., *The Documents of Vatican II* (New York: Herder and Herder, 1966), 447, in the *Decree on Priestly Formation*.
3. Ibid.
4. Ibid., 446.
5. Ibid., 71, in the *Dogmatic Constitution on the Church*. Emphasis added.
6. Ibid., 71–72.
7. Ibid., 474, in the *Decree on the Appropriate Renewal of the Religious Life*.
8. Ibid., 475.
9. The phrase "human reality and saving mystery" is from Edward Schillebeeckx's book, *Marriage: Human Reality and Saving Mystery* (New York: Sheed and Ward, 1965).
10. Abbott, *Documents of Vatican II*, The Church Today, 255.
11. Ibid.
12. Ibid., 252.
13. Ibid., 252–53.
14. Ibid., 253.
15. Ibid., 250–51.
16. Ibid., 251.
17. Ibid., 253.
18. Ibid., 256.
19. Ibid., 255.
20. Alan P. Bell and Martin S. Weinberg, *Homosexualities: A Study of Diversity Among Men and Women* (New York: Simon & Schuster, 1978), 229–30.

21. Ibid., 230–31.
22. Ibid., 207.
23. Ibid., 208.
24. Ibid., 215.
25. Ibid., 102.
26. C. A. Tripp, *The Homosexual Matrix* (New York: McGraw 1975), 153.
27. Abbott, *Documents of Vatican II*, 252.
28. ". . . ei nec definitio Ecclesiae nec certa ratio adversetur. . . ." See Adolphe Tanquerey, *Theologia moralis fundamentalis: De virtutibus et praeceptis* (Paris: Desclée, 1955), 2: 293.
29. See Chapter Sixteen, "Catholic Ethics in the Post-Infallible Church," in which I argue that it is not meaningful to say that the Church is infallible in specific issues of mortality.
30. Henry Davis, *Moral and Pastoral Theology* (London and New York: Sheed and Ward, 1949), 1: 107.
31. See Tanquerey, op. cit., 287.
32. Abbot, *Documents of Vatican II*, 17.
33. 1 Cor. 2:15.
34. *De spiritu et littera*, C 21, M.L. 44,222.
35. "Ed ideo dicendum est quod principaliter nova lex est lex indita, secundario autem est lex scripta," *Summa Theologica* I–II, q. 106, a. 1, in corp.
36. Abbott, *Documents of Vatican II*, 34.
37. See Daniel C. Maguire, "Human Sexuality: The Book and the Epiphenomenon," in *Proceedings of the Thirty-Third Annual Convention of the Catholic Theological Society of America*, ed. Luke Salm (New York: Catholic Theological Society of America, 1979), 71–75, from which this description of probabilism is taken.

CHAPTER 9

1. Quoted in Ashley Montague, *The Natural Superiority of Women*, new rev. ed. (New York: Collier Books, 1974), 28–29.
2. George F. Kennan, *American Diplomacy: 1900–1950* (New York and Toronto: A Mentor Book of the New American Library, 1951) 50. Emphasis added.
3. Rosemary Radford Ruether, *New Woman, New Earth: Sexist Ideologies and Human Liberation* (New York: Seabury Press, 1975) 25.
4. See D. B. Paintin, "The Physiology of Sex," in *Psycho-Sexual Problems: Proceedings of the Congress Held at the University of Bradford, 1974* ed. Hugo Milne and Shirley Hardy (Baltimore: University Park Press, 1975), 3–19.
5. See Daniel C. Maguire, *The Moral Choice* (Garden City: Doubleday, 1978; Minneapolis: Winston Press, 1979), ch. 9, "The Feel of Truth," 281–308.
6. See Carol Gilligan, *Harvard Education Review* 47 (November 1977): 482.
7. I borrow here the expression of R. L. Bruckberger, *God and Politics* (New York: Hawthorn Books, 1973) 33.
8. See Mark 10:14.
9. See Matt. 11:25.
10. John W. Dixon, Jr. "The Erotics of Knowing," *Anglican Theological Review* 56 (January 1974): 8.
11. See Daniel C. Maguire, *A New American Justice* (Garden City: Doubleday, 1980; Minneapolis: Winston Press, 1981).
12. John T. Pawlikowski, "Human Rights in the Roman Catholic Tradition," *The American Society of Christian Ethics, Selected Papers, 1979*, ed. Max L. Stackhouse (Waterloo, Ontario: The Council on the Study of Religion, 1979) 153.
13. Quoted in Pawlikowski, ibid.

14. Mary Daly, *Gyn/Ecology: The Metaethics of Radical Feminism* (Boston: Beacon Press, 1978), 12–13.
15. See my *The Moral Choice*, ch. 3, and also see Chapter Twenty, "The Knowing Heart and the Intellectualistic Fallacy."
16. Beverly Wildung Harrison, "The Power of Anger in the Work of Love: Christian Ethics for Women and Other Strangers," *Union Seminary Quarterly Review* 36 (Supplementary, 1981): 48.
17. Thomas Aquinas, *Commentum in Quatuor Libros Sententiarum Magistri Petri Lombardi*, Dist. 23, q. 2, a. 3; Dist. 23, q. 2, a. 1. See also *Summa Theologica* II–II q. 45, a. 2.
18. See Joannes a Sancto Thoma, *Cursus Theologicus* (Quebeci: Collectio Lavallensis, 1948) a. 3, n. 78, p. 147; n. 81, p. 150; n. 82, p. 151; et passim.
19. Marjorie Reiley Maguire, "The Status and Role of Women in Religion," an unpublished paper delivered at the 6th National Workshop on Christian-Jewish Relations, Milwaukee, Wisconsin, October 27, 1981.

CHAPTER 10

1. Aside from Marjorie, my wife, who is cited in the text, my advisory committee for this article included Judith and Bill Kelsey, who while specializing in Christology on their way to Marquette doctorates are majoring in feminism together; and Fran Leap, whose dissertation on the contributions of feminism to Christian ethics is nearing completion at Marquette.
2. On the role of belief in moral knowledge see my *The Moral Choice* (Minneapolis: Winston Press, 1979), ch. 3.
3. Beverly Wildung Harrison, "The Power of Anger in the Work of Love: Christian Ethics for Women and Other Strangers," *Union Seminary Quarterly Review* 36 (Supplementary, 1981): 57, n. 32. See also, Rosemary Ruether, *Sexism and God-Talk: Toward a Feminist Theology* (Boston: Beacon Press, 1983).
4. Chapter Nine, "The Feminization of God and Ethics."
5. Perhaps the most helpful book showing the pervasive poison of sexism infecting racism, anti-Semitism, classism, religion, even psychoanalysis and ecology is Rosemary Radford Ruether's *New Woman New Earth* (New York: Seabury Press, 1975).
6. Beverly Harrison, op. cit., p. 50.
7. Margaret A. Farley, R.S.M., "New Patterns of Relationship: Beginnings of a Moral Revolution, *Theological Studies* 36 (December 1975) and Marjorie Reiley Maguire, "Personhood, Covenant, and Abortion," in *The Annual of the Society of Christian Ethics, 1982*, ed. Joseph Allen, Council on the Study of Religion, Waterloo, Ontario, Canada N2L 3C5. Theological libraries should have *The Annual*. Otherwise, contact the author.
8. Stephen Charles Mott, *Biblical Ethics and Social Change* (New York: Oxford University Press, 1982). See also Chapter Two, "The Primacy of Justice in Moral Theology." And I do not hesitate to recommend my *A New American Justice* (Garden City: Doubleday, 1980; Minneapolis: Winston Press, 1981), especially 53–124.
9. See Chapter Twenty, "The Knowing Heart and the Intellectualistic Fallacy."
10. Madonna Kolbenschlag, *Kiss Sleeping Beauty Good-Bye: Breaking the Spell of Feminine Myths and Models* (Garden City: Doubleday, 1979), xiv.

CHAPTER 11

1. Jean LaPorte, *The Role of Women in Early Christianity*, Volume 7 of *Studies in Women and Religion* (New York and Toronto: Edwin Mellen Press, 1982), 4.

2. Carolyn Osiek, RSCJ, "Women in the New Testament Church," *Ministries* 1 (April 1980): 18.
3. Ibid.
4. Leonard Swidler, *Biblical Affirmations of Woman* (Philadelphia: Westminster Press, 1979), 290. See the whole section on the positive elements in the early Christian tradition on women, 161–328.
5. See Matt. 27:55–56; Mark 15:40; Luke 8:2–3; 23:49.
6. See Swidler, op. cit., 189.
7. Raymond E. Brown, "Roles of Women in the Fourth Gospel," *Theological Studies* (December 1975), 691.
8. See Carolyn Osiek, op. cit., 20.
9. See Leonard Swidler, op. cit., 329–351.
10. Elisabeth Schüssler Fiorenza, *In Memory of Her: A Feminist Theological Reconstruction of Christian Origins* (New York: Crossroad, 1983), 334.
11. Ibid.
12. Sandra M. Schneiders, "Did Jesus Exclude Women from Priesthood?", in *Women Priests: A Catholic Commentary on the Vatican Declaration*, ed. Leonard Swidler and Arlene Swidler (New York: Paulist, 1977) 230. See also Raymond E. Brown, *Priest and Bishop: Biblical Reflections* (New York: Paulist, 1970); Bernard Cooke, *Ministry to Word and Sacrament: History and Theology* (Philadelphia: Fortress, 1976), esp. 525–536; Andre Lemaire, *Les Ministeres Aux Origines de l'Eglise* (Paris: Cerf, 1971).
13. Sandra Schneiders, op. cit., 230–31.
14. John R. Donahue, "A Tale of Two Documents," in Swidler and Swidler, op. cit., 30.
15. See *Women Priests*, cited above, for a devastating set of commentaries by major scholars in the Church. Other documents quickly repudiated in recent memory that received similarly negative reaction from Catholic scholars were the *Humanae Vitae* of 1968 and the *Declaration on Certain Questions Concerning Sexual Ethics* in 1976. The subjects of this theologically ill-informed trio of documents: sex and women.
16. See John R. Donohue, op. cit., 25–34. See "Biblical Commission Report. Can Women Be Priests?", *Origins* 6, 6 (July 1, 1976): 92–96.
17. Jean LaPorte, op. cit., 102.
18. Ibid., 106–7.
19. Roger Gryson, *The Ministry of Women in the Early Church*, tr. J. LaPorte and M. Hall (Collegeville, Minnesota: The Liturgical Press).
20. *Didascalia Apostolorum* III, 12. See LaPorte, op. cit., 112–15.
21. Heb. 3–10. See also LaPorte, op. cit., 131 and 177, n. 231.
22. LaPorte, op. cit., 131.
23. See Elisabeth Schüssler Fiorenza, op. cit., ch. 4, "The Jesus Movement as Renewal Movement Within Judaism."
24. R. A. Norris, Jr., "The Ordination of Women and the Maleness of Christ," *Anglican Theological Review*, Supplementary Series, 6 (June 1976): 70.
25. Ibid.
26. Ibid., 72.
27. Gregory Nazienzen, *Epist.* CI Ad Cledonium (M.P.G. XXXVII, 181C).
28. Sandra Schneiders, I.H.M., "Women and Power in the Church: A New Testament Reflection," *Proceedings of the Thirty-Seventh Annual Convention: The Catholic Theological Society of America*, ed. Luke Salm (New York: Manhattan College, 1982), 124.
29. Mary Buckley, "Women, Power and Liberation," ibid., 110.
30. For a fuller explanation of justice and its place in the moral realm, see my *The Moral Choice* (Garden City: Doubleday, 1979; Minneapolis: Winston Press, 1979), especially ch. 3. See also Chapter One in this book.
31. In the old manuals of moral theology, scandal was seen as a sin against charity. However, this comes from a too narrow and juridical conception of justice. For a different and more biblical view of justice, into which scandal would fit as a species of injustice, see Chapter Two, "The Primacy of Justice of Moral Theology."
32. See Swidler and Swidler, op. cit., 46.

33. Ibid.
34. Ibid.
35. Ibid., 42.
36. Ibid., 43.
37. Ibid.

CHAPTER 12

1. See Robert M. Veatch, *Death, Dying and the Biological Revolution* (New Haven and London: Yale University Press, 1976), 4.
2. Saint Jean de la Croix, *Vie et Oeuvres* (Paris, 1893), ii, 94, 99; quoted in William James, *The Varieties of Religious Experience* (New York: Mentor Books, 1958), 240.
3. Quoted in William James, op. cit., 244.
4. Peter Fransen, S.J., *Divine Grace and Man* (New York: Mentor-Omega, 1965), 96.
5. Charles E. Curran, *Politics, Medicine and Christian Ethics* (Philadelphia: Fortress Press, 1973), 131.
6. Daniel C. Maguire, "Death and the Moral Domain," *Saint Luke's Journal of Theology*, 20 (June 1977): 197–216.
7. Henry Davis, *Moral and Pastoral Theology* (London and New York: Sheed and Ward, 1949), 1:93. See also Chapter Fifteen, "Catholic Ethics in the Post-Infallible Church." This chapter argues that it is not meaningful to say that the Church is infallible in the specific issues of morality. This is obviously relevant to the legitimacy of Probabilism.
8. Krister Stendahl, "Immortality is Too Much and Too Little." Unpublished lecture presented at Nobel Conference, Gustavus Adolphus College, St. Peter, Minnesota, January 6, 1972.
9. Schubert M. Ogden, "The Meaning of Christian Hope," in *Religious Experience and Process Theology*, ed Harry Cargas and Bernard Lee (New York: Paulist, 1976), 195–212.
10. James M. Gustafson, *Ethics from a Theocentric Perspective*, Vol. 1: *Theology and Ethics* (Chicago: University of Chicago Press, 1981), 183, 203, 252–53, 268.
11. Marjorie Suchocki, "The Question of Immortality," *The Journal of Religion* 57 (1977): 289.
12. Marjorie Reiley Maguire, "Ethics and Immortality," in *The American Society of Christian Ethics: 1978 Selected Papers*, ed. Max L. Stackhouse (Waterloo, Ontario: Council on the Study of Religion, 1978), 59.

CHAPTER 15

1. Carroll Stuhlmueller, C.P., *The Revival of the Liturgy*, ed. Frederick McManus (New York: Herder and Herder, 1963), 5–32; Gregory Baum, "The Magisterium in a Changing Church," *Concilium*, Vol. 21, 71–75.
2. It must not be presumed that the role of hierarchical figures in the early Church is the perfect paradigm for hierarchical functioning in all subsequent ages. In the process of socialization the early Christian community was inescapably influenced by the societal forms of the day.
3. Paul Hinnebusch, O.P., "Christian Fellowship in the Epistle to the Philippians," *The Bible Today*, 12 (April 1964): 793–798; G. Ricciotti, *The Acts of the Apostles* (Milwaukee: Bruce, 1958), 77–78; Nicholas Crotty, "Biblical Perspectives in Moral Theology," *Theological Studies*, 26 (1965): 587–589.
4. Cf. *Epistle to the Trallians* 13, 1, Ancient Christian Writers 1 (Westminster, Md.: New-

man, 1946), 79; cf. also J. S. Romanides, "The Ecclesiology of St. Ignatius of Antioch," *Greek Orthodox Theological Review*, 7 (1961–62): 53–77.

5. Oscar Cullmann, *The Earliest Christian Confessions* (London: Lutterworth Press, 1949).

6. Johannes Quasten, *Patrology*, Vol. 1 (Utrecht-Brussels: Spectrum Publishers, 1949), 23–29, 150–153.

7. Piet Fransen, "The Authority of the Councils," *Cross Currents* (1961), 357–374.

8. *Adversus Haereses*, 3,3,3, Sources Chrétiennes (Paris: Editions du Cerf, 1952), Livre III, 106. Cf. *Handbook of Church History*, Vol I (New York: Herder and Herder; 1965), ed. Hubert Jedin and John Dolan, 356–357. "Irenaeus' line of thought is, plainly, as follows: The apostolic tradition is found with certainty in the communities which rest on a directly apostolic foundation; there are several of these and each of them has a stronger power, grounded in its apostolic origin, for the ascertaining of truth. . . . One of these churches is the Roman church; which is even in a particularly favorable position for establishing the apostolic tradition, but not exclusively so."

9. Epistle 9, *PL* 62:66.

10. Cyprian, "Life of Caesarius," *PL* 67:1021.

11. Cyrille Vogel, *La Discipline penitentielle en Gaule des origines à la fin du VII siècle* (Paris: Letouzey et Ané, 1952), 85.

12. Bernhard Poschmann, *Penance and the Anointing of the Sick* (New York: Herder and Herder, 1964), 124–138.

13. The moral and dogmatic magisteria do, of course, face many common problems. Both face the problem of the fallibility of language and the tendency for meaning to slip fluidly from under propositional formulae so that only a new proposition could express the original meaning. Special challenges arise for the dogmatic theologian as s/he takes modern biblical exegesis and insights and faces formal magisterial pronouncements of the past on questions of original sin, the preternatural gifts, the knowledge of Christ, the reality of hell, and similar points.

14. For a fuller treatment of the Christian reaction to war and peace see my essay, "Modern War and Christian Conscience," *On the Other Side* (Englewood Cliffs, N.J.: Prentice-Hall, 1968).

15. *Contra Celsum VIII*, 68–69, Die griechischen Christlichen Schriftsteller, II (Leipzig: Heinrichs, 1889), 285.

16. *Ibid.*, 73.

17. Roland H. Bainton, *Christian Attitudes Toward War and Peace* (Nashville: Abingdon Press, 1960), 66–84; Dictionnaire de Théologie Catholique, 6, col. 1916; Ruinart, Acta Martyrum (Ratisbon, 1859), 341–342.

18. Bainton, op. cit., 72–73, 77–84; Stanley Windass, *Christianity Versus Violence* (London: Sheed and Ward, 1964), 3–20.

19. Eusebius, *Historia ecclesiastica* X, IX, 6–8, SC, 1958; *Vita Constantini* 2, 19, GCS, 1902; *Handbook of Church History,* 405–432.

20. Bainton, op. cit., 85–89.

21. *Theodosiani Libri* XVI; cf. Bainton, op. cit., 88.

22. *De libero arbitrio*, Vol. 12, PL, XXXXII, 1227; Quaest. hept., IV, 44, CSEL, XXVIII, 2, 353.

23. *Contra Faustum*, PL, XXXXII, 448–449; cf. Windass, op. cit., 20–35.

24. Bainton, op. cit., 109.

25. Windass, op. cit., 43.

26. Bainton, op. cit., 101–121; Windass, op. cit., 36–53; Steven Runciman, *A History of the Crusades*, Vol. I (Cambridge, Eng., 1951), ch. I, "Holy Peace and Holy War."

27. Poschmann, op. cit., 218.

28. Bainton, op. cit., 112.

29. *Historia Francorum*, tr. Frederick Duncalf and August C. Krey, *Parallel Source Problems in Medieval History* (New York: Newper & Brothers, 1912); quoted with permission by Bainton, op. cit., 112–113.

30. Philip Hughes, *History of the Church*, (New York: Sheed and Ward, 1952), 2: 299–300.

31. Bainton, op. cit., 115.

32. *Decretum Gratiani,* pars II, caus. XXIII, q. V, c. 46.
33. E. Schillebeeckx, O.P., *Marriage, Human Reality and Saving Mystery* (New York: Sheed and Ward, 1965); Helmut Thielicke, *The Ethics of Sex* (New York: Harper & Row, 1964).
34. The slight amount of casuistry which does appear in the New Testament must be critically appreciated. In reading Paul's remarks to the Corinthians, for example, one must consider the known cultic aspects of much Corinthian fornication as well as Paul's eschatological expectations. Only then could one decide how relevant his remarks are to modern debates.
35. *Diog. Laer.,* VII, 110.
36. Ocellus Lucanus, *The Nature of the Universe,* text and commentary by Richard Harder (Berlin, 1926), sec. 44.
37. John T. Noonan, Jr., *Contraception* (Cambridge, Mass.: Harvard University Press, 1965), 46–49, 56–91.
38. *Stromata* 3.7.57, GCS, 15:222.
39. Noonan, op. cit., 126–131.
40. "Concupiscence" is normally used by Augustine in a bad sense: "This custom of speaking obtains that if avarice or concupiscence is spoken of and no modification is added, it cannot be understood except in an evil meaning" (*The City of God,* 14.7.2., CSEL 40:14); cf. Noonan, op. cit., 134.
41. Ironically, Augustine, whose authority has been much cited in the Church's condemnation of contraception, vigorously attacked the contraceptive use of the sterile period (*The Morals of the Manichees,* 18.65, PL 32:1373), the one method approved by the extraordinary magisterium.
42. "No land could give lawful fruit which in a single year was frequently sowed. Why does one do in his own body what he would not do in his own field?" (Sermons 44.3–6, CC 103; 196–199).
43. Noonan, op. cit., 78.
44. *On the Seven Penitential Psalms* 4, PL 217:1058–1059; cf. Noonan, op. cit., 197.
45. *Le Prediche volgari,* ed. Piero Bargellini (Milan, 1936), 400.
46. Cf. above, n. 43.
47. Noonan, op. cit., 248.
48. Thomas, *On the Sentences* 4.32.1.2.2.; Raymond, *Summa* 4.2.6; Scotus, *On the Sentences,* Oxford Report, 4.32.
49. Session 24, November 11, 1563, Johannes Dominicus Mansi, *Sacrorum Conciliorum Nova et Amplissima Collectio,* ed. by H. Welter (Paris-Leipzig, 1903), 33:150.
50. Leo XIII, "Arcanum Divinae Sapientiae," *AAS* 12:385–402.
51. *The Documents of Vatican II,* Walter M. Abbott, S.J., General Editor (New York: Herder and Herder, 1966), "The Pastoral Constitution on the Church in the Modern World," no. 49, 253.
52. Ibid., 254.
53. John T. Noonan, Jr., *The Scholastic Analysis of Usury* (Cambridge: Harvard University Press, 1957); "Authority, Usury and Contraception," *Cross Currents,* 16 (1966): 55–79.
54. "Authority, Usury and Contraception," 55–56.
55. Mansi 21:529–530, 22:231; *Clementine Constitutions* 5.5., *Corpus juris canonici.*
56. "Authority, Usury and Contraception," 62–63.
57. *The Scholastic Analysis of Usury,* 346.
58. Ibid., 283–285, 289.
59. Patrick Granfield, O.S.B., "The Right to Silence," *Theological Studies,* 26 (1965), 280–298.
60. PL 119, 1010.
61. Patrick Granfield, O.S.B., "The Right to Silence: Magisterial Development," *Theological Studies,* 27 (1966): 404.
62. *Bullarum, diplomatum at privilegiorum sanctorum Romanorum pontificum Taurinensis,* editio 3 (Turin, 1858), 556.

63. Benedict XIV, *Bullarii Romani continuatio* (Florence, 1846), tom 3, pars prima, 13–17, n. 6.

64. *Regulae servandae in iudiciis apud* S.R. Rotae Tribunal, Aug. 4, 1910, *AAS* 2 (1910): 783–850.

65. "The Right to Silence," 417.

66. "Declaration on Religious Freedom," *The Documents of Vatican II*, 679.

67. Space permitting, a useful study could be done on the development of thought in the Church on questions of ecumenism and church-state relations; cf. Edward H. Flannery, *The Anguish of the Jews* (New York: Macmillan, 1965); George H. Tavard, *Two Centuries of Ecumenism* (New York: Mentor Omega, 1962); John Courtney Murray, S.J., "The Problem of Religious Freedom, *Woodstock Papers*, No. 7 (1965); and Pius Augustin, O.S.B., *Religious Freedom in Church and State* (Baltimore: Helicon, 1966).

68. Louis Bouyer, *Dictionary of Theology* (New York: Desclee Co., 1965), 237.

69. Trans. Cuthbert Butler, *The Vatican Council*, (London: Longmans, Green and Co., 1930). 2:295; cf. Denz. 1838–1840.

70. "Constitution on Divine Revelation," n. 12, *The Documents of Vatican II*, 120.

71. Mansi 52:1204. This occurs at the beginning of the *Relatio* of Bishop Gasser. The reference is to Isa. 33:7.

72. Cf. Butler, op. cit., vol II, chap. XIX; cf. also Hans Küng, *The Council, Reform and Reunion* (New York: Sheed and Ward, 1962), 161.

73. Mansi 51:1026B.

74. Mansi 52:761.

75. Mansi 52:764. "Idem Spiritus sanctus qui per charisma infallibilitatis adsistit papae et episcopis docentibus, idem dat fidelibus edoctis gratiam fidei, qua magisterio ecclesiae credunt."

76. Ibid. ". . . quoniam assistentia non est nova revelatio, sed manifestatio veritatis quae in deposito revelationis iam continetur, sanctus Spiritus agit et adiuvat papam ad veritatis conquisitionem ex fontibus divinae revelationis, quae in sacris Scripturis et traditione continetur."

77. Ibid. "Quare neque diligentiam neque curas potest omittere, quae necessario ad cognoscendam veritatem praerequirentur. Idcirco papa inquisitionem instituit sive cum clero et theologis ecclesiae Romanae, sive cum formali synodo romana, ut inquirat quid in subiecta fidei et morum materia teneat ecclesia Romana, in qua immaculata semper est servata apostolica doctrina; unde mater et magistra ominum vocatur et est. Addit etiam aliquando inquisitionem cum episcopis sive seorsum, sive in conciliis provincialibus, et quoties opportunum in Domino iudicaverit, solemniorem etiam inquisitionem instituit, convocatis simul totius orbis episcopis. . . ."

78. Mansi 52:1212.

79. Mansi 52:1213. "Sed ideo non separamus pontificem ab ordinatissima coniunctione cum ecclesia. Papa enim solummodo tunc est infallibilis, quando omnium christianorum doctoris munere fungens, ergo universalem ecclesiam repraesentans, iudicat et definit quid ab omnibus credendum vel reiiciendum. Ab ecclesia universali tam separari non potest, quam fundamentum ab aedificio cui portando destinatum est. Non separamus porro papam infallibiliter definientem a cooperatione et concursu ecclesiae, saltem id est in eo sensu, quod hanc cooperationem et hunc concursum ecclesiae non excludimus."

80. Mansi 52:1213–1214. ". . . quia infallibilitas pontificis Romani non per modum inspirationis vel revelationis, sed per modum divinae assistentiae ipsi obvenit. Hinc papa pro officio suo et rei gravitate tenetur media apta adhibere ad veritatem rite indagandam et apte enuntiandam; et eiusmodi media sunt concilia vel etiam consilia episcoporum, cardinalium, theologorum etc. . . ." "Sed nonnulli ex reverendissimis patribus, his non contenti, ulterius progrediuntur, et volunt etiam in hanc constitutionem dogmaticam inducere conditiones, quae in tractatibus theologicis diversae in diversis inveniuntur, et quae bonam fidem et deligentiam pontificis in veritate indaganda et enuntianda concernunt; quae proinde, cum non relationem pontificis,

sed conscientiam ipsius ligent, ordini potius morali quam dogmatico accensendae sunt."

81. Ibid. "Demum papam non separamus, et vel minime separamus a consensu ecclesiae, dummodo consensus iste non ponatur ut conditio, sive sit consensus antecedens sive sit consequens. Non possumus separare papam a consensu ecclesiae, quia hic consensus nunquam ipsi deesse potest."

82. Mansi 52:12.7. "Sed hoc systema aut est prorsus arbitrarium aut totius infallibilitatis pontificiae eversivum. Est arbitrarium si requireretur maioris vel minoris partis episcoporum assensus. Nam quis statuet illorum numerum? Quis faciet delectum, cum episcopi inter se sub hoc respectu sint omnino pares, et assensus quorumdam assensui et iudicio aliorum non possit praeiudicare?"

83. Cf. Mansi 52:1216–1217.

84. Mansi 52:1226. "Iam vero cum de infallibilitate summi pontificis in definiendis veritatibus idem omnino dicendum sit, quod de infallibilitate definientis ecclesiae; eadem oritur quaestio de extensione infallibilitatis pontificiae ad huiusmodi veritates in se non revelatas, pertinentes tamen ad custodiam depositi: quaestio, inquam, oritur utrum infallibilitas pontificia in his veritatibus definiendis non solum sit theologice certa, sed sit fidei dogma eodem prorsus modo sicut dictum est de infallabilitate ecclesiae. Cum autem patribus Deputationis unanimi consensione visum sit hanc quaestionem nunc saltem non definiendam, sed relinquendam esse in eo statu in quo est: . . ."

85. Mansi 52:1227. "In illis autem in quibus theologice quidem certum, non tamen hactenus certum de fide est ecclesiam esse infallibilem, etiam infallibilitas pontificis hoc decreto sacri concilii non definitur tanquam de fide credenda."

86. "Constitution on Revelation," n. 8, The Documents of Vatican II, 116.

87. "Constitution on the Church," n. 12 and n. 15, The Documents of Vatican II, 29 and 33–34.

88. Noonan, op. cit., 395.

89. Edgar Hocedez, Histoire de la théologie au XIXᶜ siècle (Brussels, 1947–1952), 1:67–69; 132.

90. See Rudolph Schnackenburg, The Moral Teaching of the New Testament (New York: Herder and Herder, 1965), 122.

91. Schillebeeckx, op. cit., 389.

92. Schnackenburg, op. cit., 249.

93. Mansi 52:1235. "Verba doctrinam de moribus insinuant, Romanum pontificem ab errore immunem non esse, quando de honestate vel pravitate alicuius actionis in concreto spectatae decernit; puta de latrocinio temporalis dominii sanctae sedis a gubernio Italico perpetrato."

94. Pius XII, Allocution "Magnificate Dominum," Nov. 2, 1954; AAS 46 (1950): 561.

95. John XXIII, Encyclical Pacem in terris, Apr. 11, 1963; AAS 55 (1963): 301.

96. Gregory Baum, O.S.A., "The Christian Adventure—Risk and Renewal," Critic 23 (1965): 44.

97. John J. Reed, S.J., "Natural Law, Theology, and the Church," Theological Studies 26 (1965): 55.

98. Richard A. McCormick, S.J., "Notes on Moral Theology," Theological Studies, 26 (1965): 614.

99. Even the strong stand of Trent on marriage and divorce is not seen today as prohibiting the growing debate concerning those matters.

100. For St. Thomas' appreciation of the essential role of circumstances, cf. Iᵃ IIᵃᵉ, q.18, a.10; ibid., q.73, a.7; Sent. 4 d.16, q.3, a.2; De malo q.2, a.6, 7.

101. Karl Rahner, S.J., Nature and Grace (New York: Sheed and Ward, 1964), 41.

102. Fransen, art. cit., 366.

103. Jan H. Walgrave, O.P., "Is Morality Static or Dynamic?" Concilium V (London: Paulist, 1965), 20.

104. Alfred North Whitehead, Process and Reality (New York: Harper Torchbooks, 1960), 297.

105. Ibid., 298.
106. John Macquarrie, *God-Talk: An Examination of the Language and Logic of Theology* (London: SCM Press, 1967), 127.
107. Butler, op. cit., I, 101; II, 215–216; Rondet, op. cit., 126.
108. Mansi 52:1133–1134; 1226–1228.
109. Richard A. McCormick, S.J., art. cit., 615.
110. Ibid., 612.
111. Ibid., 615.
112. Gregory Baum, O.S.A., art. cit., 52.
113. Decree on Ecumenism, n. 11, *The Documents of Vatican II*, 354.
114. Constitution on the Church, n. 25, *The Documents of Vatican II*, 48.
115. Encyclical *Mater et magistra*, no. 239: *AAS* 53 (1961): 457.
116. Reed, art. cit., 59. For a similar interpretation and citations from other authors, cf. Ford and Kelly, *Contemporary Moral Theology* (Westminster, Md.: Newman, 1963), 1:19–41.
117. Y. Congar, "La primaute des quatre premiers conciles oecumeniques. Origine, destin, sens et portée d'un thème traditionnel," *Le Concile et les Conciles* (Paris: Editions de Chevetogne, 1960), 76–80; cf., Hans Küng, *Structures of the Church* (Camden, N.J.: Nelson, 1963), 52–64.
118. Augustine, *Retractationes*, lib.2., c.18; *PL* 32, 637 f.
119. *Summa Theologica*, III, q.8, a.3, ad 2.
120. Karl Rahner, S.J., "The Church of Sinners," *Cross Currents*, I (1951): 68.
121. Church in the Modern World, n. 5, *Documents of Vatican II*, 204. My frequent use of the documents of Vatican II in this development is not without recognition that this council, perhaps more than most others, contains the fruit of many theologies and does not represent a synthesis of these theologies. I think it important, however, that philosophical and theological theories that support my analysis did find a place in the council.
122. Ibid., n. 54, 260.
123. Declaration of Christian Education, n. 1, *Documents*, 640.
124. The Church in the Modern World, n. 43, *Documents*, 244.
125. Ibid., n. 5, *Documents*, 203–204; n. 53–62, 259–270; and passim.
126. Ibid., n. 61, 267.
127. Reed, art. cit., 59. From here on, references to this article will be given in the text.
128. McCormick, art. cit., 613. Hereafter reference to this article will be made in the text.
129. *AAS*, 42 (1950), 568.
130. Ford and Kelly, op. cit., 32.
131. Reed, art. cit., 57.
132. Ibid., n. 30.
133. Ford and Kelly, op. cit., I:314.
134. Ibid., 315.
135. Cyprian, Ep. 55, 9; cf. *Handbook of Church History*, 380.
136. *Handbook of Church History*, 427.
137. Cf. Y. Congar, *Chrétiens en Dialogue* (Paris: Editions du Cert, 1964).
138. Constitution on the Church, n. 12, *The Documents of Vatican II*, 29.
139. This chapter was originally written in 1968. In 1976, Avery Dulles, S.J. took up the idea of multiple magisteria "complementary and mutually corrective." Avery Dulles, S.J., "The Theologian and the Magisterium," *Proceedings of the Thirty-First Annual Convention of The Catholic Theological Society of America*, Vol. 31, 1976, pp. 235–46. Dulles shows that Thomas Aquinas used the term *"magisterium"* "primarily for those who have the license to teach theology in the schools." The bishops have a qualified kind of magisterium, "concerned with preaching and public order in the Church rather than with the intricacies of theory."

CHAPTER 16

1. W. D. Davis, *The Sermon on the Mount* (Cambridge: University Press, 1966), 151.
2. Charles E. Curran, "Is There a Catholic and/or Christian Ethic?" *Proceedings of the Twenty-ninth Annual Convention: The Catholic Theological Society of America* 29 (1974): 145.
3. Charles E. Curran, *Catholic Moral Theology in Dialogue* (Notre Dame: Fides, 1972), 20.
4. Richard McCormick, "Notes On Moral Theology," *Theological Studies* 32 (1971): 74–75. Beyond the positions noted here, there is a wide gamut of response to this question ranging from the view that there is a real distinction between Christian morality and a merely human and natural morality, to the view that there can be in no sense a distinctively Christian ethic.
5. H. Richard Niebuhr, *The Responsible Self* (New York: Harper & Row, 1963), 150.
6. Franz Boas, *Anthropology and Modern Life*, 2nd ed. (New York: Norton, 1932), 227.
7. Ralph Linton, "The Problem of Universal Values," *Method and Perspective in Anthropology: Papers in Honor of Wilson D. Wallis*, ed. Robert Spencer (Minneapolis: University of Minnesota Press, 1956), 168.
8. May Edel and Abraham Edel, *Anthropology and Ethics* (Springfield, Illinois: Charles C. Thomas Publisher, 1959), 19.
9. Clyde Kluckhohn, "Universal Categories of Culture," *Anthropology Today*, ed. A. Kroeber (Chicago: University of Chicago Press, 1953). Kluckhohn does, of course, see the number of common areas. "Every culture has a concept of murder. . . . There are also common prohibitions of untruth under defined circumstances, of restitution and reciprocity, of mutual obligations between parents and children. . . ." "Ethical Relativity: Sic et Non," *Journal of Philosophy* 52 (1955): 672.
10. Morris Ginsberg, *On the Diversity of Morals* (New York: Macmillan, 1957). See especially ch. 7.
11. Linton, "Problem of Universal Values," 145.
12. Davies, *Sermon on the Mount*, 151.
13. Seely Beggiani, "A Case for Logocentric Theology," *Theological Studies* 32 (1971): 371–406. The article did elicit a serious response in a note from John Haught of Georgetown University. "What Is Logocentric Theology?" *Theological Studies* 33 (1972): 120–132.
14. Beggiani, "Logocentric Theology," 374.
15. E. Schillebeeckx, O. P., *Marriage: Human Reality and Saving Mystery* (New York: Sheed and Ward, 1965), 289.
16. Sean Freyne, "The Bible and Christian Morality" in *Morals, Law and Authority*. ed. J. P. Mackey (Dayton: Pflaum Press, 1969), 20.
17. *Contra Celsum*, 2. 27.
18. Oscar Cullmann, *The Early Church*, abr. ed., ed. A. J. B. Higgins (Philadelphia: Westminster, 1966), 50.
19. Cullmann, *Early Church*, 50.
20. Charles E. Curran, *Catholic Moral Theology in Dialogue* (Notre Dame, Indiana: Fides, 1972), 47.
21. Alan Richardson, "Kingdom of God" in *Theological Word Book of the Bible*, ed. Alan Richardson (New York: Macmillan, 1962; paperback edition), 119. Raymond E. Brown, S.S., writes: "In the New Testament, the establishment of God's kingdom is to a certain extent identical with Jesus' coming, for His ministry opens with the announcement that the kingdom of God is at hand." *New Testament Essays* (Milwaukee: Bruce Publishing, 1965), 233. As John L. McKenzie says noting that the term is frequently used in the synoptics "to designate the central theme of the mission of Jesus. . . ." "The abandonment of the term in the apostolic writings is probably due to the heavily Jewish coloring of the term, which was not easily intelligible to Greek-speaking Christians." John L. McKenzie, *Dictionary of the Bible* (Milwaukee: Bruce Publishing, 1965), 479. The theology of God's special action and our call to respond is not abandoned in subsequent writing.

22. Schnackenburg, *Moral Teaching*, 145.
23. T. W. Manson, *Ethics and the Gospel* (New York: Scribner, 1960), 65.
24. Richardson, "Kingdom of God."
25. Richardson, "Kingdom of God."
26. Herbert Marcuse, *One Dimensional Man* (Boston: Beacon Press, 1964), 123.
27. Eric Voegelin, *The New Science of Politics* (Chicago and London: Univsersity of Chicago Press, 1952), 100.
28. Gabriel Marcel, *The Philosophy of Existentialism* (New York: Citadel Press, 1964; 4th paperbound edition), 33.
29. *Summa Theologica* I–II, q. 91, a.2. ". . . rationalis creatura excellentiori quodam modo divinae providentiae subiacet, inquantum et ipsa fit providentiae particeps, sibi ipsi et aliis providens."
30. My book *Death By Choice* (Garden City: Doubleday, 1974) defends the morality of doing this in certain qualified circumstances.
31. H. Richard Niebuhr, *The Responsible Self* (New York, Evanston, and London: Harper & Row, 1963), 165–166.
32. Hannah Arendt, *The Human Condition* (Garden City: Doubleday Anchor Books, 1958), 289–291.
33. Schnackenburg, *Moral Teaching*, 95, 98.
34. The idea of prophet is not univocal in the Bible. I am selecting the social conscience aspect as special and salient.
35. Schnackenburg, *Moral Teaching*, 32.
36. Johannes Pedersen, *Israel: Its LIfe and Culture* (London: Oxford University Press, 1926), I–II, 263–325; quoted by C. F. Evans, "Peace," *Theological Word Book of the Bible*, ed. Alan Richardson (New York: Macmillan, 1950), 165.
37. James M. Gustafson, *Can Ethics Be Christian?* (Chicago and London: University of Chicago Press, 1975), 80, 62. Reviewing Gustafson's book Norbert J. Rigali, S.J., cites Gustafson's "tendency to exercise caution" and laments that "The question of whether there is a material difference between Christian and non-christian, secular ethics is thus left in suspension." *Theological Studies* 30 (September 1975): 551–553. However, as even the two quotes given here from Gustafson show, Gustafson theoretically escapes the artificality of the *intentionality-material content* dichotomy. He does not, however, spell out thematically the differences that should mark Christian moral experience.
38. The unnaturalness of divorcing attitudes and dispositions from "material content" can be seen by reference to the notion of *habitus* in Thomas Aquinas. *Habitus*, he says, is a principle of operation. One acts in accordance with one's *habitus* so that *habitus* can be called *actus primus*, and behavior (or *operatio*), *actus secundus*. (*Summa Theologica* I–II, q. 49, a.3 c; ad 1.) *Habitus* will be informed by one's intentions, attitudes, goals, etc. and one will make even practical judgment according to *habitus*. Thus it is artificial to speak of a material content existing in one's ethics beyond the reach of one's "habitual" disposition. The ethics of character proceeding from Kantian and other inspirations points to a similar conclusion.

CHAPTER 17

1. See my *A New American Justice* (1979, 128–53), where I argue that we mistakenly and self-servingly lump black problems among those of the disadvantaged in general, missing the unique difficulties black persons face in the United States.

CHAPTER 19

1. Thomas Aquinas, *Summa Theologica* I–II, q. 90, a.1. ". . . imperare est rationis . . ." See also ibid., q. 17, a.1.

2. Unless otherwise noted, quotes from Thomas Aquinas will be from the *Summa Theologica*. These phrases are from I–II, q. 90, a.1 of that work.
3. Thomas Aquinas, I–II, q. 94, a.4.
4. In operativis autem non est eadem veritas vel rectitudo practica apud omnes quantum ad propria, sed solum quantum ad communia." Ibid.
5. Thomas Aquinas, I, q. 105, a.6 ad 2. See also II–II, q. 64, a.5, ad 4; II–II, q. 154, a.2, ad 2; *De Malo*, q. 3, a.1, ad 17; *De Potentia Dei*, q. 1, a.6, ad 4; In III Sent., d. 37, a.4. On the question of absolutes in Thomas, see John G. Milhaven, "Moral Absolutes and Thomas Aquinas," in *Absolutes in Moral Theology?*, ed. Charles E. Curran (Washington, D.C.: Corpus Books, 1968). On the inconsistent terminology in Thomas and the difficulties this presents, see Eric D'Arcy, *Conscience and Its Right to Freedom* (New York: Sheed & Ward, 1961), 69–71.
6. I–II, q. 18, a.1, in c.
7. Ibid., a.3, *Sed contra*.
8. "Ergo circumstantia constituit actum moralem in aliqua specie boni vel mali." Ibid., a. 10, *Sed contra*.
9. Thomas Aquinas, *Summa Theologica* II II q. 83 a. 1. Ratio vero practica est non solum apprehensiva sed etiam causativa.
10. Ibid., The terms used for the functioning of practical reason are *imperare, petere, deprecari, ordinare* toward some *finem seu bonum*.
11. See ibid., I–II, q. 90, a.1.
12. Ibid.
13. See *De Malo*, q. 16, a. 6, ad 13, and ad 8.
14. I–II, q. 90, a.1, in c.
15. I–II, q. 57, a.5, in c.
16. See Josef Pieper, *The Four Cardinal Virtues* (New York: Harcourt, Brace & World, 1965), 3–40, 155–58.
17. Ibid.
18. Ibid. ". . . virtuosus enim recte iudicat de fine virtutis quia qualis unusquisque est, talis finis videtur ei, ut dicitur in III Ethic."
19. Rectitudo autem iudicii potest contingere dupliciter: uno modo, secundum perfectum usum rationis; alio modo, propter connaturalitatem quandam ad ea de quibus iam est iudicandum. Sicut de his quae ad castitatem pertinent per rationis inquisitionem recte iudicat ille qui didicit scientiam moralem: sed per quandam connaturalitatem ad ipsa recte iudicat de eis ille qui habet habitum castitatis. . . . Hierotheus est perfectus in divinis non solum discens, sed et patiens divina. Huiusmodi autem compassio sive connaturalitas ad res divinas fit per caritatem, quae quidem unit nos Deo . . . Sic igitur sapientia quae est donum causam quidem habet in voluntate scilicet caritatem: sed essentiam habet in intellectu . . . *Summa Theologica* II–II, q. 45, a.2.
20. Ibid., ad 1.
21. See Daniel C. Maguire, *The Moral Choice* (Garden City: Doubleday, 1978; Minneapolis: Winston Press, 1979), 288–90. The literature on Thomas, of course, is replete with arguments on the priority of intellect over volition in Thomas. Some texts seem to leave no doubt about that. For example in *Summa Contra Gentiles*, Book 3, Chapter 26: "unde apparet intellectum simpliciter esse altiorem voluntate, voluntatem vero intellectu per accidens et secundum quid." And, ibid., Chapter 25: "Deo autem assimilatur maxime creatura intellectualis per hoc quod intellectualis est; hanc enim similitudinem habet prae caeteris creaturis, et hoc includit omnes alias." However, in Thomas the comparison of the intellectual and the affective is not in our terms, is incomplete and unsystematized even in his terms, and is in any text conditioned by the contextual agenda. Like any great thinker, Thomas was on to more than he had time to develop and systematize. Note too that in *Summa Theologica* I–II, q. 27, a. 1 Thomas seems to imply that connaturality comes before love. "Amor importat quandam connaturalitatem . . . ad amatum." He is talking there, however, about the cause of love and parallels *connaturalitatem* with *complacentiam*. In II–II, q. 45, a.2,

where he is involved in theological epistemology, "connaturalitas ... fit per caritatem."

22. ". . . dona Spiritus Sancti connectuntur sibi invicem in caritate . . . quorum nullum sine caritate haberi potest." I–II, q. 68, a. 6 in c.

23. Ibid., a.3. in c.

24. I–II, q. 31, a.4.

25. I–II, q. 31, a.1, ad 1.

26. Aristotle, *Nichomachean Ethics*, Bk. X Chap. 5, 1176a.

27. See Daniel C. Maguire, *The Moral Choice* (Garden City: Doubleday, 1978; Minneapolis: Winston Press, 1979), 290–93.

28. Another neglected corner of Thomas; epistemology is the subject of ecstasy. This is not much developed in Thomas but he does recognize that ecstasy can obtain in our knowing and in our willing capacities "secundum vim apprehensivam, et secundum vim appetitivam." I–II, q. 28, a.3. It is possible for us to know in a way beyond our normal modes of knowing. Thomas does not underestimate the un-chartable reaches of the mind.

29. *Commentum in Quatuor Libros Sententiarum Magistri Petri Lombardi*, Dist. 23, q. 2, a.1 ". . . cognitio fidei ex voluntate procedit quia nullus credit nisi volens . . ."

30. ". . . fides autem habet certitudinem ab eo quod est extra genus cognitionis in genere affectionis existens." Ibid., Dist. 23, q. 2, a.3.

31. ". . . vis appetitiva et apprehensiva sunt quidem diversae partes, sed unius animae." *Summa Theologica* I–II, q. 33, a.4, ad 2. In this place Thomas is noting that diverse "Parts" or faculties can distract one another, but his seeing them as parts of the one soul militates against objectification of faculties.

32. See Joannes a Sancto Thoma, *Cursus Theologicus* (Quebeci: Collectio Lavallensis, 1948), a.3, n. 78; n. 81, n. 82, n. 45, a. 5, n. 9, a. 4, n. 15, n. 19.

33. Unde fit quod homo unitus Deo per amorem fiat bene mobilis a Spiritu Sancto, tum ad intelligendum et judicandum de divinis, tum ad judicandum de creatis." Ibid., a. 4, n. 26.

34. Ibid., n. 33.

35. ibid., 42. ". . . experimentaliter cognitum in affectu et juxta experientiam et gustum internum cognoscibile et judicabile."

36. Ibid., n. 42, 43.

37. W. D. Ross, *The Right and the Good* (Oxford: Claredon Press, 1930), 39.

38. Daniel C. Maguire, *The Moral Choice*, 84.

39. Ralph Linton, "The Problem of Universal Values," in Robert F. Spencer, ed., *Method and Perspective in Anthropology: Papers in Honor of Wilson D. Wallis* (Minneapolis: University of Minnesota Press, 1954), 169.

40. Arnold Toynbee, *Change and Habit* (New York and London: Oxford University Press, 1966), 13.

41. Daniel C. Maguire, op. cit., 89.

42. Teilhard de Chardin, *Writings in Time of War* (New York: Harper & Row, 1969), 290.

43. Marjorie Reiley Maguire, "Ethics and Immortality," *Selected Papers from the Nineteenth Annual Meeting of The American Society of Christian Ethics*, ed. Max L. Stackhouse, distributed by The Council on the Study of Religion, 42–61.

44. Blaise Pascal, *Pensées* (New York: Washington Square Press, 1965), Nos. 282 and 277. Pascal relates faith to affectivity. "This then is faith: God felt by the heart, not by reason" (No. 278).

45. Henri Bergson, *The Two Sources of Morality and Religion* (Garden City: Doubleday, Anchor Books, 1956), 58.

46. John Macquarrie, *Principles of Christian Theology* (New York: Scribner, 1966), 88.

47. Regarding the criteriology of affect, I attempted in my *The Moral Choice* not only to assess the workings of affect (*Gemüt*) in moral thought, but to probe the normative implications of ideology, myth, class consciousness, cognitive mood, nationalistic tribalism, and social roles. Regarding the idea of a Center for the Study of Moral Values in a university, see ibid., 181.

Postlogue

Most of the chapters published in this book were previously published, in whole or in part, over some seventeen years. Some were interred in journals or volumes that did not have the virtue of accessibility. The updating and indexing of them here will, I hope, bring them to a new life and a new audience.

In the assembling of these chapters, I made many changes. I purged out the sexist language that was considered normal in my earlier writing. I disagreed with my younger self at times. The order of the chapters is not sacred. The chapters on "The Knowing Heart and the Intellectualistic Fallacy" and the "Service on the Common: A Portrait of the Ethicist" could claim priority of place, but they are not the simplest articles to read, and I hated to greet the reader with them.

All writers have favorite ideas and references. I eliminated most repetition but at times found that some redoing served a new argument and a new context.

Index